WOMEN IN NEW RELIGIONS

WOMEN IN RELIGIONS
Series Editor: Catherine Wessinger

Women in Christian Traditions
Rebecca Moore

Women in New Religions
Laura Vance

Women in New Religions

Laura Vance

NEW YORK UNIVERSITY PRESS
New York and London

NEW YORK UNIVERSITY PRESS
New York and London
www.nyupress.org

References to Internet websites (URLs) were accurate at the time of writing.
Neither the author nor New York University Press is responsible for URLs that
may have expired or changed since the manuscript was prepared.

Library of Congress Cataloging-in-Publication Data
Vance, Laura Lee.
Women in new religions / Laura Vance.
pages cm. — (Women in religions)
Includes bibliographical references and index.
ISBN 978-1-4798-4799-0 (cl : alk. paper) — ISBN 978-1-4798-1602-6 (pb : alk. paper)
1. Women and religion. 2. Mormon women. 3. Seventh-Day Adventist women. 4. Family
International (Organization) 5. Wicca. I. Title.
BL458.V36 2015
200.82—dc23   2014040531

New York University Press books are printed on acid-free paper,
and their binding materials are chosen for strength and durability.
We strive to use environmentally responsible suppliers and materials
to the greatest extent possible in publishing our books.

Manufactured in the United States of America

10 9 8 7 6 5 4 3 2 1

Also available as an ebook

To my students,

for their passion in engaging ideas

and for caring to what ends those ideas are used.

CONTENTS

ACKNOWLEDGMENTS

Growing up as a Mormon girl in the 1970s, I encountered questions of gender and religion early and often. That they persisted is not surprising, but their growth into a life's work required the encouragement and contributions of many people.

I could not have done this work without women and men in religions—especially Mormonism and Seventh-day Adventism—who were willing to share their experiences. To all of the Latter-day Saints and Seventh-day Adventists who have talked with me, answered questions, and provided insights, I am deeply grateful.

My students provide ongoing opportunities for me to experience the joy of discovery. For your interest, eager participation, hard work, and creativity, thank you. Most of all, thank you for sharing a love of sociology.

Questions become a conversation only with others, and I am fortunate to be part of an incredibly inspiring and engaged academic community at Warren Wilson College. I am especially grateful to Siti Kusujiarti, who is captivated by ideas regardless of the hour; Marty O'Keefe, for her unshakable honesty; Ben Feinberg, Christey Carwile, and David Moore, who are wonderful colleagues and simply good people; Paula Garrett and Gary Hawkins, who support faculty research with unfailing humor and enthusiasm; Heather Stewart Harvey, librarian extraordinaire; Julie Wilson, fellow dog lover and willing listener; and Katherine Burleson, Jeff Keith, Jennifer Mozolic, Lucy Lawrence, and everyone who haunts Jensen at odd hours.

I am indebted to more scholars than would be possible to list here. Terrie Aamodt, Gary Land, Ronald L. Numbers, Julius Nam, and the participants in the Ellen White Project provided better insight into Ellen White. Lavina Fielding Anderson offered much-needed perspective for me as both a researcher and a Mormon woman at a critical juncture. Kendra Haloviak Valentine, Bert Haloviak, Gordon Shepherd, Gary Shepherd, and D. Michael Quinn have all inspired and influenced me with their work.

The Appalachian College Association provided funding for the sabbatical that allowed time to write this book. Thank you, ACA, for all that you do for liberal arts institutions in the Central Appalachian Region. The Andrew W. Mellon Foundation provided monies that made it possible to travel to the Graduate Theological Union to access Mo Letters in the library's Special Collections. I am especially grateful to the library staff at GTU for their help.

To Kate Kelly and James A. Kelly, I appreciate your willingness to allow me to use photographs depicting the efforts of Ordainwomen.org. Gerry Chudleigh, communication director of the Pacific Union Conference and publisher of the PUC *Recorder*, generously shared his photographs, and willingly read and responded to a lengthy selection of this work pertaining to Seventh-day Adventism. Thank you, Gerry. I only regret that I did not find you earlier.

Two anonymous readers provided me with thorough comments on both the form and substance of this work. I thank them for sharing their obvious knowledge and skills. Any errors that remain are my own.

Catherine Wessinger's vision, intellect, and determination make this series possible. I have been impressed by Cathy's prodigious and brilliant work for decades, and this book would have suffered a great loss without her expansive knowledge and graceful guidance.

Jennifer Hammer, senior editor at New York University Press, saw the possibility in this series early on, and I appreciate her expertise and support. Constance Grady, editorial assistant, and Dorothea Stillman Halliday, managing editor at the press, provided me invaluable and timely assistance. I am grateful to them, and to all of those at the press who contributed to this project.

I owe a great debt to my grandmothers, Janet Vance and Thelma Stewart, whose lives told of a Mormon history more complicated than its official rendition. I would not have spent a lifetime trying to make sense of the gendering of religion were it not for my family; they inform the experiences that shape this work. I thank them all, especially my brother Scott, who is always ready to engage questions, regardless of where they lead.

Last, Jennifer Langton and I have now spent more of our lives together than we have apart. More than anyone, Jennifer, you ignite my thinking and inspire me. My thanks to you can only be lived.

Introduction

Why Study Women in New Religions?

Media and other popular depictions of new religions often highlight the bizarre: the mass suicide/murders of members of Peoples Temple at Jonestown, Guyana, polygamous marriages among Fundamentalist Latter Day Saints, the group suicide of Nike-clad followers of Heaven's Gate, or collective weddings featuring hundreds of followers of Sun Myung Moon simultaneously repeating wedding vows. New religions, however, are more varied—and often more mundane—than these images suggest. Indeed, because of the almost exclusive media focus on the more surprising aspects of atypical new religions, in the popular imagination new religions are strange and dangerous, their leaders are treacherous or deceitful, and their followers are brainwashed dupes. This image emerges from a particularly narrow focus on extreme practices, actions, and beliefs of a few new religions or sometimes an extreme reaction of the surrounding culture to the religion, as in the case of the aftermath of the Bureau of Alcohol, Tobacco, and Firearms raid on David Koresh's Branch Davidians on 28 February 1993.

This focus on the bizarre is misleading. Most religions began as new religions—by breaking away from an existing religion, through new insights of charismatic leaders, by being imported from another context, or by some combination of these. Christianity emerged from Judaism as followers coalesced around a charismatic leader who eventually came to be called Jesus Christ. Early Christians formed a number of groups that promoted and accepted diverse interpretations of Jesus's teachings, including varied explanations of the resurrection, the nature of God, and the role of women in the movement.[1] Two main streams of Christianity dominated until the Protestant Reformations of the sixteenth century. Catholic Christianity in the West used Latin in its worship, recognized the primacy of the bishop of Rome (the pope) and emphasized Jesus's

1

role in atoning for human sin. Orthodox Christianity in the East, in contrast, used Greek or national languages in its worship, recognized the independence of autonomous state or national churches, and emphasized Jesus's role as the incarnation of God. Martin Luther (1483–1546) posted the *Ninety-Five Theses* in 1517, which criticized Roman Catholic practices such as the sale of indulgences;[2] in 1536 John Calvin (1509–1564) first published *The Institutes of the Christian Religion*,[3] his influential exposition of Protestant theology, and other interpretations and innovations followed.

More recently, a plethora of religious movements have been birthed in the United States. The United States has an especially varied history of new religions, at least in part due to the country's cultural and religious pluralism, constitutional protections of religion, geographic expansion, lack of governmental control of religion, historical-social emphasis on religion, including religious dissent, and the "built-in tendency for cycles of renewal, reform, and schism" in the Jewish and Christian traditions.[4] Ann Lee (1736–1784), an English immigrant, was accepted by her American followers as the female incarnation of Jesus Christ; Jemima Wilkinson (1752–1819) proclaimed herself the "Publick Universal Friend" and led followers in upstate New York; William Miller (1782–1849) preached that the world would end in 1843 (and later 1844); the Perfectionists of John Humphrey Noyes (1811–1886) helped to create the Oneida community; and Mary Baker Eddy (1821–1910) taught a system of spiritual healing and founded the First Church of Christ, Scientist. Such a plethora of religions were, and continue to be, born in the United States that the sociologist and historian of religions Douglas E. Cowan and the sociologist David G. Bromley cite approximately 2,500 different religions in the nation, making it one of the "most religiously diverse countries both in the world and throughout history."[5]

Only a scant few new religions ever garner media attention. These are the most unusual, and media attend to them at moments of conflict or crisis—a failed prediction of the end of the world, mass suicide, or sexual abuse. Though scandals can occur in established religions— witness accusations of sexual abuse in Catholicism, for example—the details may seem more salacious, more novel, in the context of an unfamiliar religion, which also holds potential promise of peculiar beliefs and strange practices.

That most religions begin as new religions renders them indispensable for understanding patterns of religious development, belief, or practice. Although gender, when examined, is almost always considered as an addendum to studies of religion, including studies of new religions—in a section, a chapter, or one book in a series, for example—it is a central and often contested site of cultural meaning. As the historian of religions Ann Braude notes, "Women constitute the majority of participants in religious activities and institutions," including in new religions.[6] Gender is not fixed by biology, though differences such as those of genitalia, chromosomes, or sexual dimorphism may serve as starting points from which cultures build and seek to legitimize concepts and implications of gender—often around notions of gender difference or opposition, a gender binary. Some cultures generally recognize and accept more than two genders, such as two-spirit people among some indigenous North American groups, hijras of South Asia, and others. When gender is constructed as binary, those who are perceived as gender-nonconforming often face pressures to comply with extant gender categories. Cultures create ideas about gender that pervade virtually every aspect of life—from clothing and hairstyles to speech and nonverbal communication; to appropriate work and play; to how one is expected to sit, stand, move, or occupy space. Gender shapes human interactions, relationships, work, remuneration, and family roles and obligations—everything from the trivial to the profound, from the personal to the public.

The sociologists Candace West and Don H. Zimmerman build on the work of the sociologist Erving Goffman to theorize that gender is a "routine accomplishment embedded in everyday interaction,"[7] something that we do in social interactions when we play sports, talk with colleagues, have sex, or engage with others in various other contexts. Aspects of interaction such as how we present ourselves and perceive others, whether and how we touch others, our tone of voice and word choice, topics and types of conversation, and so on are influenced by gender. Francine M. Deutsch emphasizes that people may also "undo" or transgress gender by doing gender in a way that disrupts social patterns and expectations.[8] The philosopher Judith Butler asserts that although gender may appear to be natural, or even biologically based, it is better conceptualized as emerging from stylized acts. The repetition of these stylized acts—what she calls performance—Butler argues, is not freely chosen, but is structured inside regulative "discourses," such as systems of meaning provided by religions, schools, and media, that organize and define possibilities for the individual.[9] The sociologist Lynn Weber provides a conceptual framework for making sense of the ways macro- and mezzo-level social systems, structures, and institutions work in conjunction with micro-level interactional processes to create patterns of gender, economic, racial and ethnic, and sexual inequalities. Her approach indicates that these patterns are at once systematic and complex; that they are historically patterned, but may change over time; and that they vary regionally and in other ways.[10] These and other contemporary feminist theorists assert that gender is not biologically determined, but socially constructed, evidenced especially by variation in gender categories and definitions of appropriate gender norms over time and between cultures. Though biological patterns may provide a starting point, and biological and physiological factors interact with cultural forces in complex ways, feminist theorists note that cultures develop varied gender distinctions, as well as meanings and rules associated with those. Patterns of gender emerge and, as with other social norms, are taught and reinforced, even as they may be contested.[11]

Religion, as the social institution in which meaning is connected to ultimate, often divine, explanations, plays a central role in informing and perpetuating cultural notions of gender, as well as of sexuality. Sex, reproduction, and socialization are essential components of social control, and all cultures inform and seek to influence human reproduction and socialization, largely through ideas about gender, and concomitant behavioral prescriptions and proscriptions: "All religions have addressed the theme of human sexuality and gender roles because sexuality is a potent force in human life and because gender is, in most societies, a major factor in social stratification."[12]

Religion does this within the larger social context, in a manner that is influenced by that context, even if just in response to it. Patriarchal distribution of power in a society generally—in politics and government, media, law, education, work, and family—influences distribution of power in religion. Social scientists point out that there is a complex and dynamic relationship between institutions and individuals, in which each influences the other. Individuals are educated, fed, cared for, and otherwise socialized within institutions such as the family and schools.

We learn about ourselves, about our place in the world, about how to act, about gender categories, about what it means to be male or female, in and from these social institutions. Yet social institutions are made up of individuals, all of whom are capable of not only acting according to social rules and norms, but also acting in opposition to them. Pressures to conform are great, and there are punishments if one violates social rules, as well as rewards if one follows them, but actors can reinterpret, challenge, and resist social patterns. Religion, as a site of ultimate meaning, plays an important role in legitimating social ideas. Religions may generally reflect societal arrangements and reinforce dominant ideas about everything from the distribution of wealth in the society to ideas about gender roles, or they may challenge them.

Individuals not only shape ideas through social institutions, but also—often concomitantly—seek to influence allocation of resources. Leaders of political parties, corporations, unions, interest groups, or religions, for example, do not only promote ideas, they also endeavor to justify certain ways of distributing resources valued in the society. In modern societies, ideas are promoted to attempt to shape allocation of wealth through such things as wage or tax policies, regulations, or allocation of funding for programs in childcare, education, health care, or corporate subsidies.

Influencing ideas is generally easier to do with more resources (by purchasing more and better advertising, for example). Any advantage in shaping ideas, in turn, can allow still better control of resources. This is not to say that those who have more resources exclusively control ideas, but that greater control of resources often provides an advantage in attempting to shape them. This is not predetermined; resources and ideas are contested. Still, greater access to resources may improve ability to sway ideas, including in patriarchy, where men share some advantages, though access to these varies significantly by race, sexual orientation, and in other ways.

The specific content of gender—whether gender is constructed as a binary; how clothing, colors, or objects are gendered; how one should sit, stand, interact, and speak; what activities are appropriate to each gender—varies across culture, history, and geography. Gender expectations and normative performance also often vary by class, sexual orientation, and ethnicity or race. These variations all demonstrate the malleability of gender. The social construction this malleability points to is potentially dangerous. If recognized as social creations, phenomena can be intentionally and more easily re-created, done differently. Given this, sociologists point out that social constructs are not presented or generally understood as such, but seek to be taken for granted, and are imbued with stability via their connection to larger systems of meaning and morality,[13] including—in the case of questions of meaning with widespread cultural implications, as is the case with gender—cultural cosmology. Those in power in society may use religion, media, political discourse, formal educational curricula, and other avenues to promote some ideas over others, and to attempt to establish those ideas as truth.

Because religion is the institution most responsible for answering questions of ultimate meaning, notions of gender intersect with virtually every aspect of religion—including images and characteristics of the divine, access to the divine, accounts of creation, sacred texts and stories, moral norms, access to religious authority, roles in ritual, and religious history. Moreover, religion intersects with gender in the secular realm, informing social discourse and rules regarding sex, whether and when people should marry, reproduction and reproductive control, divorce, gendered violence, proper participation in education and work, reasonable remuneration, work in the family, and participation in politics, among many other aspects of social life. Religion is therefore an important site for legitimating and for *challenging* ideas about gender in any society, including in patriarchal societies.

Religious socialization, which has as its goal the individual's internalization of religion—its rituals, beliefs, and practices—so as to locate social control internally, is intimately connected to internalization of gender. The child is taught primarily by parents and teachers what to do, what to believe, how to act, what is right, what is forbidden, what is evil; in short, the social order and her and others' place within it. Her psychological and physical dependence on primary agents of socialization, particularly parents or caretakers, heightens the individual's motivation to internalize religion and other components of socialization. Additionally, religious socialization connects ideas about good and bad, right and wrong, to the cosmos. Behavior and belief are not just encouraged or discouraged, they are often linked to notions of eternal meaning, death, and what happens following death. Gender in religious socialization is

Figure I.1. Congregants of the Glendale City Seventh-day Adventist Church, in Glendale, California, watch as Cherise Gardner is ordained on 27 April 2013. Religion, which helps people to answer questions of ultimate meaning, can play an important part in legitimizing social ideas and rules, including those about gender. Photograph by Gerry Chudleigh.

not only connected to how one should believe and act in this life, but is also often connected to notions of the divine, of ultimate meaning, and of eternity.

Despite all of this, socialization is neither ever completed nor absolute, and the individual, capable of resistance and agency, can respond to agents of socialization. Additionally, as social actors negotiate meaning, they sometimes participate together in structuring meaning in new ways. In religions we sometimes see social actors debating and reinterpreting sacred texts, challenging restrictions on religious authority, imbuing stories of creation with new meaning, and reshaping religion in other ways. Contestation of gender occurs in these interactions, as in deliberations, conversations, and debates about whether to ordain women or trans people, whether wives should be submissive to husbands, whether women should teach in seminaries, or whether men should be active fathers.

These complex phenomena are on display in all religions, but new religions are especially well suited for their examination as they allow us to explore developmental processes through which religions pass. Certainly the sociohistorical context in which a particular religious movement emerges is unique, as are each movement's leaders and its circumstances of birth or schism (breaking away from an established religion, usually in order to return to truths perceived to have been lost by the tradition). Nonetheless, new religions provide us our best opportunity to study processes of religious emergence. Moreover, a growing body of scholarship suggests that ideas about gender are central to the process of religious emergence, and that if we wish to understand gender and religion, we must consider new religions, especially their leadership and their relationships with the larger sociocultural context.[14] This is in large part because new religious movements often afford women access to possibilities not available in more established religious traditions and in the wider social context. New religions provide a break from tradition, defining themselves in opposition to established patterns, and so they may allow women positions of authority and other opportunities generally denied them. New religions—which often form around a charismatic leader or leaders, as a schism movement breaking away from an established religion, and/or when a religion is imported that is radically different in its new cultural setting—define themselves through their difference.

Part of this difference emerges from a new religion's leader(s). The sociologist Max Weber (1864–1920) defines charisma as a "certain quality of an individual personality by virtue of which he is set apart from ordinary men and treated as endowed with . . . specifically exceptional powers or qualities . . . [which] are not accessible to the ordinary person."[15] The charismatic leader is *extra*ordinary, and breaks with tradition.[16] She says, in effect, "you have heard . . . but I say to you"; she introduces new truth.[17] Weber suggests that charismatic leaders claim, and are recognized by adherents as possessing, unique access to the divine, and are able to accrue and motivate followers. Charismatic leaders are perceived by followers as divinely appointed, and they are consequently able to inspire adherents, who not only accept the leader's message but also "carry out the normative pattern or order proclaimed by the leader."[18] The historian of religions Catherine Wessinger indicates that charisma is rooted in followers' belief that their leader has "access to and is imbued with the qualities of an unseen source of authority," and only "when a person claiming charisma gains followers [can] she or he . . . be said to be a charismatic leader."[19] As the sociologist of religion Bryan Wilson notes, charisma is defined more by the relationship between leader and follower than as a personal attribute.[20]

All of the religions examined in this volume—Mormonism, Seventh-day Adventism, The Family International, and Wicca—emerged as religions largely through some combination of divine insights, innovations, and leadership. Most important, each of these new religions emerged, at least in part, by introducing—and asking adherents to embrace—beliefs that were heretical, that is, "severely at variance with the authority of established orthodoxies."[21] As the charismatic leader introduces a new truth, she represents a break from tradition. Religious movements that form as schism movements breaking away from or reviving truths perceived to be lost by an established religion, and/or religions that are imported that are radically different in their new cultural settings also define themselves through their difference.[22] The differences between these—new religions formed *de novo* around a charismatic leader or leaders (termed new religious movements [NRMs] by new religions scholars); schism movements (termed sects, in the English language); and imported religions (also called new religious movements)—are based in the primary component of their formation, but many new religions have elements of more than one.[23] New religions are to some degree at odds with the social context into which they emerge.

The term "new religions" is used here to denote religions that emerge and exist in tension with their social context, not to indicate age per se. Indeed, many new religions assert a connection to earlier religious traditions, claiming to provide a corrective to a tradition that has gone astray, and thus define themselves as part of a longer religious tradition. Sociologists do not dispute truth claims, but attempt to understand religions in part via examination of their evolving relationship with the world. The sociologist Benton Johnson asserts that an essential point of analysis of new religions is their relationship—specifically, the degree of tension they maintain—with the surrounding society, or the degree to which a new religion accepts or rejects its surrounding sociocultural context.[24] The sociologists William Sims Bainbridge and Rodney Stark contribute to this approach by providing direction for empirical examination of a religious movement's tension with its sociocultural context.[25] More recently, David G. Bromley and J. Gordon Melton have built on these insights to propose a way to conceptualize the immense religious diversity that we see in new religious traditions based on analysis of a religion's relationship "to established institutions (including religion)."[26] Their framework focuses on the extent to which a religious tradition is aligned with or diverges from the cultural (symbolic) and/or social (behavioral) patterns and norms of dominant institutions.[27] As Bromley and Melton point out, however, religious traditions are dynamic, as are the sociocultural contexts in which they exist, and so are "unlikely to occupy a stable niche."[28] Instead beliefs, organizational structure, leadership configuration, practices, and other characteristics may change over time and may therefore be variously more or less aligned with dominant institutions. Religious traditions experience more or less cultural and social tension with dominant institutions and with their sociocultural context over time.

Gender—which plays a central role in systems of meaning, perhaps especially in religions—is an important factor in this evolving relationship with the sociocultural context. Gender, particularly construction of women's place within a movement, allows a religion to define and express itself vis-à-vis its sociohistorical context, to demonstrate its difference or similarity regarding such things as family norms, sexuality, ideas about work, division of labor, politics, and so on. Gender permeates so many aspects of life that in constructing women's place, a religious movement may convey its identity in things from the mundane to the profound.

The four movements examined here are in no way exhaustive of new religions, nor would it be possible to provide an all-inclusive discussion of women or gender in new religions. Instead, these movements are selected to provide diverse and interesting cases via which to examine women in new religions. Two of the movements—Mormonism and Seventh-day Adventism—grew rapidly and significantly after their founding, while The Family International originally experienced significant growth, but has a declining membership in recent years. The movements' origins are in the West, but the membership of each is international, and in three—Mormonism, Seventh-day Adventism, and The Family International—a majority of members currently reside outside the United States. Each of the religious movements examined here has a unique origin. Seventh-day Adventism, for example, emerged in response to millennial expectations that originated with William Miller and spread to become the Millerite movement, found a charismatic leader in Ellen G. White (1827–1915), and incorporated some beliefs and practices of mainstream Protestantism alongside religious innovations into its theology. Mormonism, too, clearly a religious movement founded by a charismatic leader, Joseph Smith Jr. (1805–1844), integrated both novel beliefs and elements of established Christianity. The Family International grew from the prophecies of David Berg (1919–1994), and Wicca was birthed in the writings of Gerald Gardner (1884–1964). All emerged in tension with dominant religious and other institutions, and although each of these movements incorporates a binary definition of gender (though this is more complex in Wicca), tension with the wider social context may have encouraged the movements to define women's position in a way that was at variance with definitions provided by dominant institutions.

In the space created by the new religion's break from tradition, Max Weber saw opportunities for women. In an insight he never fully elaborated, Weber noted that "the religion of the disprivileged classes . . . is characterized by a tendency to allot equality to women."[29] The sociologist Meredith B. McGuire explains that new religions "are more amenable to alternative gender roles because they are based on alternative sources of authority. . . . not bound by tradition."[30] Max Weber's theory of religion of the nonprivileged classes notes allotment of equality to women in a new religion's early years as an outgrowth of charismatic leadership that is not bound by rules. Charismatic religious leadership generates alternative ideas and fosters new rituals. A new religion most often promotes distinctive beliefs and practices—belief in a living prophet; a claim to access to the divine; unusual teachings, rituals, symbols; unique access to truth—as it emerges. These serve to set the new religion apart from other religions and from the larger society (established religions being seen as less distinct from the wider society by the new religion, and rendered suspicious by their proximity to it). Thus, the distinction of a new religion is defined in reference to its social context and by the religious movement's perception of that social context, and will change over time.

Analysis of gender in new religions is complicated because as a new religion's relationship with its social context shifts, so may its definition of appropriate gender roles. No generalization regarding gender will be true for all new religions at all times. Not only do new religions change over time, they are too numerous to enumerate, highly varied in their origins and characteristics, and dynamic. Gender resides, is contested, and evolves in this mix. Some new religions "focus on gender roles but generally reassert traditional rather than new ones. . . . The Jesus People, neo-Pentecostal movements, evangelicalism, Hare Krishna (International Society for Krishna Consciousness), and the Unification Church (of Reverend Moon) define women's roles very conservatively."[31] The sociologist Janet Jacobs points to women's experiences of "attachment, rejection, sexual exploitation, and violence" in her studies of new religions, and men's experiences "jockeying for positions of power, access to women, and ideological differences with the religious leadership."[32] The sociologist Elizabeth Puttick found that in the Osho movement, Bhagwan Shree Rajneesh (later known as Osho) discouraged feminism, encouraged submissiveness in both male and female followers, and sought sexual submission from female followers. At the same time, he asserted that women's natural passivity provided them a spiritual advantage, and placed women in positions of leadership within the movement.[33] Thus, even in one new religion at one time, gender is complex. In spite of this complication and variation—perhaps because of these—new religions may illuminate patterns of gender in religion.

A new religion is ordinarily most distinct as it emerges—when the charismatic leader heads the movement or directly following schism or importation. Distinction is sharpened, during this period, in a variety of ways. Not only is the movement differentiated by its unique beliefs or its adherence to the prophecies of the charismatic leader, but practices and rituals emerge from these that further its distinction from the larger society. Most critically, the new religion claims unique access to truth. The larger society, "the world," and other religions are perceived to some extent as lacking complete truth. The new religion cultivates a sense of peculiarity that grows from the belief that followers have exclusive access to the truth: it is not strange to be distinctive if difference embodies what believers have that others do not. New religions may incorporate a variety of strategies to set themselves apart from the social context, including different dress, diet, and vocabulary; rejecting and/or withdrawing from the secular economic system; rejecting political symbols and refusing to participate in the state's political process; and creating different sexual and marital norms and new family forms. Gender, which pervades ideas about dress, language, work, politics, sexuality, and family, is perhaps the most potent potential symbolic marker of identity for the new religion. And because gender can crosscut every aspect of life, to do gender differently is to potentially do everything differently.

Weber asserted that charismatic authority, which exists in a state of *originating*, is inherently unstable, and that if a new religion is to survive it must move from charismatic (not bound by rules, breaking from established patterns) to bureaucratic (rule-bound) authority and leadership.[34] To persist, according to sociologists, religions must establish institutions and patterns for doing such things as socializing children, recruiting and training converts, codifying and enforcing rules, expelling dissidents, accumulating and transferring property, and training and credentialing leaders.

The sociologists Thomas F. O'Dea and J. Milton Yinger call this move from the "insights of founders" to establishing bureaucracy the most necessary but most perilous transition for a religion.[35] Moreover, religious movements gain a sense of urgency and identity through distinction, but too great a distinction can make it difficult for a new religion to retain members, especially children born into the movement who have not made the personal sacrifice that their parents made by choosing to join it. If a religion is *too different* from its sociocultural context it will also face difficulty in attracting and retaining recruits. Religions must avoid distinguishing themselves out of existence by adhering to beliefs and practices so offensive and threatening to outsiders that they render the movement a pariah. Still, via routinization and institutionalization the religion may gain what is necessary to continue, but lose sight of its original message and enthusiasm. Weber asserted that increased opportunities for women

> only in very rare cases . . . continue beyond the first stage of a religious community's formation, when the pneumatic manifestations of charisma are valued as hallmarks of a specifically religious exaltation. Thereafter, as routinization and regimentation of community relationships set in, a

reaction takes place against pneumatic manifestations among women, which come to be regarded as dishonorable and morbid.[36]

McGuire elaborates, observing that in new religions, as the "emphasis on charisma fades and the movement becomes established," as new religions become more "formalized and bureaucratic,"[37] opportunities allotted to women generally decline. Women's authority may be increasingly seen as inappropriate, most especially if their authority and leadership are seen as inappropriate in the wider society.[38] "Religious movements have historically returned to traditional, hierarchal, or bureaucratic forms of authority as they become settled—and in so doing have reverted to less innovative and more submissive roles for women."[39]

It is important to note that the process of developing bureaucracy, while critical to a religious movement's long-term survival, does not preclude some level of religious distinction being maintained by the movement. Yinger conceptualized the "established sect" as a new religion, especially a schismatic one, that has developed qualities of established religions, such as a trained ministry, but also has retained distinction from the larger society for several generations.[40] Stark and Bainbridge draw from the sociologist Benton Johnson to note that new religions may "disagree" with society about "proper beliefs, norms, and behavior" and thus experience a degree of "tension" with the "surrounding sociocultural [environment]."[41] Bryan Wilson asserts that the bureaucracies that new religions create may potentially even be used to maintain distinction to the extent that they promote the group's unique identity, norms, beliefs, and practices.[42] In short, the development of bureaucracy, necessary for new religions to survive over generations, consolidates decision making and thereby may lead the religion to accommodate to and become aligned with the wider society, but it does not portend that end, and may even be used to align the religion with its sociocultural context in some ways while signaling distinction in others. This maintenance of distinction even after routinization occurs may be connected, as we will see, with ideas about appropriate roles for women that are more conservative than those adopted in the religion's early decades. Though women are allotted greater equality in the movement's initial form, routinization often sees limitations of opportunities for women, but these are generally perceived, after they are adopted, as normal, as the way that things have always been for women in the religion.

Jackson Carroll, professor emeritus of religion and society, and his coauthors the sociologists Barbara Hargrove and Adair Lummis note that not all religions seek to maintain distance from the society, that some mature into religions *not* at odds with their social-historical context. These religions are generally consistent with Bromley and Melton's "dominant" religious traditions, which they see as *"constitutive of,* rather than *accommodated to,* the dominant institutional structure."[43] Consistent with this notion that these religious traditions may help constitute the dominant institutional structure, Carroll, Hargrove, and Lummis assert that when a religion "no longer must seek respectability, when its boundaries blur into the general social structure," it may "now tolerate mildly prophetic expressions of social conscience, and attempt to lead rather than adapt to the larger society."[44] Indeed, Carroll, Hargrove, and Lummis assert that development of the religious movement into a well-established denomination may provide the religion freedom to once again allow women leadership opportunities.

As Weber noted, movement away from dependence on charismatic leadership and toward routinization is often accompanied by a decline in opportunities for women. Carroll, Hargrove, and Lummis help explain this initial limitation, noting that to the extent that the children of the movement's founders become invested in norms of the wider society, they may restrict opportunities for women in a way that is in keeping with social norms: "If adherents of the movement become active participants in the status system of the wider society, organization and respectability become important goals; and the role definitions of the society at large become the natural order to which the group would grant religious legitimacy."[45] But as a religion continues to develop, it may gain the confidence to challenge social norms from a position of maturity. No longer compelled by the uncertainty of a less mature religious movement, established religions may dispute social restrictions of gender and create conditions that allow women to emerge as visible leaders. Whereas a new religion is likely to allot opportunities to women in an effort to *distinguish* itself from its social context, however, a mature religion is likely to allot women authority in order to attempt to *influence* the larger society. Even in a patriarchal society, established religions may attempt to lead the society toward greater equality—of gender, race, and sexuality—as in the Episcopalian, Unitarian Universalist, and other traditions.

Here again, gender is critical to our understanding of new religions. Audre Lorde (1934–1992) and other feminist theorists note that in binary cultural constructs, as when gender is constructed as a male/female dichotomy, one side of the binary is defined as normative and subsequently valued more, while the other is defined as nonnormative and devalued.[46] Simone de Beauvoir (1908–1986) wrote that one is not born a woman, but becomes a woman.[47] The processes involved in being made a woman—objectification and sexualization, for example—reinforce social and individual conceptualization of male/man as normative and female/woman as "other." Religion, which seeks to answer questions of ultimate meaning, imbues doctrine, ritual, and practice with strands of ideas about gender. These may complexly incorporate components of the larger cultural systems of meaning into new combinations, and integrate new ideas or practices. Although masculinity is also socially constructed, because it is so deeply culturally ingrained as normative, valued, and fixed, it is less often a contested category. New religions, whose origins are premised on access to complete truth, use gender, most especially and most consistently definitions of femininity and prescription of women's roles, to define themselves, to demonstrate their difference, and to display their truth.

Just as new religions change over time, though, so too does the sociocultural context in which they exist. Not only are new religions in flux in regard to their creation of structures for survival and the ways they define and represent themselves to the world, but also "the world"—their sociocultural context—shifts around them. The sociocultural context evolves in regard to its plurality, politics, economy, social mores and norms, and the like. A new religion defines itself vis-à-vis its sociocultural context, and so faces constantly shifting boundaries, both from within and without. Its struggle is to maintain enough distinction to allow members a sense of discrete identity and the rewards that come from participating in a clearly defined religious community—such as heightened commitment, a strong sense of community and belonging, greater certainty regarding questions of ultimate meaning, and enhanced spiritual rewards—without making costs of participation so great as to deter significant numbers of potential recruits, or to cause members or those born into the movement to fall away. Gender, especially the definition of women and femininity, is crucial to sociocultural context and change, and remains a critical site for definition of difference as well as efforts at alignment with the larger society for new religions as they attempt to negotiate boundaries over time. Furthermore, as McGuire notes, religious histories are full of a variety of diverse raw materials, allowing religious movements to remember and rethink history in a manner in keeping with changed definitions of gender over time—a phenomenon that is imperative for understanding the evolution of gender ideals in Mormonism and Seventh-day Adventism.[48] Though history is cited by official religious sources as evidence of continuity and consistency, like gender, it is contested, and helps a religious movement form a sense of identity and formulate its place as bearer of truth.

Gender is vital both to religious movements as they originate and evolve in defining truth and establishing and maintaining identity, and in social scientists' attempt to make sense of religions and religious phenomena.

1

Mormonism

Gendering the Heavens

Origin of Mormonism

Nineteenth-century America saw the birth of numerous religions—the Christian Science of Mary Baker Eddy (1821–1910); the Oneida Community of John Humphrey Noyes (1811–1886); the Bible Student movement (from which the Jehovah's Witnesses later emerged) of Charles Taze Russell (1852–1916); the Church of Jesus Christ of Latter-day Saints, commonly called the Mormons; and the Seventh-day Adventists. The Mormons and the Adventists, two of the most successful religions to emerge from nineteenth-century America, at least in terms of number of adherents, were born from prophetic visions dated to the 1820s and 1840s.[1] Each was led by a young, apparently unlikely prophet, had a millennial message—meaning that they expected Jesus Christ to come to earth soon—and provided female members with leadership and other opportunities denied them in the wider society at the time. The first of these to emerge, Mormonism, was born in western New York when a young man named Joseph Smith Jr. (1805–1844)—after being visited by God, Jesus, and an angel—translated golden plates containing a record of an ancient civilization that had once lived in the Americas into a book of scripture: the Book of Mormon. The other, Seventh-day Adventism, coalesced under the guidance of a seventeen-year-old girl of frail health—Ellen Gould Harmon White (1827–1915)—who experienced a lifetime of religious trances, visions, and dreams.

At first glance neither Joseph Smith nor Ellen White seems a likely charismatic founder of a large and long-lasting new religion. Joseph Smith was the fourth child of Joseph Smith Sr. (1771–1840) and Lucy Mack Smith (1775–1856), who by all accounts were hardscrabble farmers in Vermont and later western New York. Following their marriage in 1796, Lucy and Joseph farmed the rocky hills of Vermont, moving often, and never managing to get very far ahead of their debt. After snow fell in June 1816, they abandoned Vermont for Palmyra, New York, where they opened and operated a small shop.[2] By 1818, having saved some money, the Smiths purchased one hundred acres of woodland between Palmyra and Farmington, on which they eventually began to build a wood-frame house.[3] They fell behind in their payments, though, and by 1825 were forced to sell the farm and continue on as tenants on the land that they formerly owned.[4]

For Joseph, place was significant. As it would be for Ellen White, the locale of his childhood was critical in exposing him to religious ideas that would help set Joseph on a path to prophetic leadership. Western New York was rich with religious revival in the 1820s: the Second Great Awakening was spurred by the enthusiastic preaching of Charles Grandison Finney (1792–1875); several Shaker communities and a band of followers of Jemima Wilkinson (1752–1819) could be found in western New York at the time;[5] and the number of Presbyterians nearly doubled between 1816 and 1817 in the same area.[6]

In this context Joseph Smith received a divine visitation. There is some variation in Smith's written accounts of his first vision.[7] The version of events accepted by most Mormons as authoritative is provided in his "history" that he began dictating in the late 1830s. In it, Smith describes himself as a teenager consumed by religious questions. His mother began attending a Presbyterian meetinghouse after the family moved to Palmyra, but out of loyalty to his father, who was religious but did not attend church, Joseph also chose not to attend. Family disagreements about worship were accentuated, according to Smith's account of his life, by contention among the churches in Palmyra.

Smith describes himself as a fourteen-year-old boy who retired to the woods near his home in the spring of 1820 to pray for religious guidance, and thereupon received a vision. "Two personages," God the father and Jesus Christ, stood above him in the air.[8] These personages were corporeal, with human-like bodies. God, gesturing to Jesus, said, "This is my beloved son. Hear him."[9] Smith was informed that no existing church was true, and that he should join none. According to his account, an angel named Moroni appeared to Joseph when he was seventeen, told him that his sins were forgiven, and informed him of records written on "plates of gold" along with an instrument to be used in their translation consisting of "two transparent stones attached like eyeglasses to a breastplate."[10] These gold plates, Joseph was told, contained the history of ancient inhabitants of the Americas and were buried near his home. The angel quoted Bible verses about the end of days, and ascended in a conduit of light until Joseph could no longer see him. Joseph's account describes two more similar visits by Moroni that same night, and one the next morning, in which the angel repeated what he had said, and added that a great judgment was coming, and that Satan would tempt Joseph.[11] When Joseph went to the Hill Cumorah and attempted to retrieve the plates after the vision, he describes himself reaching out to take the plates and being shocked; he was unable to obtain them. He was told that his desire to use the plates for his own monetary gain prevented him from being able to take them. He would have to wait.

Mormonism's detractors—and, more recently, some Latter-day Saint (LDS) historians—have attended to Smith's time spent searching for buried treasure around the same time that he was led to the gold plates. Court records indicate that Smith was hired to search for buried treasure in western New York, where Native American burials, containing what would have been perceived as treasure, dotted the landscape. Smith is also described in numerous historical accounts using seer stones, a practice not uncommon at a time when divining rods and dreams were also thought to lead people to things they wished to find.[12]

In 1825, after hearing of Joseph's abilities, Josiah Stowell (1770–1844) hired Joseph to locate an abandoned Spanish silver mine he believed to be hidden on his land, and the following year Stowell's neighbor swore in a warrant for Joseph's arrest that he was a disorderly person. Under oath Joseph acknowledged having used a seer stone to locate coins and lost property.[13] Joseph never found the silver mine, but he met Emma Hale (1804–1879), whose father, Isaac, helped subsidize the search on Stowell's land. Joseph was smitten with Emma, and over objections from her father (who seems never to have fully trusted Joseph), married her in January 1827. On 22 September of the same year Joseph took Emma with him on a carriage ride to the Hill Cumorah, where he left her at the carriage and returned with a cloth-draped box in which, he told her, lay the gold plates. The contents of that box changed the lives of Emma and Joseph, as well as millions of others.

After moving to Harmony, New York, where Emma's father provided them with a cabin, Joseph commenced a process of translating the plates with a series of scribes, including Emma as well as Martin Harris (1783–1875), a local farmer.[14] When Harris's wife, who resented her husband's financial support of the young prophet, repeatedly questioned the enterprise, Smith reluctantly agreed to allow Harris to take 116 pages that had been translated to show his wife as evidence of the veracity of the book. The pages were lost. Smith—convinced that if he provided a new translation of the same section, an altered version of the lost pages might be presented in an attempt to prove him a fraud—was divinely admonished, and instructed to commence translation of a different part of the plates.

The stories that emerged from Smith's translation of the plates told of a family that left the Middle East and traveled by boat to the Americas in approximately 600 BCE. The family was led by a patriarch, Lehi, and eventually split into two groups: the Nephites, descendants or associates of Lehi's righteous sons, Nephi and Samuel; and the Lamanites, descendants of Lehi's less-righteous sons, Laman and Lemuel.[15] The translation, eventually published as the Book of Mormon, provides an account in which the two groups are often at war. It is a cyclical narrative of the groups in which, variously, the Nephites and Lamanites live according to God's dictates, are righteous, and are consequently blessed, only to become vain and sinful in the riches of God's abundance. There is then a fall and suffering, after which, chastened, the people repent and return to righteousness, only to see the cycle begin anew. The Book of Mormon—filled with accounts of massive battles, secret criminal gangs, a visit by Jesus to the Americas, and other epic events—provided a new book of scripture, and attracted followers to Smith after it was published in 1830.

Though the original membership of the church when it was organized on 6 April 1830 consisted of Smith's family members and close associates, membership quickly grew. A critical component for the new religion was restoration of the priesthood, something that Smith told his followers had been lost in other religions as Christianity went astray. An angel conferred the priesthood—the "keys," the authority to act in the name of God on earth, and the power, therefore, to perform religious rituals such as baptisms and marriages—on Smith and Oliver Cowdery

(1806–1850), who would serve as second elder in the church upon its organization, and the two baptized each other on 15 May 1829.[16] By the 1830s, with the priesthood conferred on virtually all men in the church, Smith sent some priesthood holders out as missionaries, a practice that has never ceased.

In 1830, as Mormons in New York faced resistance from their neighbors, Smith received a revelation telling him to relocate the church to Kirtland, Ohio. Thus began a period of religious resettlement accompanied by intense growth in members concentrated first in Kirtland and, later, Far West, Missouri, and Nauvoo, Illinois. As converts joined the church—soon from as far away as Europe—they were encouraged to sell their belongings and migrate to one of the burgeoning Mormon settlements. In Kirtland some Latter-day Saints began to purchase land and build businesses and farms. Most significantly, within two weeks of arriving in Kirtland, Smith declared a revelation, the Law of Consecration, which encouraged members to voluntarily deed (consecrate) their property to the church. After members gave all of their belongings to the church, leaders would return to each family what was needed, and then use the rest for maintenance of the church and for distribution to the poor within the church. In addition, each family was to turn over whatever surplus they had at the end of the year to the church's storehouses, from which church leaders made distributions.[17] In June 1831, just as he was helping to establish Kirtland, Smith and a small group of followers traveled to Independence, Missouri. Smith declared that a temple would be built there, and instructed followers to begin buying land, which they did.

Rapid growth of these Mormon settlements disquieted their neighbors. The new religion preached a soon-coming Jesus, practiced a form of religious socialism, and was growing quickly, and buying up land as it did. As more and more Mormons flocked to Mormon settlements, land prices increased and neighboring communities began to fear that if Mormons voted as a block they could dictate the outcomes of local elections. Tensions boiled over into violence as non-Mormons near various settlements burned Mormon property and robbed Mormons, following an 1838 order signed by the Missouri governor Lilburn Boggs (1796–1860) calling for Mormons to be "exterminated or driven from the State if necessary for the public peace."[18]

In the August 1838 election, Mormons attempted for the first time in five years to vote in the village of Gallatin, and Missourians tried to stop them. Angry words were exchanged, a fight broke out, and some Mormon men, who happened to be standing near a pile of lumber, picked up pieces and used them as weapons. The Mormons prevailed in the fight, but a warrant for Smith's arrest was issued. In an especially tragic incident, non-Mormons attacked Mormon residents of Haun's Mill. Under siege, most of the town's men sought refuge in the blacksmith shop, the widely spaced logs of which provided no protection from bullets. Seventeen of those in the blacksmith shop, including some young boys and elderly men, were shot and killed.

The history of violence against the Mormons is one in which Latter-day Saints were dragged from their homes, stripped, tarred and feathered, and driven from the communities they had built through exhausting work; but it is also one in which the Mormons regrouped each time they were displaced and, even after Smith was killed in 1844 and Mormons decided to settle outside the then-contiguous states, Mormons resisted. In Nauvoo Smith formed a militia, the Nauvoo Legion, with himself as lieutenant general, as well as endorsing the founding of a secret society, the Danites, for protection. Smith even ran for president of the United States in 1844. Nonetheless, Mormon settlers were dogged by violence until Smith's assassination that year on 27 June by a mob and the group's subsequent retreat two years later to the valley of the Great Salt Lake.

One of the issues that inspired the antipathy of outsiders was the rumored practice of Mormon men marrying multiple women. Although publicly Smith and other church leaders adamantly denied their practice of polygamy until well after Smith's death, historical evidence indicates that Smith was practicing polygamy by the 1830s. Though originally Smith did not tell most other church leaders of the practice, by 1837 Oliver Cowdery suspected Smith of having an affair with Fanny Alger (1816–1889), a teenage servant in his home. Smith denied having committed adultery, but never denied a relationship with Fanny.[19] The historians Fawn M. Brodie and Todd Compton note that Smith's early polygamous relationships were informal, but that they eventually became more elaborate. In Nauvoo Smith developed complex temple marriage ceremonies in which initiates were ceremonially washed, anointed with oil by someone of the same sex, and dressed in a sacred garment; swore an oath of secrecy; watched a dramatic enactment depicting the creation of the earth and Adam and Eve's expulsion from the Garden of Eden; received their endowments; and were told their heavenly sacred names (husbands learned their wives' names so they could call them into heaven, but a woman knew only her own), and the words and gestures they would need to know in order to be admitted to heaven.

Smith's revelations laid out a new understanding of heaven as including three levels, or kingdoms, to which nearly everyone would be admitted. The highest of these, the Celestial Kingdom, was reserved for those who were baptized and followed the tenets of the church, including participation in temple ordinances. Moreover, Smith taught that "sealing" ordinances (religious rituals) performed by priesthood holders in temples would withstand death. Marriage did not end with death, but could last through eternity if performed in a temple. Thus men and women needed each other to attain the highest level of salvation in Mormon cosmology, and if they did so, following death men would become gods and women goddesses.

As Smith unfolded the new vision of temples, eternal ordinances, families, and divinity, he also hesitantly and selectively began to reveal his doctrine of plural marriage. In 1841 Smith told his twelve apostles about the practice, and "they began marrying other women soon after."[20] About a third of the women that Smith married were married to other men already, and Compton provides evidence that eleven of those Smith married were teenagers.[21] Compton also finds other patterns in Smith's later marriages: the women Smith approached were sworn to secrecy; they were initially shocked and sometimes repulsed by Smith's proposal of marriage; potential wives viewed Smith as a prophet; Smith told prospective wives that through revelation God had commanded them to marry him; plural wives were never publicly acknowledged as wives; Smith had sexual relationships with most of his wives; Smith's plural wives lived in isolation, sometimes finding emotional support in friendships with Smith's other wives (their sister wives); and most of Smith's wives married other LDS leaders following his death.[22] (As Smith was sealed to his plural wives in ceremonies in homes or temples, he understood them as eternal marriages, though several ended without fanfare.)

Emma never accepted Joseph's plural marriages, and was jealous of Smith's relationships with other women when she knew of them. She kicked Fanny Alger out of their home when she became suspicious of her husband's attention to the teenager, and "sometimes sought to separate Joseph from his plural wives."[23] In response to Emma's hatred of the practice, Smith received a revelation on plural marriage, which he wrote down at the urging of his bother Hyrum (1800–1844) in 1843: "If any man espouse a virgin, and desire to espouse another, and the first give her consent, and if he espouse the second, and they are virgins, and have vowed to no other man, then he is justified; he cannot commit adultery for they are given unto him."[24] The revelation called Emma by name and threatened her with destruction if she did "not abide this commandment."[25] When Hyrum shared the revelation with Emma she abused him as, he claimed, he had "never been . . . abused by a woman," and when Joseph brought the revelation to her again, she put it into the fireplace, where she lit it and watched it burn. After Emma burned the revelation—a "purely symbolic victory," as Joseph had copied it beforehand—Emma ceased "badgering" and "threatening" Joseph, and Joseph never again discussed plural marriage in her presence.[26]

The Mormon women's organization—the Relief Society—was created about the same time that Joseph began to reveal plural marriage to close confidants, including his wife and some church leaders. Sarah Granger Kimball (1818–1898) had initiated a Ladies' Society in Nauvoo in the early 1840s to undertake charitable work. When the group's bylaws and constitution, written by Eliza R. Snow (1804–1887), were presented for Joseph's approval, he called them the "best he had ever seen," but told the women that he had something more important for them, an organization of women "under the priesthood after the pattern of the priesthood."[27] As with the priesthood, the Relief Society was led by a president with two counselors (advisors and assistants to the president, the common leadership model in Mormonism). Emma was unanimously elected president by women at the initial meeting in March 1842, and she selected Sarah M. Cleveland (1788–1856) and Elizabeth Ann Whitney (1800–1882) as her two counselors, and Eliza Snow (who would be married to Joseph by June of that year) as secretary. John Taylor (1808–1887) ordained the counselors. Relief Society minutes of the meeting record Smith saying, "I now turn the key to you in the name of God and this society shall rejoice and knowledge and intelligence shall flow down from this time."[28] The significance of this language is important for women's role in Mormonism, as Mormon feminist scholars such as Linda King Newell, Maxine Hanks,[29] Maureen Ursenbach Beecher, and Lavina Fielding Anderson[30] see in it evidence that women had access to priesthood authority. It is important to note that women in the Relief Society began to participate in many of the religious rituals that before that time had been restricted to priesthood holders—men—such as consecrating believers with sacred oil, healing via the laying on of hands, and speaking in tongues.[31]

Religious leaders of the Second Great Awakening allowed women to participate publicly in religious prayers and worship, and in the nineteenth century women's clubs, charitable groups, and evangelistic societies, such as the Woman's Missionary Union, became more common, but the Mormon Relief Society conveyed exceptional religious authority to women. Joseph Smith told the members of the newly formed Relief Society in the spring of 1842 that he would "make of this Society a 'kingdom of priests' as in Enoch's day—as in Paul's day."[32] Later that spring, as polygamous marriages continued and Smith took additional wives, he began secretly instructing a select group of nine men in the "principles and order of the priesthood"; soon afterwards women and men began to be sealed in temple rituals that were to bind marriages beyond death, and women were trained in and performed temple washing and anointing rituals for women as part of the process.[33] In addition, female temple workers performed washing and anointing healing rituals in the temple, and "performed these ordinances outside the temple for the same purposes."[34]

The historian Linda King Newell documents numerous instances of early Mormon women washing, anointing, and laying hands on the sick for healing, rituals the contemporary church reserves for male priesthood holders, and argues that the Relief Society—until the 1970s a mostly autonomous women's organization—was critical to Mormon women's religious participation. Indeed, unlike contemporary Mormon women, countless early Mormon women shared the gifts of the Spirit, not only administering to the sick and speaking in tongues, but sealing blessings and conferring blessings on their children by laying on of hands with their husbands. Nineteenth-century discussions in church publications—including the *Woman's Exponent*, an independent Mormon women's periodical published from 1872 to 1914—focus attention on whether women's performance of these ordinances was proper (most authors agreed it was) and fell under the purview of the priesthood (most asserted that women performed ordinances as members of the church, often in conjunction with their husbands as priesthood holders). The *Young Woman's Journal*, published between 1889 and 1929, in 1896 stated a belief "common" among church members that a "missionary wife 'bears the priesthood of the Seventy, in connection with her husband, and shares in its responsibilities more closely and effectively than any other office of the priesthood entails upon womankind.'"[35] The historian D. Michael Quinn insists that Mormon women performed these healing rituals "by virtue of the priesthood they held,"[36] while others, most notably the historian Richard Bushman, claim that Mormon women never held the priesthood, and had access to its powers only through men.[37] This point, critical to contemporary Mormons in defining the propriety of women's roles today, is less important than the historical documentation of women's active participation in gifts of the Spirit in the early church to a degree and in a manner that was clearly not available to Mormon women by the middle of the twentieth century.

Mormon women in the church's early decades performed religious rituals, controlled an autonomous women's organization, oversaw the publication of periodicals (for which they wrote and which they edited), and participated in temples. Some of them also participated in plural marriages with church leaders. We will probably never know for certain how many wives Smith married. Brodie places the number near fifty; more recently, Compton documents more than thirty marriages. By the time of Smith's death, up to twenty-nine other church leaders had also taken "at least one additional wife under his direction."[38]

By the summer of 1843, rumors of Smith's polygamy were spreading in Nauvoo. Smith and other church leaders denied the practice (some of them did not know of it) and excommunicated those caught publicly teaching or practicing plural marriage. The issue came to a head when Smith's trusted associate, William Law (1809–1892), who had served as Smith's second counselor, learned that Smith had approached his wife, Jane, with an offer of marriage. Law had been unhappy with what he saw as Smith's financial mismanagement and abuse of power, and he approached Smith to ask him to repent. Law was an idealist who believed in Smith's message and thought that Smith could be corrected and the church set back on its correct path.

Unable to elicit any acknowledgment of wrongdoing from Smith, Law printed an editorial in the first (and only) issue, dated 7 June 1844, of the *Nauvoo Expositor*, a publication he created with other disaffected Mormons, describing a hypothetical case of a young convert coming to Nauvoo only to be approached by a church elder with a proposal of plural marriage. Though the editorial also criticized church leaders' financial decisions and abuse of power, the charges of polygamy—given church leaders' long public denial of the practice—were most damning.[39] The Nauvoo city council passed an ordinance calling the *Expositor* a public nuisance, and Smith ordered it destroyed. The city marshal and a mob carried out the order, after which a Carthage, Illinois, grand jury indicted Smith for inciting a riot.[40] Though a Nauvoo court dismissed the count, in the turmoil following destruction of the press Smith declared martial law, an act that resulted in a charge of treason.

Smith initially considered fleeing, but eventually turned himself in. Although he feared (and eventually seemed resigned to the idea) that his incarceration meant death, Smith—with his brother Hyrum and a few other church leaders—surrendered. Some of the members of the group were released on bail, but Joseph, Hyrum, Willard Richards (1804–1854), and John Taylor (1808–1887) were in jail in Carthage when, in spite of personal assurances from the Illinois governor, members of a mob, faces painted black, attacked the second-floor cell in which the four were held, shot and killed Hyrum, and shot Joseph. Joseph fell out of a window, held onto the window ledge for a few moments, and fell to his death.

After a struggle and religious split over the question of successorship, the group that would eventually become the contemporary Church of Jesus Christ of Latter-day Saints accepted Brigham Young (1801–1877) as its new prophet and, in 1846 and 1847, began traveling in companies of wagons and handcarts under Young's leadership to what would become the Utah Territory. There, after the public announcement of the practice in 1852 by Orson Pratt (1811–1881), a member of the Quorum of Twelve Apostles, polygamy was practiced openly.

Mormon women's religious participation extended to arenas and activities reserved in established churches for men, but opportunities for women did not end there. In the early decades of Mormonism, the Relief Society was essential to development of women's skills and influence— for example, through publication of an independent journal, and autonomy in financial matters—and Mormon women perceived their influence as being in tandem with men in spiritual matters.[41] In fact, Mormon women, especially after westward migration, were encouraged to engage in a variety of activities. Mormon women were encouraged by church leaders to attain college and postcollegiate education; to train to become teachers, lawyers, and doctors; to work outside their homes as well as within them; and to vote.

Although the campaign to enact suffrage in Utah was initiated by "anti-polygamy forces" that believed that giving Mormon women the vote would end polygamy,[42] leaders of the Relief Society staunchly promoted suffrage, and Susan B. Anthony (1820–1906) made several excursions to the territory to work with Mormon women. The Utah territorial assembly voted unanimously to extend suffrage to women in 1870 (shortly after the Wyoming Territory enfranchised women), and both Mormon church leaders and the Relief Society leadership supported the move.[43] In contrast, the Nineteenth Amendment enfranchising American women was not formally introduced until 1878, and was not ratified until 1920. When national leaders saw that voting Mormon women did not use their vote to end polygamy, Congress repealed women's suffrage in Utah in 1887 as part of the Edmunds-Tucker Act. In response, a Utah branch of the National Woman Suffrage Association was formed in 1889, and Mormon women, many working in conjunction with their local Relief Society, coordinated to fight for suffrage, a cause enthusiastically advocated by the *Woman's Exponent*, a publication closely tied to the Relief Society. Suffrage was eventually ratified in Utah in 1895, after polygamy was repealed in 1890.[44]

More broadly, the *Woman's Exponent* reprinted articles from secular publications, informed Mormon women about national affairs, and promoted gender equity in a variety of arenas—publishing articles in support of expanded educational opportunities, improved working conditions in American sweatshops, and equal pay and opportunities for women.[45] Indeed, the *Exponent* sometimes used language not dissimilar from that of second-wave feminists almost a century later.[46] The journal's second editor, Emmeline B. Wells (1828–1921), for example, wrote,

"Let [woman] have the same opportunities for an education, observation, and experience in public and private for a succession of years, and then see if she is not equally endowed with man and prepared to bear her part on all general questions socially, politically, industrially, and educationally as well as spiritually."[47]

A similar emphasis on women's participation in activities in addition to those of the domestic sphere (wifehood and motherhood) was advocated by Mormonism's primary official periodicals, including *The Improvement Era* (1897–1970).[48] These publications represent a primary link between church leaders and members, and carry leaders' instructions to members (including in biannual issues that include the General Conference talks of Mormon leaders). Nineteenth-century American law, grounded in the English common law principle of coverture, subsumed a married woman's legal position under her husband's in a way that denied women equal property, divorce, employment, custody, or other rights. In a sociocultural context still influenced by what historians call "the Cult of True Womanhood," the *Era* offered an expanded definition of appropriate activities for women.

Although the Cult of True Womanhood represented an ideal not available to all women, especially not to women of color, immigrant women, and poor women, its ideals—promulgated in the pews of many established religions, in books and popular periodicals, and in formal education and socialization—had enormous cultural influence.[49] Gender ideals advanced the idea that men were primarily responsible for activities in the public sphere—in the economy, in politics, and in religious leadership—and women should be confined to and responsible for the private, domestic sphere, their work there necessary for the well-being of society. Women were to preserve the home as a haven, and to remain within it educating their children in Christianity and exercising a subtle Christianizing influence over their husbands, protected in their isolation from the corrupting influences of politics, paid work, and other arenas thought to be rife with vice.[50] The sociologist Christine E. Bose finds that the ideal of gendered spheres influenced women's labor force participation in the nineteenth and early twentieth centuries.[51] Even as colleges and universities opened their doors to women in the nineteenth century, first at Oberlin College in 1833, and more broadly by the late nineteenth century, female students were often expected to perform domestic work for male students, and faced resistance and hostility.[52]

In this context the *Era* instructed Mormon women that "there is no limit prescribed as to the subjects that [women] shall consider. The whole world[s] of science, religion, philosophy, politics, history, art, and literature are open to them, and they may wander in these limitless fields of knowledge when and how and to what extent they choose."[53] The *Era* credited Joseph Smith's founding of Mormonism with ushering in important advancements for women, including participation in religious leadership, formal education, and professional work. Susa Young Gates (1856–1933), a writer, editor, women's rights advocate,[54] and daughter of Brigham Young and his twenty-second wife, Lucy Bigelow (1830–1905), insisted in 1907 that "it would be impossible to find on the earth a community where women as a class are more independent in thought, word and action than Utah."[55] Mormon women, she asserted, studied and taught equally with men, "acted in nearly every civil [political] capacity," and, "from the organization of the Church to the present day, equal religious franchise is given to the man and to the woman." "The girls of the Church," she wrote, "have imbibed the modern monetary independence, and thousands of them are typewriters, clerks, artists, and school teachers. Some are doctors." And girls could succeed in professional endeavors as they were provided opportunities to prepare for them: for Mormons, in formal education there was, Gates claimed, "no distinction . . . made on sex lines."[56]

Reshaping Gender in the Twentieth and Early Twenty-First Centuries

In the twentieth century, especially after the Second World War (1939–1945), the propriety of Mormon women's participation in economic, political, and religious leadership (particularly participation in the gifts of the Spirit) was called into question, and even by the early twentieth century, women more rarely anointed the sick or conferred blessings. During World War II, as American women generally were encouraged to enter the wage labor market in jobs normally reserved for men, Mormon women were told, for the first time in the *Era*, to restrict their activities to homemaking. Indeed, not only did women cease to participate in performing religious rituals (at least outside the temple; Mormon women continue to perform temple washing and anointing for other women), by the mid-twentieth century the church's gender ideology began to reframe women's role in the history of the movement in a way that emphasized their contributions as mothers and homemakers, to the exclusion of their participation in anointing, laying on of hands, or performing blessings, all of which came to be more explicitly defined as appropriate only for priesthood holders—men. The notion that women's first—even exclusive—priority is to be wives, mothers, and homemakers became more prominent in Mormon leaders' prescriptions for followers by the 1950s, though alternative messages about women's participation in activities outside the domestic sphere did not disappear entirely.

President David O. McKay (1873–1970) told Mormons in the late 1940s that "home is the center from which woman rules the world. . . . A married woman who refuses to have children, or who having them neglects them for pleasure or social prestige, is recreant to the highest calling and privilege of womanhood."[57] By the 1950s Mormon women were encouraged by church leaders to withdraw from paid labor and concentrate on their families, pursuits that before had not been presented as mutually exclusive for women.

When the second-wave feminist movement emerged in the early 1960s, the message of women's primary domestic obligations was only repeated more often and vociferously by church leaders, and with less ambiguity. In the 1970s, faced with a societal movement for gender equality that penetrated Mormonism,[58] Mormon leaders told women that their obligations were as wives and homemakers, and if it was possible for them to have children, as mothers. Thomas S. Monson (b. 1927), then an apostle (later president of the church), accused feminists of "deceiving" women, of "cunningly [leading] them away from their divine role of womanhood down that pathway of error."[59] "God made it clear," instructed N. Eldon Tanner (1898–1982) of the First Presidency in 1974, "that woman is very special and he has also very clearly defined her position, her duties, and her destiny in the divine plan."[60] Mormon church leaders identified the family as the foundation of society, and defined women's role within it—as wife, mother, and "helpmeet"—as critical to the success or failure of society. While Mormonism stood in sharp contrast to dominant gender ideals in the movement's early decades, by the 1970s Mormon church leaders emulated ideals of that model that were, at that time, being challenged and abandoned in the larger culture, turning away from its more gender-equal model at the same time that many in the wider society sought such a model.

Mormon opposition to women's participation in extra-domestic activities was stated most explicitly in the 1987 fireside address, "To the Mothers in Zion," by then-president Ezra Taft Benson (1899–1994), delivered during the priesthood session of the General Conference. In it Benson called "the mother's role" "God-ordained," counseled church members "not to postpone having . . . children," explained that able-bodied husbands are "expected to be the breadwinner[s]," and cited the call to "wives" by former church president Spencer W. Kimball (1895–1985) to "come home from the typewriter, the laundry, the nursing, come home from the factory, the café." According to Benson,

> No career approaches in importance that of wife, homemaker, mother—cooking meals, washing dishes, making beds for one's precious husband and children. Come home, wives, to your husbands. Make home a heaven for them. Come home, wives, to your children, born and unborn. Wrap the motherly cloak about you and, unembarrassed, help in a major role to create the bodies for the immortal souls who anxiously await.[61]

Some Mormon periodical articles allowed for exceptions to this model (such as those authored by *Ensign* associate editor Lavina Fielding Anderson in 1976), and church leaders did note that in "unusual circumstances" women might not be able to have children, or might have to work for a time to help support their families.[62] The decades that saw the burgeoning of the modern feminist movement, however, saw the phenomenon described by the journalist Susan Faludi as a "backlash"[63] among Mormon church leaders. These leaders, especially the president/prophet, his counselors, and members of the Quorum of the Twelve, are believed to have access to divine revelation, particularly when they speak in their official capacities as church leaders, as they do in semiannual General Conference addresses and in official periodicals. Church leaders in these venues were most consistent in their insistence on a narrowing of women's role to the domestic sphere.[64]

Moreover, church leaders implemented the priesthood Correlation Department beginning in the early 1970s, which brought all church auxiliaries, programs, and publications—including those formerly financially autonomous auxiliaries led by women (the Relief Society, and children's and young adult auxiliaries)—under control of the highest level of priesthood leadership.[65] Though in planning for decades, this reorganization not only streamlined religious authority—systematizing LDS publication content, doctrine, and policies, for example—it deprived Mormon women of one area of control that they had held since Joseph Smith led the church, and this occurred just as women in the society saw possibilities opening before them.[66] The journalists Robert Gottlieb and Peter Wiley argue that implementation of priesthood correlation at the time and in the manner manifested was an outgrowth of anxiety about social changes, including changes in the nuclear family, especially women's roles.[67] The sociologist Marie Cornwall calls women "innocent bystanders" of priesthood correlation, not intentional targets of the program.[68] Regardless, the consequence of the reorganization was to consolidate decision-making power and eliminate such things as women's direct control of periodical publication, religious curricular materials, and independent fund-raising. According to the historian Martha Sonntag Bradley, correlation "positioned [Mormon] women in a clearly defined place and regulated their activities according to standards and policies rather than local talents or interests. In the process, the autonomy and independence that nineteenth-century women had experienced were reined in more tightly and regulated in the name of efficiency and internationalization."[69]

Some Mormons resisted this narrowing of women's role. In the 1970s a "dozen or so matrons in the Boston area" began meeting to discuss their experiences as Mormon women and realized that, while they did not identify with the more "militant" aspects of the feminist movement, they were nonetheless "not always completely satisfied with [their] lives as housewives."[70] The group—which included some who would become prominent Mormon feminists, such as Claudia Bushman and Laurel Thatcher Ulrich—eventually published what became known as the "pink issue" of *Dialogue: A Journal of Mormon Thought* in 1971 on questions of gender equity in Mormonism. The pink issue pointed to the "formidable, intelligent, resourceful, and independent" Mormon women of the nineteenth century as precedent for expecting more diverse gender ideals in Mormonism.[71]

Modern feminism was a diverse movement that changed over time, and included some Mormons. During the second-wave feminist movement, Mormon feminists taught women's history at the LDS Institute of Religion in Cambridge, Massachusetts, in 1972 (the same year that the Catholic feminist scholar Rosemary Radford Ruether first taught feminist theology at Harvard Divinity School). In 1974 Claudia Bushman, Laurel Thatcher Ulrich, and other Cambridge Mormon feminists founded *Exponent II*, a Mormon-themed feminist quarterly magazine named for the *Woman's Exponent* (1872–1914). Elouise Bell delivered an address on feminism at Brigham Young University in 1975, and in 1976 Bushman published her edited volume *Mormon Sisters: Women in Early Utah*.[72] While church leaders have tolerated some dissent by modern Mormon feminists, they have sometimes disciplined feminists and scholars who expressed views out of keeping with contemporary church teachings or official history. None of the Boston-area Mormons involved in publishing the pink issue was excommunicated (though in 1992 Brigham Young University's board of trustees vetoed a proposal to invite the Pulitzer Prize–winning historian Laurel Thatcher Ulrich to speak at the university's annual women's conference), but in 1979, following a nationally publicized speech critical of Mormon patriarchy to the American Psychological Association, Sonia Johnson (b. 1936), cofounder of Mormons for ERA, was excommunicated.

Mormon leaders' reaction to second-wave feminism was not restricted to reactions to feminism within the church. Martha Sonntag Bradley has carefully documented lobbying efforts, use of church resources, and other efforts of Mormon church leadership to mobilize members to help defeat the proposed Equal Rights Amendment (ERA).[73] In May 1993 Boyd K. Packer, a member of the Quorum of the Twelve, called "feminists, homosexuals, and so-called intellectuals . . . a danger to the church."[74] Later that year, the Mormon church excommunicated a number of scholars, a significant portion of whose works examine the roles of nineteenth-century Mormon women. In a few weeks in September of that year, six writers and intellectuals—dubbed the September Six in the press—were either excommunicated or disfellowshipped. Feminists in the group included Lynne Kanavel Whitesides, known for her writings on the Mormon concept of a Mother in Heaven; Maxine Hanks, editor of *Women and Authority: Re-emerging Mormon Feminism* (1992); the historian D. Michael Quinn, a former Brigham Young University professor and author of "Mormon Women Have Held the Priesthood since 1843" in *Women and Authority*; and Lavina Fielding Anderson, former associate editor and writer at the *Ensign*, and coeditor of *Sisters in Spirit: Mormon Women in Historical and Cultural Perspective* (1992).

Modern official Mormon gender ideology, rooted in assertion of binary gender difference, asserts the necessity of heterosexual marriage and concomitant gender roles, and discourages gender ambiguity. As articulated in "The Family: A Proclamation to the World," a document adopted as official church policy in 1995 and which members are asked to display in their homes, contemporary Mormon church leaders call heterosexual marriage "ordained of God," and the family "central to the Creator's plan for the eternal destiny of His children." The proclamation tells Mormons that they are "command[ed]" "to multiply and replenish the earth," and "declare[s] that God has commanded that the sacred powers of procreation are to be employed only between man and woman, lawfully wedded as husband and wife." Though spouses are called "equal partners," the document instructs fathers "to preside over their families in love and righteousness," and holds them "responsible to provide the necessities of life and protection for their families." On the other hand, "mothers are primarily responsible for the nurture of their children." Gender is called an "essential characteristic of individual premortal, mortal, and eternal identity and purpose"—something fixed by God, unchanging.[75] Rooting women's and men's appropriate gender roles, the family, and social order in divinely ordained gender distinction extends Mormon interest to social policy (as in the church's opposition to the ERA), and the church was instrumental in some fights against same-sex marriage, as in its explicit support for Proposition 8 in California.[76]

Despite this, some contemporary Mormons use electronic media to consider questions raised by feminism, and to explore the boundaries of gender within church policy and individual religious expression. For example, beginning in the winter of 2012, the self-identified Mormon feminists Stephanie Lauritzen and Sandra Durkin Ford of All Enlisted used Facebook to inaugurate "Wear Pants to Church Day."[77] Although

LDS policy does not prohibit women from wearing pants to church, tradition and community practice discourage it. It is impossible to know how many LDS women have participated in the event (or men, by wearing purple ties to demonstrate support), but electronic media have been employed to promote it, and have generated significant numbers of responses, including more than two thousand "likes" and many negative comments.[78] In October 2013 more than a hundred LDS women, led by Ordainwomen.org founder Kate Kelly, sought and were denied entrance to the priesthood meeting of the semiannual General Conference.

The web—sometimes called the Bloggernacle—allows Mormon feminists to communicate, organize, share information, and provide one another support in a way never before possible: Mormon feminists post blogs, employ social media, and use pages at sites like Feminist Mormon Housewives, Young Mormon Feminists, I'm a Mormon Feminist, and Ordain Women to do things such as request clarification from church leaders regarding whether women and girls may be baptized for the dead when they are menstruating,[79] and call for the ordination of women to the LDS priesthood.[80] Ordainwomen.org, for example, makes the case publicly that barring women from the priesthood results in their "exclusion from almost all clerical, fiscal, ritual, and decision-making authority" in the church. Moreover, the group focuses attention more broadly on gender inequality in the church, pointing to the 1995 proclamation as an "antiquated and unequal model in both domestic and ecclesiastical realms." Instead, Ordainwomen.org founders seek a

> spiritual community in which women can once again offer blessings of healing and comfort, as did our 19th-century foremothers, or have their pastoral and administrative gifts fully recognized, or join their husband in blessing or baptizing their children, or lend their voices and experience to our decision-making councils, regardless of child-bearing ability or marital status.[81]

In the face of this burgeoning and readily available discussion of LDS gender policies and norms, leaders have taken some recent steps to emphasize and expand things Mormon women may do, by clarifying that women may open or close religious meetings with prayer, allowing women to pray in General Conference, and lowering the age at which

Figure 1.1. Kate Kelly, founder of Ordainwomen.org, and more than a hundred other Latter-day Saints seek entrance to the October 2013 general priesthood session of the church's semiannual General Conference. Mormon women and men came from as far away as Europe to seek entrance for women, and were told that the event is only for boys and men. Kelly was excommunicated in June 2014. Photograph by James A. Kelly.

LDS women may serve missions (see below).[82] While especially the last of these is significant—encouraging a woman to serve a mission at age nineteen suggests that she should perhaps prioritize going on a mission prior to marriage—there is no indication that more substantive reforms (to ordain LDS women, for example) will be implemented in the near term. Current calls for ordination of women were met by the church spokeswoman Jessica Moody's observation that while Mormon women and men have equal access to spiritual guidance, "faith and revelation," and prayer, the church's male-only priesthood was "established by Jesus Christ himself," and the decision not to ordain women is "not a decision to be made by those on earth."[83]

In June 2014 Kate Kelly was excommunicated, and the highest leaders in the church issued a statement reaffirming that only men may be ordained to the LDS priesthood. John Dehlin, Mormon Stories podcast host and a researcher who advocates for LGBT Mormons, faced disciplinary action at the same time. Several other, less well-known Mormons, who posted online comments exploring gender, women's place in the church, same-sex marriage, and church history and doctrine also reported being called in for questioning by their bishops, and at least some faced excommunication.[84] Nonetheless, the web allows a public conversation that is impossible to contain. Public sanction delimits acceptable dissent within the movement, and will certainly discourage some devout followers from engaging in public (especially open electronic) conversations about topics rendered volatile by church censure. Church punishment of feminists once again serves to delimit religious boundaries and, for those who are not targeted and who do not identify with targets of censure, enumerate and enhance individual and group religious identity. However, it may also increase interest in Mormon feminist websites and the issues that they raise. For example, Ordain-women.org featured around two hundred "I support ordination" profiles prior to Kelly's excommunication, and about five hundred in the weeks after, many submitted by active Mormons. Another site, Mormonfeminist.org, highlights pictures of Mormon feminists holding statements explaining why they are feminists. Such sites are proliferating in number, participants, and viewers. Kelly's excommunication may be an attempt to quash public dissent regarding church gender policies, but there is no indication that discussion of gender or women's roles in Mormonism unleashed by electronic media will be contained.

Living as a Mormon: Eternal Families, Eternal Gender

Mormon culture provides cohesive and consistent structures to support parents in religious socialization of children. Mormonism is hierarchal, with the president/prophet at the head assisted by the First Presidency (his first and second counselors), the Quorum of the Twelve Apostles, the Quorums of the Seventy (and the Presidency of the Seventy), regional representatives, stake presidents, and bishops, as well as general presidencies of each of the church's auxiliary organizations. Every member of the church is part of a congregation, a ward headed by a lay bishop (or a branch, if the congregation is small, under the jurisdiction of a branch president), and several wards are organized into larger stakes, headed by a stake president. Mormon culture, which affects aspects of life ranging from dress to diet to marriage and family life, is reinforced in wards, which offer structured religious activities almost every day of the week. On Mondays, families hold Family Home Evening, in which they socialize and study religion. Members are encouraged to read scriptures and pray every day, both individually and as a family. Friday or Saturday evening is likely to see a dance at the stake meetinghouse, and Sunday meetings include Sunday school (organized by age), auxiliary and priesthood meetings (organized by age and gender), and a sacrament meeting, which all attend together, usually sitting in families.

Religious culture infuses the daily lives of Mormons. The Word of Wisdom calls on Mormons to avoid alcohol and tobacco and provides other dietary guidelines. Mormons who have received their temple endowments wear undergarments that provide standards for hem lengths. Mormons participate in secular education, but often leave campus for one course period during high school to attend religious classes, and young Mormons (until recently, especially men) are encouraged to prepare to serve a mission, and to attend one of the campuses of Brigham Young University, a church-affiliated school.

This pervasive religious culture is permeated with ideas about gender.[85] Mormon boys and girls are both taught to prepare for marriage and parenthood, and the priesthood is integral to both. Priesthood rituals at important life junctures create bonds that may withstand death, and priesthood power is the prerequisite to all positions of religious authority, from bishop to president. Even positions in the Relief Society or the young women's organization, which women and girls hold, require being called and set apart by priesthood holders. Contemporary Mormon culture teaches not that boys and girls hold priesthood together, but that males hold the priesthood and females support priesthood holders. In both the family and in the church generally, girls are socialized to confirm, follow, and encourage male priesthood holders, while boys are socialized to lead as priesthood holders—to head their families, their congregations, and the church. Some recent emphasis in church addresses encouraging men to help their wives with childcare or housework does not fundamentally reframe these roles. Not only is this religious socialization intensive in a religion that permeates many aspects of life for the devoted, but the individual is taught that her place in the family, the church, and eternity is premised on adherence to the teachings of the gospel. Admission to the temple is necessary for access to the Celestial Kingdom, families are together eternally only in the Celestial Kingdom, and admission to the temple is premised on adhering to church doctrines. One's place is gendered now and eternally.

The nexus of Mormon theology is the family, which plays a critical role in framing what Mormons call the "plan of salvation."[86] Drawing from the Book of Mormon, the Bible, and *The Doctrine and Covenants* and *The Pearl of Great Price* (collections of revelations received by Joseph Smith), as well as widely accepted and shared (including over generations) folk theology, Mormons have developed a unique theology.[87] Latter-day Saints believe that God, the literal father of all spirits, determined that all souls should live in bodies to be tested to determine their righteousness, their worthiness of salvation. A pre-mortal battle followed, in which all spirits—of those who would later live on earth and those who would not—fought on one of two sides: with Jesus, the son of God (and distinct from God in Mormon theology), or with Satan, also a son of God, but a fallen son. The battle in heaven centered, Mormons believe, on implementation of one of two possible plans of salvation. Jesus advocated God's plan that spirits be given a body and a chance to live, and be granted agency—the freedom to choose between right and wrong—and be judged based on their actions, while Satan advanced the notion that people be denied freedom to choose so that all would be saved. The spirits who sided with Jesus (two-thirds of them) were victorious, and thus God implemented the plan of salvation. Mormons believe that Eve's decision to eat the forbidden fruit in the Garden of Eden was necessary to this plan to introduce knowledge of good and evil to humans, and they see Eve not as a temptress, but instead, with Adam, as essential to God's plan.[88]

Outsiders often find it interesting that Joseph Smith's version of the afterlife includes no hell. The highest level of salvation in the Mormon afterlife, the Celestial Kingdom, also has within it levels of glory. Here reside the most righteous, those who completed Mormon ordinances (or who accepted the ordinances completed on their behalf by living proxies in a temple on earth), and lived according to gospel principles. God reigns over the Celestial Kingdom, and people within it live for eternity in patrilineal families formed originally on earth. An intermediate level of salvation is found in the Terrestrial Kingdom, which Mormons describe as much like the heaven of mainline Christianity—beautiful, peaceful, and harmonious. People who did not adhere to the ordinances and covenants of the church but who nonetheless lived honest lives without committing serious sins spend eternity here, receive the presence of Jesus, but not God, and do not live in families. The lowest level of salvation, the Telestial Kingdom, is where "liars, and sorcerers, and adulterers, and whoremongers" reside.[89] There is no hell or hellfire in Mormon theology, but there is outer darkness, a place from which God is absent, reserved for those who "knew the truth" and rejected it, and for the pre-mortal spirits that sided with Satan in the heavenly battle.

The Mormon concept of Godhead includes three distinct entities—God, the father, not triune; Jesus Christ, his literal son; and the Holy Ghost, a spirit entity that moves within people to comfort and help them to know the truth of the gospel. Mormon belief stipulates that God—with at least one heavenly consort, Heavenly Mother—is the literal *father* of Jesus Christ and all spirits that will ever live on earth.[90] God and Heavenly Mother (or mothers) provide the model for Mormon families. Earthly parents give birth to children in part to provide bodies for those spirits waiting for a chance to come to earth and be tested. Heterosexual marriage and reproduction are thus rendered divine in Mormon theology. Just as God lived, and through righteous living, became a deity, so too all individuals who will live may prove themselves righteous—participate in necessary religious rituals and practices such as baptism, temple marriage with endowments, and holding the priesthood for men—and become gods or goddesses themselves.[91]

As gospel ordinances are necessary to salvation, Mormons believe that they have an imperative to share their beliefs throughout the world. At its October 2012 General Conference, the church lowered from nineteen to eighteen the age at which men who are worthy may serve a two-year mission, and from twenty-one to nineteen the age at which women may serve eighteen-month-long missions.[92] Church leaders had, before 2012, emphasized marriage over mission as a priority for women, but the lowering of women's age of entry suggests more emphasis on missions for women, who are often more successful in evangelizing than men.[93] Mormons are also encouraged to follow the adage "every member a missionary," and to share the message of the gospel with those they encounter in their lives. Since so many people lived on earth before Joseph Smith restored the gospel, Mormons believe that they also have a responsibility to perform ordinances for the dead.

Temple ordinances, initially introduced by Joseph Smith, bind families patrilineally through eternity. The details of temple work are considered too sacred to discuss with those not worthy to participate (including members) in temple rituals, but they have been discussed in the media and by scholars (such as in the HBO series *Big Love* [2006–2011] and the journalist Deborah Laake's 1993 book *Secret Ceremonies*).[94] In order to be able to enter the temple, a member participates in a one-on-one interview with her bishop and a member of her stake presidency and, if deemed worthy (that is, if she adheres to the tenets of the religion, such as having been baptized for at least a year, being a full-tithe payer, and following the law of chastity), is issued a temple recommend, which allows her admission to any temple (though not to all parts of any temple).[95] Only white clothing and underclothing is worn in the temple, the only jewelry worn is a wedding ring, and makeup is minimized.

Most important, temple work is believed to withstand death; marriages performed in the temple may be binding after death, and if someone died before being baptized, a proxy, in the temple, could be baptized for her.[96] Male priesthood holders are primarily responsible for performing temple rituals, though women play an indispensable function, especially in the endowment ceremony, when they wash and anoint female participants. The endowment ceremony helps prepare initiates for their roles as kings and queens, priests and priestesses. After the initiate is washed and anointed by someone of the same sex, the couple (together with other couples) watches a reenactment of the Genesis story, and each learns his or her sacred name (shared only in one part of the ceremony in the temple and otherwise kept secret). The initiates learn sacred, secret gestures and words that will be used to gain entrance to the Celestial Kingdom, are given temple garments that they will wear in place of conventional underclothing, and make several promises (covenants).[97] As temple marriage is ideally for eternity, divorce is strongly discouraged. Additionally, if a man's spouse dies, he may marry another woman in the temple; no such contingency exists for LDS women. In this theological sense, plural marriages for men are still allowed after death.

Mormon theology locates individual salvation in family relationships and in access to rituals performed by priesthood holders. The individual is the child of earthly parents, and through participation in temple endowments and adherence to religious prescriptions, she may be "sealed" to them forever; at the same time, she is the child of God, as are her parents. Mormons use "brother" and "sister" as terms of address for those Mormons outside their biological family to reflect the notion that they are all children of God. For Mormons, marriage and parenthood are part of the plan of salvation, and Mormons are strongly encouraged to marry and to have children. Tasked with raising these children "in righteousness," according to church teachings, parents are encouraged to prepare their children to be baptized by immersion at the age of eight, to be confirmed in the church shortly thereafter, to receive the priesthood (if they are boys) at age twelve, and to marry in a temple and become parents themselves.[98]

Every stage of life is gendered, in part because of the emphasis in Mormon theology on the eternal family and gender roles within it. Ideally, women are wives and mothers, and fathers lead with the priesthood. The heterosexual family is key; everything is connected to it, including sexuality. Mormon literature portrays sexuality as a powerful force to be controlled through heterosexual marriage. Mormons are encouraged not to date until they are sixteen years old, and to date in groups so as to avoid sexual temptation. Formerly church leaders published materials for distribution to young Mormons calling masturbation a sin, and providing advice on ways to avoid it.[99] Most especially, Mormon leaders call homosexual sex a sin, though they have tempered their rhetoric somewhat, beginning with a 1995 address by President Gordon B. Hinckley (1910–2008), who told gay Mormons ("those who struggle with feelings of affinity for the same gender"), "We remember you before the Lord, we sympathize with you, we regard you as our brothers and sisters. However, we cannot condone immoral practices on your part any more than we can condone immoral practices on the part of others."[100]

Prior to Hinckley's address, Mormon church leaders published materials that encouraged lesbian and gay Mormons (Mormon teachings did not usually specifically address bisexual or trans people) to participate in programs—such as Evergreen International or an aversion therapy program commenced at Brigham Young University in the late 1950s—to "cure" or "reorient" homosexuality, almost exclusively among men, by applying electroshock and other "treatments."[101] A 1992 LDS instruction manual for ecclesiastical leaders asserts that "sexual contact, including fornication, adultery and homosexual and lesbian behavior, is sinful" and that "those who persist in such practices or who influ-ence others to do so are subject to Church discipline."[102] Church leaders were instructed that "these problems [homosexuality] can be controlled and eventually overcome. Members can be helped to gain self-mastery, adhere to gospel standards of sexual purity and develop meaningful, appropriate relationships with members of both sexes."[103] Mormon church teachings advocate adherence to the law of chastity, which de-fines any sex outside the heterosexual marital relationship as threatening salvation:

> Heaven is organized by families, which require a man and a woman who together exercise their creative powers within the bounds the Lord has set. Same-sex relationships are inconsistent with this plan. Without both a husband and a wife there would be no eternal family and no opportu-nity to become like Heavenly Father.[104]

Church leaders and publications stopped referring to homosexuality as a "disease" in the early 1990s, by 2007 had stopped calling homosexu-ality a "problem," and now more specifically emphasize abstinence from same-sex sexuality rather than reorienting those with what church lead-ers prefer to call "same-sex attraction" (SSA) or "same-gender attrac-tion" (SGA). The 2010 church handbook removed language sanctioning homosexual "thoughts or feelings" while maintaining proscriptions against engaging in "homosexual behavior,"[105] and in late 2012 the church launched Mormonsandgays.org, a webpage that emphasizes re-sponding to "our gay brothers and sisters" with "love and acceptance."[106] Church leaders continue to suggest, via the church's official publications and website, that "many Latter-day Saints, through individual effort, the exercise of faith, and reliance upon the enabling power of the Atone-ment, overcome same-gender attraction in mortality," but now acknowl-edge that "others may not be free of this challenge in this life."[107] For the latter, sexual abstinence and religious participation are encouraged, so that their "bodies, feelings, and desires will be perfected in the next life so that every one of God's children may find joy in a family consisting of a husband, a wife, and children."[108] Church leadership resists use of medical procedures by transgender people to transition: the 2010 church handbook continues to inform stake presidencies and bishoprics that "elective transsexual operations . . . may be cause for formal Church discipline" and to call "homosexual activity" a "sexual perversion" and a "serious sin."[109] Heterosexual marriage, the centerpiece of Mormon theology, makes acceptance of open expression of homosexuality, bisexuality, or nonconforming gender identity unlikely in the foreseeable future, though the church may continue to moderate its tone in some ways.[110]

Mormon life is not simply gendered, it is eternally gendered.[111] Even in the contemporary Mormon church, where there is increased recognition that some women "must" work, fathers and husbands are "responsible to provide the necessities of life . . . for their families" and mothers are deemed primarily responsible for work in the domestic sphere.[112] At the 2012 General Conference young women's session, Mormon girls were told to "bless your children and your future home by learning as much as you can now." They were encouraged to "learn a marketable skill," as a contingency in case they needed to support themselves or their families, but they were reminded—via a quote from the 1995 proclamation on the family—that women should be primarily responsible for nurturing children.[113]

Though contemporary church leaders explicitly acknowledge that this ideal is not attainable by all Mormon women, it remains the ideal. In her 2007 inaugural General Conference talk to Mormons worldwide, the Relief Society general president, Julie B. Beck (b. 1954), called on Mormon women to "stand strong and immovable." She called on Mormon women to: "(1) Understand and defend the divine roles of women; (2) Embrace the blessings of the priesthood; (3) Form eternal families; (4) Maintain strong marriages; (5) Bear and rear children; (6) Express love for and nurture family members; (7) Accept responsibility to prepare a righteous rising generation; [and] (8) Know, live, and defend the doctrine of the family." She went on to quote President Benson's "To the Mothers in Zion" and insist that "as a disciple of Jesus Christ, *every* woman in this Church is given the responsibility for upholding, nurturing, and protecting families. Women have distinct assignments given to them from before the foundation of the world."[114] In his October 2013 General Conference address, D. Todd Christofferson (b. 1945), a member of the Quorum of the Twelve, asserted that women have an "innate moral power" that allows them to serve as a "civilizing influence in society." This "moral influence," he claimed, "is nowhere more powerfully felt or more beneficially employed than in the home."[115] Even given some moderation of tone by church leaders on gender and sexuality, contemporary Mormons are encouraged to marry heterosexually, to marry in the temple, to have children, to participate in Mormon culture and rituals, and, by doing these, to become a family forever; and gender roles within this process are binary, are preordained, and have eternal consequences.[116]

2

Seventh-day Adventism

Women's Changing Role in an Endtime Religion

Origin of Adventism

Walking the streets of Portland, Maine, in 1836 as a child less than ten years old, Ellen Harmon picked up a scrap of paper about a man in England who predicted that the world would be destroyed in about thirty years.[1] She was already a pensive and deeply religious child, and the announcement focused Ellen's spiritual quest on the soon-coming end. Ellen and her family were Methodists, and Ellen and her mother were among their congregation's "shouters," enthusiastic worshipers who shouted "amen" and participated fervently in religious meetings. Ellen's identical twin, with whom she shared a bedroom, described Ellen as sometimes praying throughout the night without ceasing. In her later life, Ellen described her childhood as one consumed with uncertainty about her religious worthiness and salvation. Moreover, Ellen was a sickly child whose pronounced spirituality was intensified as a result of the isolation from her peers to which her poor health contributed.[2]

Another pivotal event in Ellen's life occurred when, walking home from school, she was hit in the head by a stone thrown by a classmate "angry at some trifle."[3] Ellen's family described her as falling into a coma for three weeks and being so misshapen by the injury that her father, who had been out of town when the incident occurred, did not recognize her upon his return. Ellen was already in poor health and imbued with the spiritual, and these two incidents concentrated her spiritual quest even more intensely.

The roots of the religion she was to coalesce extended beyond Ellen to an existing movement convinced of Christ's soon return, the Millerite millennial movement. The Millerites followed an unlikely religious leader, William Miller (1782–1849), who had been a deist early in life, but was convinced by events he witnessed in the War of 1812 at the Battle of Plattsburgh (New York) on Lake Champlain—where 1,500 American troops and 4,000 volunteers defeated 15,000 British troops—that God intervened in human affairs.[4] Studying the Bible after the war in an effort to persuade his deist friends of his new view, Miller applied the year-day principle (the idea that every "day" in the Bible is one year in length) to the 2,300 days of Daniel 8:14 and discovered that the world would end and Christ would return in 1843.[5]

Not by nature drawn to public speaking or emotional religious display, Miller originally did not share his startling conclusion widely. But the weight of responsibility to warn others of the impending end wore on him. When he received an invitation from his nephew to preach in Dresden, New York, shortly after praying for guidance as to whether to share his message, Miller began to preach of Christ's soon return. Even so, Miller's preaching was contained in Low Hampton, New York, and he would likely have remained mostly unknown had it not been for Joshua V. Himes (1805–1895).[6]

A Christian Connection pastor in Boston, Himes was a highly skilled publicist who had honed his skills in the temperance, abolitionist, and other reform movements, in which he and his congregants were active. After hearing Miller speak, Himes devoted himself to promoting Miller's message. Publishing and widely distributing periodicals, then bringing Miller to preach in a large, rented auditorium—or eventually a "great tent"—proved immensely successful, and as Miller preached from town to town, religious revival followed in his wake.[7] Protestants, especially Baptists and Methodists, were attracted to Miller's message, though they did not at first sever their existing denominational ties, and as pastors saw the religious excitement that Miller's message generated, he became a sought-after speaker.

Estimates of the number of Millerites vary widely, in part because so many remained within their congregations that their numbers are difficult to gauge. Still, historical press reports and other documents agree that at least tens of thousands of listeners accepted Miller's prediction. Probably between twenty-five thousand and fifty thousand Protestants considered themselves committed to Miller's message.[8] As Miller's following grew, some of those—who began to be called Millerites—used prophetic charts with graphic illustrations of scenes described in Daniel and Revelation to evangelize, contributing to the growth of the movement.

Himes's Christian Connection, the Millerites, and later the Adventists were among nineteenth-century religious movements that allowed women to preach in public. At a time when mainline religious groups "forbade women to preach," the historian of religions Catherine A. Brekus notes, some upstart religious movements allowed women access to the pulpit and organizational leadership.[9] These movements' dramatic growth necessitated more pastoral labor than men could provide; the urgency of the Advent heightened believers' desire to spread the message before the End; belief in direct communication between God and the individual led followers to believe "it was possible for God to inspire women as well as men to proclaim the gospel"; and high levels of emotionalism in religious worship "made anything [seem] possible—even female preaching."[10] Two of these movements—the Christian Connection and the Millerite millennial movement—would help spark the largest religion ever coalesced by a woman, and the largest religion to emerge from nineteenth-century America, Seventh-day Adventism.

No one knows exactly what was depicted on the piece of paper that Ellen found in 1836 that ignited her religious journey, but its effect was profound. Ellen convinced her parents to attend a Millerite camp meeting in Portland, Maine, in March 1840, and the Harmons eagerly embraced William Miller's message and were eventually asked to leave their Methodist congregation.[11] The Harmons, who refused to withdraw their memberships voluntarily, were forced out of their Methodist congregation in 1842, and Ellen turned her attention even more to Christ's soon return.[12]

The Harmons were not alone in being asked to leave their congregation; as 1843 drew near, tension increased between Millerites and the more mainline congregations in which they worshipped. When 1843 passed and the world did not end, Millerites adjusted their expectations. Miller had not set a specific date for Christ's return, and he came to believe that, by the Jewish calendar, 1843 extended into the spring of 1844. The stage was set for profound disappointment when a Millerite, Samuel S. Snow (1806–1870), introduced a specific date for the end—22 October 1844—which spread rapidly and heightened both Millerites' expectations and tensions with their denominations.[13]

Although press accounts of preparations made by Millerites for the end of the world were no doubt exaggerated, at least some Millerites did quit their jobs, settle their debts, or fail to plant crops in anticipation of the Second Coming. Some sat on rooftops or climbed hills to glimpse Christ's return. William Miller climbed a hill near his home where he watched through the night on 22 October 1844.

Believers were bitterly disappointed when 23 October dawned. Among these was Ellen Harmon, who, no longer rooted in her Methodist congregation, spent time in the fall and winter of 1844–45 with other disappointed Millerites trying to make sense of their failed expectations. In December 1844, while praying with four other female believers in the Advent, Ellen had her first vision. "Wrapt in a vision of God's glory," she "seemed to be rising higher and higher from the earth" and saw the "travels of the Advent people to the Holy City."[14] That winter, through additional visions, Ellen saw that Millerites who remained committed to the message of Christ's soon return were the 144,000 of the book of Revelation (Rev. 7:4–8, 14:1, 14:3). About sixty Portland, Maine, Millerites soon became convinced of the divinity of Ellen's message, and following a vision confirming her prophetic role, Ellen began to share her message in small, private religious gatherings. After a letter to a follower was published in an Advent paper in Cincinnati, Ellen became more widely known among believers in the soon-coming Advent, many of whom received her gift as the spirit of prophecy foreseen in the book of Revelation (Rev. 12:17, 19:10). Seventeen years old and often in poor health, she accepted the responsibility of prophet, and began to travel to share the news that Millerites must persist in their millennial expectations.[15]

One of Ellen's early advocates was James White (1821–1881), a Millerite itinerant lay preacher who joined Ellen in her travels after becoming convinced that she was a prophet. The two married in August 1846 to circumvent rumors sparked by their unchaperoned travel. Ellen and James together shepherded what would be officially organized as the Seventh-day Adventist Church in 1863. Ellen received visions in which she would exclaim, "Glory! G-l-o-r-y! G—L—O—R—Y!" and walk about, eyes open, describing what she saw.[16] These were replaced, as Ellen matured, by visionary dreams. James played a more sedate role as Ellen's promoter and as a religious organizer, administrator, and publisher. With James as her advocate, Ellen's visions fanned the flames of disappointment into the formation and burgeoning of Seventh-day Adventism.

Adventist Eschatology

Adventism remains a deeply millennial movement. Even in Ellen White's lifetime, however, as millennial expectations went unfulfilled, Adventism structured beliefs and institutions both to help explain the delay and hasten the Advent. Ellen White called herself a "messenger," not a prophet, and as a woman, she was subjected to tests of authenticity not faced by nineteenth-century male prophets like Joseph Smith, such as having believers cover her nose and mouth to see whether she could retain consciousness.[17] From the age of seventeen, when her waking visions began to provide direction for struggling Millerites, until old age, when night dreams provided guidance to the Seventh-day Adventist Church, Ellen White played a vital role in drawing together a remnant of believers in the Parousia (the Second Coming) and shaping Adventist belief, especially by helping to settle questions of theology and practice.

The most obvious problem facing a failed millennial movement is an explanation of the continuation of time. In Adventism, Ellen White confirmed a belief, introduced earlier by Hiram Edson (1806–1882) and O. R. L. Crosier (1820–1912), that Miller's prediction was not wrong, it just inaccurately represented the event. Although Christ did not return to the earth on 22 October 1844, he did commence the work of "cleansing the sanctuary," the final work of Christ's atonement—the "investigative judgment." Ellen White described people's lives passing "in review before God" and being "registered for faithfulness or unfaithfulness."[18] When that work was complete, she explained, Jesus would return; thus for Adventists the End remained "soon," but White avoided further date setting.

The overarching eschatological framework of Seventh-day Adventist belief is the Great Controversy, and the soon-coming Advent is framed within this. Adventists believe that the universe was initially without sin, and that Lucifer, originally "next to Christ, [and] . . . most honored of God," began to desire to rule in God's place and rebelled, introducing sin into the universe.[19] Satan and his followers were cast out of heaven because God understood that their destruction would have led some to serve "God from fear rather than love."[20] Satan perpetuated the Great Controversy on earth by tempting Eve, whereafter God introduced a plan of redemption in the form of the antediluvian church, led by Adam and other biblical prophets. Christianity fell astray after the apostles died, however, and, although some Protestant reforms attempted to set it back on the correct path, it remained mostly lost until Millerism emerged and later Seventh-day Adventism was formed. Seventh-day Adventism is God's church; Adventists are performing the work necessary to usher in the Second Coming.

That work is captured in the three angels' messages: (1) that judgment is come and Adventists must carry their message to the world; (2) that people should come out of Babylon and separate themselves from the world; and (3) that people should keep the commandments, including the seventh-day (Saturday) Sabbath (Rev. 14:6–12). Some Adventist beliefs do not diverge from mainline Protestantism, but others set Adventism apart—for example, the seventh-day Sabbath, vegetarianism, the belief that Ellen White possessed the "spirit of prophecy," and the belief that Christ's atonement was not completed on the cross but continues in the work of the investigative judgment that commenced in 1844.

Ellen White's voluminous prophetic writings helped to settle questions of belief in Adventism, especially in its early decades. There has been some tension within Adventism regarding the place of White's writings vis-à-vis the Bible, especially since the 1970s, when Adventist scholars, including the American historian of science Ronald L. Numbers, wrote about White's tendency to borrow words from others in her writings. But Adventists—though they call Ellen White's writings the "lesser light"—continue to cite Ellen White in religious worship and discussion, and to see in her writings guidance for living. Adventism asserts belief in "present truth," the idea that biblical revelation continues to unfold, especially as demonstrated in White's writings.[21]

Much of the counsel of Ellen White's writings is not unlike advice of some of her contemporaries, such as those in the nineteenth-century health reform movement.[22] She encouraged Adventists to be modest, especially in their attire, and many contemporary Adventists do not wear jewelry (some exchange watches rather than rings upon engagement and marriage, while others wear modest wedding rings) or cosmetics. She advocated dietary guidelines outlined in her health message—to eat two vegetarian meals, one at morning and one in the afternoon; to avoid tobacco, alcohol, coffee, and tea; to avoid spicy condiments (which, she wrote, could inflame sexual passions); and to incorporate hydropathy in one's routine. Some aspects of her message that are more controversial in a contemporary context—especially the notion that people are born with a limited supply of "vital force," which is lost when they experience orgasm, and the depletion of which contributes to health ailments—are not emphasized in modern Adventism.[23]

One of Ellen White's most significant and lasting contributions was her insistence that Adventists build institutions to complete the work necessary to hasten the Advent. In keeping with her health message, she encouraged construction of Adventist sanitariums—most notably that led by John Harvey Kellogg (1852–1943) at Battle Creek, Michigan— many of which eventually became Adventist hospitals.[24] She also encouraged the construction of schools so that Adventist children could avoid secular education, resulting in the second-largest parochial school system in the world, and promoted the creation of extensive publication and media enterprises, resulting in numerous Adventist presses, Adventist book centers (ABCs), and eventually, radio and television shows and stations.

Adventists are often educated in SDA schools and, as adults, work at Adventist institutions, which results in Adventist enclaves around these institutions. These communities have grocery stores and fast-food restaurants that provide extensive vegetarian offerings, Adventist schools and often colleges, ABCs, and other services and businesses that cater to Adventist needs. These Adventist ghettos—which generally support group beliefs, dietary guidelines, and dress—reinforce Adventist distinction and shared identity.[25] Indeed, so many Adventists are educated in SDA schools and employed in SDA institutions, that the fear of being cast out of the Adventist community (and possibly fired from one's church-affiliated job) can serve as a deterrent for Adventists who might otherwise oppose the church more easily with regard to questions such as the ordination of women or the place of lesbian, gay, bisexual, and transgender (LGBT) people within the movement.

The basic unit of salvation in Adventism is the individual, and individuals are organized into local churches—congregations that vary from as few as twenty-five members to those, especially those associated with an Adventist institution, that number in the thousands. Several congregations constitute a local "conference" or local "mission," which together, in turn, form a "union conference" or "union mission." Union conferences together form a division, and all of the divisions make up the General Conference. Each of these is loosely structured along geographical lines. The president, whose name the General Conference nominating committee puts forward, and who is accepted or rejected by a voice vote of General Conference delegates, leads the global General Conference. Although Adventists believe in present truth—that biblical truth continues to be revealed, and that God can and does inspire individuals—they do not have a belief in prophetic revelation since Ellen White, and so are governed by a form of democratic representation similar to the Presbyterian organizational system.

Adventists are encouraged to participate in formal and informal worship. Many Adventists gather for a vespers ceremony on Friday evening around sunset to welcome the Sabbath, and on the Sabbath—Saturday—Adventists are to refrain from secular work and generally also from secular leisure activities such as attending films or watching secular sports. Sabbath worship entails participation in group study (Sabbath school) and congregation-wide worship not unlike that found in evangelical Christian churches, with a sermon delivered by a pastor, prayers, scripture reading, singing, and collection of offerings. Adventists participate quarterly in an open communion that begins with a foot-washing ceremony, the "Ordinance of Humility," in which people of the same sex wash one another's feet. After corporate worship, Adventist congregations often share a vegetarian meal. Individuals are encouraged to continue worship throughout the week with daily devotions.

Gender, Sexuality, and Family in Adventism

Numerous early Adventist leaders, including Ellen White, advocated women's active participation in public aspects of the emerging religion's work. During decades in which the larger culture embraced and encouraged a gendered distinction of spheres, and those women who worked for pay outside the home were often restricted in their work by gender (either through protective legislation or by custom), Adventist women were told—mostly in the *Second Advent Review and Sabbath Herald* (the *Review*, published under variations of this title), the group's primary periodical—that Christ's soon return necessitated participation of *all* in God's work.[26] As early as the 1850s, less than a decade after the Seneca Falls Convention in 1848, the first women's rights convention in America, *Review* readers were told that the Bible supported women's public ministry, that biblical references to "men" included men and women, and that although in other churches "prejudice against women's efforts and labors in the church have crushed her usefulness," Adventism should not "neglect the use of gifts designed to edify the church and glorify God," for the "promise of the Father was as much to the female as the male disciples of Jesus."[27] Defense of women's public religious work accelerated in the next decade, as the Adventist pioneer S. C. Welcome encouraged women's participation in "preaching, prophesying, exhorting or praying in public."[28] Women were equally qualified, insisted Welcome, who demanded, "Where is the authority for saying that females should not receive a gift of the Holy Spirit in the last days? Verily God hath promised it" (see Acts 2:17). Women should be allowed to fill the place that "God wants them to fill," including public participation in worship and public ministry.[29]

Before 1860, Ellen White said "virtually nothing about the role of female ministry."[30] Instead, other Adventist leaders defended women's participation in public religious work, and by extension, Ellen White's claim to the spirit of prophecy. Following formal organization of Seventh-day Adventism in 1863, the church instituted a course of training and study for ministers, and women participated. After Adventism defined and established ministerial training programs beginning in 1865, especially under the guidance of Ellen's husband, James, Adventist women began to participate in ministerial training, and some were licensed as ministers. The Adventist archivist Bert Haloviak and Kit Watts, former assistant editor of the *Review*, point out that women were trained and licensed as ministers between 1865 and 1871.[31] Around the same time, women also served in positions of institutional leadership, such as General Conference treasurer, licensed minister, and editor of *Youth's Instructor*.[32]

By the 1870s, women served in pastoral roles in Adventism.[33] In 1878 and 1879 Ellen White published a three-part series in the *Review* calling for women's increased participation in religious work, focusing on their work as colporteurs (literature evangelists), but also calling for their contributions in ministry. "I was shown" she wrote, that there must be with men and women a general waking up to the needs of God's cause. There is a wide field in which our sisters may do good service for the Master in the various branches of the work connected with his cause. Through missionary labor they can reach a class that our ministers cannot.

She continued, "Women of firm principle and decided character are needed. . . . Nothing will deter this class from their duty. Nothing will discourage them in the work. They have faith to work for time and for eternity."[34] White suggested that women's public religious work was critical to Adventism, but also important for women, as it allowed the "minds of our sisters [to] be expanded and cultivated."[35]

Increasingly insistent in her support for women's participation in public religious work, Ellen White repeatedly claimed in the late nineteenth century that all Adventists were needed to hasten the Parousia. "The Lord has a work for women, as well as for men," she wrote. Further, she asserted, the

Savior will reflect upon these self-sacrificing women the light of his countenance, and will give them a power that exceeds that of men. They can do in families a work that men cannot do, a work that reaches the inner life. They can come close to the hearts of those whom men cannot reach. Their labor is needed.[36]

"I have felt recently," wrote White, "that it should be so arranged that women have greater responsibilities. It is their privilege to be educated in some lines of work just as thoroughly as the men are educated."[37]

The 1884 *SDA Yearbook* listed several women licensed as ministers, and in 1895 Ellen White called for women to be set apart for religious work by "prayer and laying on of hands" and asked that they be paid from Adventist tithes, as were men involved in this type of work.[38] Beginning in the early 1890s, as White increasingly emphasized beneficent ministry—evangelical work entailing practical assistance, by providing health care, for example—she concomitantly increased calls for women's participation in religious work outside the home. Bert Haloviak notes, "It was the 'ministry of compassion' that naturally brought women to a prominent role in . . . ministerial team efforts."[39] In 1898 the first women's ministry department was instituted, and in 1900 Ellen White participated in an Australian service that included ordaining deaconesses.[40]

Although Ellen White was never ordained (she indicated that ordination by men was not necessary for her, as she was ordained by God), and said "virtually nothing" about women's ordination during the 1850s and 1860s, historical evidence indicates that by the late 1870s she not only encouraged women's participation in lines of religious and other institutional leadership, but also advocated their equitable remuneration.[41] In the late 1870s, for example, White called upon women to "extend their missionary work beyond neighborhood welfare work to a more public form of ministry."[42] Indeed, White called for women to work as colporteurs, physicians, teachers, missionaries, Bible instructors, and with their husbands in ministry, and asserted that "whenever a great and decisive work is to be done, God chooses men and women to do this work, and it will feel the loss if the talents of both are not combined."[43] Nonetheless, when a resolution supporting women's ordination was introduced in the General Conference in 1881 Ellen White, mourning the recent death of her husband, James, was absent. The resolution—that "females possessing the necessary qualifications to fill that position may, with perfect propriety, be set apart by ordination to the work of Christian ministry"—was discussed, but tabled and never voted on. Despite that, the "Adventist church encouraged women to enter the ministry, and made it relatively easy for them to do so."[44]

Adventism's failure to ordain women is not surprising. Like nineteenth-century Mormon women, Adventist women who engaged in religious work did so in a larger social context in which women lacked many legal rights or equitable opportunities. White commenced her religious work when women's ordination was anomalous. Congregationalists became one of the first denominations to fully ordain a woman, Antoinette Brown, in 1853.[45] Within a decade of when the Disciples of Christ became the first American denomination to change denominational rules so as to include women in ordination (in 1888), White wrote that women in the "service of the Lord" should "be set apart to this work by prayer and laying on of hands."[46] In 1895 women—still discouraged from public speaking—in Adventism were told by White, "not a hand should be bound, not a soul discouraged, not a voice should be hushed; let every individual labor, privately or publicly, to help forward this

grand work. Place the burdens upon men and women of the church."[47]
At a time when it remained unusual for women to participate in higher
education, Ellen White encouraged Adventist women to "take advantage
of schools that have been established for the purpose of imparting the
best of knowledge."[48] Most significantly, White called women to varied
forms of religious work, public and private.

In spite of this, Ellen White did not explicitly challenge the
nineteenth-century notion of essential gender qualities, though she
taught that these should not prevent women from participating in public religious work.[49] She cautioned, "Wives and mothers should in no
case neglect their husbands and their children," but insisted, "women
can do much without neglecting home duties; and there are many who
do not have these responsibilities."[50] Though she encouraged, especially
in her later years, men to be active and nurturing participants in the
household, and proposed that women might hire domestic labor to free
them for activities outside the home (as *she* did), she still suggested that
domestic work was primarily women's work.[51] Still, Adventist theology
includes no imperative for women to marry or have children. White
warned Adventists not to "belittle women's work" and insisted numerous times that women in the work of ministry should be paid as much
as men. "I was instructed," wrote Ellen White, "injustice has been done
to women who labor just as devotedly as their husbands. The method
of paying men laborers and not their wives is a plan not after the Lord's
order. Injustice is thus done. A mistake is made."[52] When equal pay for
women workers was not forthcoming, she withheld her tithes from the
movement, depositing them instead into a fund she established for pay-
ment of women in ministry.[53]

Interestingly, by the late nineteenth century the *Review* provided men
with an ideal of masculinity that, while not entirely out of keeping with
popular notions of masculinity, emphasized men's roles as fathers and
husbands. Men were encouraged to be loving and empathetic fathers
and house-bands and to "do all in your power to make your wife pleas-
ant and happy."[54] They were told to share with their spouses in taking
responsibility for childcare and housework—to be a "man *of* the house."
A man should "invite his wife to participate in the management of his
work," "divide burdens evenly," "prepare vegetables, lay a table, sweep
a floor or cook a meal." To this end, boys, Adventists were informed,

should learn "to wash clothes and dishes, . . . [and] plain cookery and housekeeping."[55] While boys and men were told that they had responsibilities in the home, a girl was advised to be "self-reliant" and do what was necessary to prepare to "feed and clothe herself, so that if left alone, she can stand upon her own two feet, dependent upon no human being."[56]

Historical data from the *SDA Yearbook* indicate that Adventist women did assume numerous and varied leadership roles in the movement's early decades, as women served in leadership in virtually every type of Adventist work—in the education and Sabbath school departments, as conference secretaries, and as conference treasurers. In all cases, women's participation in these positions declined dramatically following Ellen White's death in 1915. Without a defender at the movement's head, women's access to public leadership opportunities diminished.

Early Adventist gender ideals, which stand in contrast to those of the dominant sociocultural context, began to shift noticeably following the turn of the last century, toward emphasis on gendered separation of spheres. By the early 1900s the *Review* began to identify homemaking as women's exclusive "vocation" and to present women as the "central figure of the home."[57] Calls for women's participation in public religious work did not disappear from the pages of the *Review*, however: Luella B. Priddy wrote in 1910, "There are many kinds of work in which women can successfully engage, and the spirit of prophecy tells us that their work is needed."[58] These admonitions were increasingly outnumbered by calls for women to confine their work, including religious work, to the home. As late as 1921, six years after Ellen White's death, the General Conference asserted that "in all cases, so far as possible, strong, capable men or women be chosen to head our departments, being selected with reference to their ability as real soul winners, sound in the doctrines of the message and able to teach them, and qualified by experience for the special work of their departments." Despite this, in 1924 the General Conference called on divisions to select department heads who were ordained when possible (only men were ordained), and in 1932, in the context of the Great Depression, Adventist leaders pointed to economic conditions and the need to "spread" employment among members to request that "both the husband and wife should not be remuneratively employed" within Adventism. Moreover, if "for special reasons" it was deemed necessary to remunerate both a "man and his wife, the wife shall be paid on the basis of a greatly reduced wage."[59] Thus Adventism instituted a gendered system—termed "head of household"—that favored male workers both in access to Adventist employment and in higher pay. This system would remain in place until it faced a successful Equal Employment Opportunity Commission class-action legal challenge by Adventist employees, Merikay Silver (McLeod) (b. 1946) and Lorna Tobler (b. 1933), in the 1970s.

It is important to note that Adventists' promotion of women's extra-domestic activities prior to Ellen White's death (and shortly thereafter) was at odds with then-prominent secular trends. When Adventist leaders took steps to remove women from positions of public religious work in the mid-1920s and 1930s, they did so in opposition to the movement's prior support of women's active religious participation, but the move was generally not in opposition to the social context. On the other hand, when the secular world encouraged women to enter the paid workforce during the Second World War (1939–1945), at least some *Review* articles concurred, and Adventist women, though still deemed responsible for domestic work, were also encouraged to participate in paid work and public religious work outside the home.

That changed dramatically after the war ended.[60] Even though most American women employed during the war wanted to keep their jobs, layoffs targeting women commenced just weeks after V-E Day (Victory in Europe Day). As experts and popular culture began to pressure women to leave paid work and return home, gender ideals in Adventism shifted once more to focus on the domestic sphere to the almost complete exclusion of women's broader work or contributions. Although White had praised her own domestic staff and wrote that women could employ others in their homes with perfect propriety, by the 1950s *Review* authors accused working mothers who placed their children in childcare of "farming [them] out" and asserted that to do so threatened the happiness of the home. Moreover, the "breakup of the home" was attributed to the "'emancipation' of women, where women go into competition with men."[61] "'Others' can never give the child the motherly interest and care the child deserves and requires."[62] Adventist admonitions echoed popular secular rhetoric in claiming that women's work outside the home was unnecessary and threatened the family, and therefore society.[63] Women and men were explicitly depicted as homemakers and breadwinners; women were "created . . . to be a helpmeet"[64] and men "[work] untiringly, that [they] may provide well for those in [their] care."[65] Gone were calls for women to participate in all avenues of Adventist work; in their place were appeals for women to devote themselves to housework and childcare,[66] and warnings that if they did not, their children would suffer.[67] *Review* authors, in contrast to White, claimed that participation in paid work outside the domestic sphere was, for mothers, "selfish."[68] Faced with changed religious expectations and policies, by 1950 women had disappeared from positions of leadership in SDA departments.[69]

Adventist advocacy of women's domestic work was in keeping with secular gender ideology following the Second World War and through the early 1960s, when feminists challenged confinement of women to the domestic sphere following Betty Freidan's publication of *The Feminine Mystique* in 1963. In fact some Adventists, especially initially, framed women's potential departure from the domestic sphere as threatening the family:

> Many mothers today are spending their energies trying to reach that "higher sphere," all the while neglecting the important task at hand, that of rearing their families. We do not have to look far to see mothers who, while trying to satisfy their own personal ambition and hunger for unnecessary praise, are leaving their families to suffer for want of a real mother![70]

Throughout the 1970s, Adventists mostly reiterated gender norms idealized in the movement since the 1950s. June Strong, for example, asserted in 1975 that "woman was born to soothe a troubled child" and complete other aspects of homemaking and childcare.[71] Working mothers were deemed selfish and "materialistic."[72] Still, a few Adventists defended mothers' work outside the home, insisting that it provided opportunity for children to learn skills and independence.

Adventist conversations about gender, work, and family roles continued in the late twentieth and early twenty-first centuries, with an increasing focus on the propriety of women's ordination. Unlike Mormons, however, for Adventists, salvation is not gendered, nor is it connected to marriage. Consequently, Adventists' discussions about domestic obligations focused on mothers, not on women generally. Some Adventists continued to define women's roles as mothers and homemakers as primary and critical to their children's well-being and salvation, but others increasingly encouraged Adventists to support women who worked outside the home, and by 1990 at least some Adventists writing in the *Review* seemed to applaud changing gender norms: "If the traditional concept of the husband as sole breadwinner is disappearing then it is time that the traditional concept of the woman as exclusive caretaker of the home disappear with it. And we'll all be better for it."[73]

Questions of gendered work crystallize in contemporary Adventism around the propriety of women's ordination. Although the denomination was founded by a female prophet, ordination of women remains a contentious issue in modern Adventism since at least the 1970s. Opponents of women's ordination point to Ellen White's lack of ordination as evidence that she must have opposed ordination of women. On the other hand, proponents note that White received her ministerial credentials (sometimes with the word "ordained" included, and sometimes omitted); frequently left her children for long periods to complete her ministerial work; and called for women's participation in public religious work, setting women apart for the work by the "laying on of hands,"[74] and equitable remuneration for women from Adventist tithes.

Despite this—and despite the historical record indicating that early Adventist women were ordained as deaconesses, received ministerial licenses, and served in a variety of capacities in departmental leadership—as women were removed from employ in departments in the 1920s and 1930s, they mostly disappeared from ministry as well. As the "formal acknowledgement and authentication of one's call to service ministry,"[75] ordination is an official credential that has been traditionally denied to women, but lack of ordination has not prevented Adventist women from making vital contributions to religious work. Local conferences select candidates for ordination, who are then approved by unions. Although Adventism has never had a formal policy forbidding the ordination of women, and although women have served in ministerial capacities without being ordained, Adventist world leaders currently insist that the General Conference controls ordination policy, and have resisted ordination of women. Consequently, Adventist women, who never left ministerial work entirely, serve in pastoral positions most often without being ordained, and so with lesser credentials than their male colleagues (see below).

In spite of Adventism's early advocacy of gender ideals at odds with those of the sociohistorical context (and explicit emphasis on the way this distinguished the movement from "Babylon," a term used in Adventism to refer to sinful and worldly society), after the shift toward gender norms more consistent with those of the larger secular context (from the mid-1920s to the late 1960s), *those* norms became accepted enough in the movement that some Adventists defended them in resisting later calls for women's public religious work. A small number of women did continue to serve in pastoral roles in Adventism during the mid-twentieth century—Maybelle Vandermark earned a ministerial degree from Washington Missionary College in 1932 and went on to serve as an associate and later the sole pastor of churches in Virginia; Jessie Weiss Curtis received a license as an Adventist minister and "raise[d] up several churches in Pennsylvania"; and Margarete Prange served as co-pastor in Biclefeld district, Germany, from 1970 to 1976.[76] Nonetheless, compared to women's active role in the early decades of the movement, as well as the vociferous defense of that role by Adventist leaders, women had mostly disappeared from public religious roles by the middle of the twentieth century.

As early as 1950, General Conference vice president Albert Victor Olson (1884–1963) and a handful of other General Conference officers quietly requested a study of the question of women's ordination after noting that a statement penned by Ellen White in 1895 "has been understood by some to provide for the ordination of certain sisters in church service."[77] No policy change resulted, and in 1968 officers of the Northern European Division called for the General Conference to study women's ordination, a committee was appointed, and the question was discussed in 1970. In 1973 Josephine Benton became associate pastor at the Sligo Seventh-day Adventist Church in Takoma Park, Maryland, and Kitt Watts joined the pastoral staff. Additional Adventist women began to train for and serve in pastoral positions in the following years. In 1973, after the Far Eastern Division (now the Southern Asia-Pacific Division) made a request for the General Conference to provide direction on women's ordination, a General Conference committee considered the question in a meeting at Camp Mohaven, Ohio.[78] After study, the group recommended women's full ordination, participation in other religious work, and valuation of women's work in the home. Despite approval of the recommendations by two General Conference Annual Councils, the recommendations were accepted in principle only, and restrictions on women's ordination remained. Two additional years of study followed, and in 1975 the General Conference urged that the "greatest discretion and caution be exercised in the ordaining of women to the office of local elder, counsel being sought in all cases by the local conference/ mission from the union and division committees before proceeding," and indicated that the church would grant women only missionary licenses, ending a century-long practice of granting them ministerial licenses.[79] Despite continued study, between 1976 and 1981 more than thirty women graduated from the Andrews University seminary program, and some local congregations moved to place women in positions of pastoral leadership.

As a worldwide church with a minority of members in the North American Division (NAD), Adventism incorporates diverse cultures, some of which are strongly opposed to women's ordination. In 1977, in response to disapproval from some divisions outside Europe and North America, ordination was dropped from the General Conference agenda. By the 1970s, calls for women's broader participation in the Seventh-day Adventist Church—especially calls for women's ordination—had come to be associated by many critics of women's ordination with secular feminism. Supporters of women's ordination, on the other hand, often made reference to nineteenth-century Adventists in attempting to justify change in General Conference policy to allow ordination. Despite earlier findings of no biblical basis to preclude women's ordination, the General Conference continued to call for study of the issue, and to deny women access to ordination.

A major official action on issues of gender and pastoral work taken by the General Conference was the creation of a two-tiered, gendered system of pastoral credentials. A new pastoral position, the associate in pastoral care, was created in 1977 for those serving in pastoral positions who were not eligible for ordination. Unordained men had been allowed by the General Conference to perform baptisms since 1979, and in 1984 the Potomac Conference voted to allow eight local elders, three of whom were women, to perform baptisms. The response of some General Conference officers in attendance in Maryland, where Marsha Frost baptized a young woman, was to reprimand the conference. In the summer of 1984 the General Conference ordered North American Division women to cease performing baptisms, and promised further study of the issue of women's ordination.

Still, pressure to ordain Adventist women grew. By the mid-1980s, the Camp Mohaven documents finding no biblical obstacle to women's ordination were distributed in the church. In 1980, then General Conference president Neal C. Wilson (1920–2010) asserted that "the church must find ways to organize and utilize the vast potential represented by our talented, consecrated women."[80] Adventists in a number of capacities pointed out that women constituted the large majority of Adventist membership, and that many congregations lacked pastoral leadership. Allowing women access to ordination, they argued, could both bridge the gap in pastoral care and better utilize Adventism's human potential. Neal Wilson noted, for example, "I am not only urging that women be represented in the administrative structure of the church, but also that we harness the energies and talents of all the women so as to better accomplish the task of finishing the work assigned by our Lord."[81] By the 1980s, Adventist women were earning more graduate theology degrees at SDA seminaries; in 1982 the Association of Adventist Women (AAW) was established with the goal of "empowering women for leadership and ministry in the Seventh-day Adventist Church"; and in 1983 the North American Division created a Women's Division. General Conference officers, however, advised the newly created Women's Division not to discuss women's ordination.[82]

The 1984 Annual Council created a Commission on Women in the Church to decide definitively the issue of women's full ordination.[83] In 1985 the commission recommended further study of women's ordination, but also recommended that Adventism take affirmative action to increase the number of women in SDA leadership positions not requiring ordination. At its October meeting of the same year, the General Conference decided *not* to allow women to solemnize marriages or perform baptisms.

In the 1980s, women in new leadership positions called for more positive articles about women in Adventist publications, such as the *Adventist Review*, and Adventist presses, as well as the *Review*, began to comply, especially by the 1990s, in spite of the request by some General Conference officers that Adventist editors not publish on the question of women's ordination.[84] Women's role in the pastorate became an increasingly divisive issue as congregations took up debate and votes on the question of ordination, and more congregations ordained women and allowed them to baptize. The Southeastern California Conference, for example, determined that it would treat women and men equally; that as nonordained men had been allowed to baptize since 1979, so too, now, could women.

Calls for women's ordination only increased in number and intensity, despite the General Conference's continued study of the issue. In 1989 the Ohio Conference and Columbia Union Conference endorsed Leslie Bumgardner for full ordination; the Pacific Union Conference passed a resolution calling to "eliminate gender as a consideration for ordination to the gospel ministry"; and North American Division presidents unanimously endorsed a resolution supporting women's ordination "in those divisions where it would be deemed helpful and appropriate."[85] The Southeastern California Conference passed a resolution calling for women's ordination by 1990. A 1988 Institute of Church Ministry study from Andrews University in Berrien Springs, Michigan, found 960 ordained women serving as elders in the North American Division, compared to 14,495 men. Women now made up a significant and quickly growing part of Adventist lay ministry.[86] Still, by the close of the decade, the General Conference Commission on the Status of Women in the Church remained opposed to full ordination, though it voted to extend authorization for women to solemnize marriages and baptize, a recommendation adopted by the General Conference at its October 1989 meeting. Nevertheless, the NAD requested in 1990 and 1995 that the General Conference officially approve ordination of women. At both of those sessions, delegates voted against women's ordination.

The General Conference of Seventh-day Adventists, which has studied the question of women's ordination for more than four decades, continues to resist women's full access to ordination, but has also granted incremental access to alternative credentials and pastoral opportunities to women over the same period. In 2000, the designation "associate in pastoral care" was replaced with "commissioned minister," and women may baptize and solemnize marriages, and serve as senior pastors. Divisions

Figure 2.1. Velino A. Salazar, executive secretary of the Southern California Conference, presents ministerial credentials to Cherise Gardner at her ordination on 27 April 2013 at the Glendale City Seventh-day Adventist Church. Glendale City Church is part of the Pacific Union Conference, which voted in 2012 to authorize ordinations without regard to gender. Photograph by Gerry Chudleigh.

may, since a 2010 General Conference vote, ordain women as deaconesses, a position that corresponds to that of Adventist deacon. Also in 2010 the North American Division voted overwhelmingly to extend a 2009 working policy to allow either "an ordained or a commissioned minister" to lead North American Division conferences and missions, opening the way for women to serve in these positions. The General Conference pressured the North American Division to rescind the decision, however, which it did in the spring of 2012. That year, the General Conference established the Theology of Ordination Study Committee to examine ordination issues. After several unions voted to call special sessions to address the question of women's ordination, the General Conference clarified that the study would include women's ordination, something that had also been requested during the 2010 meeting of the General Conference.

Some conferences acted without waiting for more study. In 2012 the North German Union and delegates of the Netherlands Union

ₐually to their male
…n the North American
…erence, the Pacific Union Con-
Conference—voted to authorize or-
gender, as did the executive committees of
Conferenc… …fornia Conference and the Potomac Conference.[88]
coll… …these votes, Ted N. C. Wilson (b. 1950), president of the
…Conference, issued an "appeal for unity," in which he suggested
…at "recent actions by constituent union conferences on the question of the ordination of women are 'causing considerable distraction,'" and called for "submission to the collective decisions of the world Church."[89] President Wilson and other Adventist leaders recognized the "vital role that women play in the life, ministry and leadership of the church," but called votes to ordain women "serious mistakes" that "directly challenge two world church decisions," and "a serious threat to the unity of the worldwide Seventh-day Adventist Church."[90]

Less than a year later, in October 2013, delegates of the Southeastern California Conference elected Pastor Sandra E. Roberts conference president. Before the vote, a message to delegates from President Ted N. C. Wilson warned that the move would put the conference in direct confrontation with the world church, and that the world church would not recognize a female conference president.[91] After Pastor Roberts's election, General Conference officers released a statement indicating deep concern that a "local conference constituency elected as a conference president an individual who is not recognized by the world church as an ordained minister,"[92] and in his November 2013 State of the Church address, Wilson called the "danger of disunity" a major challenge to Adventism.[93] In the following weeks, the North American, Inter-European, South Pacific, and Trans-European Division executive committees voted to endorse reports recommending women's ordination.[94] The Southern Africa–Indian Ocean Division reached a conclusion in opposition to women's ordination.

All thirteen world divisions reported to the General Conference Theology of Ordination Study Committee in January 2014. In addition to divisions already in favor of women's ordination, the Northern Asia-Pacific Division indicated support,[95] and the Inter-American Division reported that it would support women's ordination so long as the church made the

Figure 2.2. Delegates applaud Sandra Roberts following her election as president of the Southeastern California Conference of Seventh-day Adventists. With her election on 27 October 2013, Roberts became the first female president of a Seventh-day Adventist conference. Photograph by Gerry Chudleigh.

decision at a plenary session. Four divisions—the East Central Africa Division, the Euro-Asia Division, the South American Division, and the Southern Asia-Pacific Division—voted against women's ordination, but all either agreed to go along with a world church decision to ordain women, allowed that other divisions might decide the question for themselves, or conceded points in favor of women's ordination. Southern Asia reported that it was not ready to ordain women, but would support the world church if it moved to ordain women. In all, only one division issued unqualified opposition to women's ordination—the Southern Africa–Indian Ocean Division. The world church's Theology of Ordination Study Committee prepared a final report for General Conference executive committee officers based on these reports in June 2014, and the 2014 October Annual Council approved a 2015 General Conference vote on whether each division may itself decide the question of women's ordination to ministry.[96]

Unlike in Mormonism, Adventist women's salvation is not premised on their family roles. Adventist women and men may marry or not, have children or not, with no threat of eternal consequences. Adventists are encouraged to pursue education, including higher education, more as *Adventists*—in private SDA schools—than as per gender expectations. Gender norms in Adventism are much like those of the surrounding communities, if a bit more conservative. Adventist women have options regarding marriage, reproduction, and family, but this is not to say that all choices are equal. If Adventists marry, most believe that they may use contraception, but abortion is generally discouraged. Women may work, but if they have children, childcare is still seen by most as mainly women's work. Divorce is discouraged, and should an Adventist divorce and remarry, s/he may be considered to have committed adultery. This general similarity to wider sociocultural gender norms points to the import of the question of ordination: lack of access to ordination to ministry is the major obstacle to full religious participation and leadership for Adventist women, and the major barrier to symbolic equality for Adventist women and girls.

Ordination of Adventist women is divisive largely because of the symbolic value attached to the question. As the sociologist Mark Chaves points out, women's ordination was originally, especially during the Second Great Awakening, justified by proponents based on the "extraordinary abilities of the few women who wanted to preach," the "special religious sensibilities of women," or the "practical need for effective workers for Christ."[97] Only later, in the context of the first-wave women's movement—in the United States beginning with the first women's rights conference in Seneca Falls, New York, in 1848 until around 1920 with the ratification of the Nineteenth Amendment to the Constitution granting women the right to vote—did women's ordination become associated with gender equality, and this association became even more explicit in the late twentieth and early twenty-first centuries as women's ordination was associated with feminism. This association led the question of women's ordination to have symbolic resonance and contributed to its divisiveness. Indeed, Adventists Affirm, a group established to defend what participants perceive as traditional Adventist values, decries the

> systematic and aggressive lobbying *by liberal and feminist groups* for the church to issue unisex ordination credentials for ordained and nonordained employees of the church; the hijacking of official church publica-

tions, institutions, departments, and certain other organs and events of the church for pro-ordination propaganda; and the silencing, coercion, or persecution of individuals who challenge the un-Biblical practice of ordaining women as elders or pastors.[98]

In both Adventism and Mormonism, reactions to women and definitions of gender can be understood as part of the religions' reactions to their broader social context. In the nineteenth century, when the sociocultural context limited women's legal rights, including their access to more remunerative and public roles, for a religious movement to encourage women's public participation was to take a position—vis-à-vis "the world"—of distinction. For Mormon periodicals to call for equal working conditions for girls and women, for Mormon church leaders to call for women's participation in higher education and paid work in fields normally reserved for men, served to distinguish the movement from its social context. For Adventists to not only adamantly defend Ellen White's role as prophet, but call on all women to engage in the work necessary to hasten the Parousia set Adventism apart from its broader social milieu. As these movements became more routinized and bureaucratic during the twentieth century, both generally became more like other Protestant movements and less distinct from the world, in part in order to attract converts, and as a result of the maturation of generations subsequent to the founding generation.

This shift—this alignment with the wider society—coincided, in both movements, with the mid-twentieth-century American emphasis on domesticity for women that followed the end of the Second World War. We see some variation in these religions regarding ideals for women in the 1920s, 1930s, and 1940s, but as the secular world—including psychologists, popular literature and magazines, television, mainline religious leaders, politicians, and others—encouraged men to be breadwinners and women to remain inside the home as wives, mothers, and homemakers, Mormon and Adventist leaders and official periodicals concurred. Especially in Mormonism, these ideals became so connected to religious ideals and theology that church leaders came to defend them as integral to the movement. Thus, when the second-wave feminist movement in the 1960s and 1970s challenged those ideals, some leaders and adherents in both movements portrayed the challenge as threatening

core tenets of the movement. Mormon leaders resisted feminist movement by restating gender ideals previously most explicitly advocated in
the movement during the 1950s, using church resources to oppose the
proposed Equal Rights Amendment, naming "feminists" a "danger" to
the church, and excommunicating some feminists.[99] Adventist leaders
have taken a somewhat more conciliatory approach, attempting to sat-
isfy both opponents and supporters of women's ordination by perpetu-
ally studying the issue, and allowing the creation of a two-tiered pastoral
system that provides women most of the privileges of pastoral work,
while at the same time avoiding the symbolic shift that endorsement of
full ordination of women would entail. Recent votes to ordain Adventist
women have been met with resistance, but the General Conference lacks
the concentration of institutional power that Mormon church leaders
enjoy, and so Adventist world leadership discouraged the votes for ordination, and called them "mistakes," but did not expel proponents of
women's ordination. As Chaves notes, "Women's ordination symbolizes
liberal modernity, and that is why it is so deeply resisted by religious
organizations defined centrally by their antiliberal spirit."[100] On the
question of women's ordination, Adventism is a religion largely divided:
North American Division, European, and Australian Adventists—and
within these urban, younger, and more highly educated Adventists—
tend to be more comfortable with modernism, including women's ordination; Adventists in Latin America, Africa, and other parts of the
developing world have generally been more resistant to liberal modernism, including women's ordination.

As in other denominations, in Adventism, "rules about women's ordination . . . have less to do with women clergy than with symbolizing cooperation with or resistance to a much broader social project."[101] Indeed,
women in Adventism may perform functions of an ordained pastor,
with the exceptions of administrative capacities that require ordination,
such as organizing a church, ordaining others, or serving in "leadership,
committee and delegate posts."[102] Rules precluding their ordination
symbolically distinguish women's religious leadership and make it more
difficult for them to secure pastoral, especially full-time senior pastoral,
positions. They sometimes also face resistance from congregants, especially initially.[103] Still, as commissioned ministers, women serve as de
facto pastors: it is no longer novel in many North American Division

congregations for women to preach, baptize, or marry, and Adventist women in China have been ordained since the 1980s.[104] The two-tiered pastoral system Adventism has evolved in its response to calls for women's ordination mostly placates opponents of women's ordination, while at the same time allowing women to participate in most pastoral work. It is unclear for how long this compromise will remain viable. Recent votes to ordain women in some unions and conferences, as well as the election of a female conference president, suggest fault lines, and support for women's ordination in the North American, Trans-European, and South Pacific Divisions—divisions that make significant financial contributions to the General Conference, and from whom most church leaders are drawn—create pressure for full ordination.

3

The Family International

Sexualizing Gender

Origin of The Family International

The Family International (TFI or "The Family," which has been called various names, including Teens for Christ, the Children of God, The Family of Love, and others) is one of the most controversial new religions to emerge from the Jesus Movement of the late 1960s and 1970s. The Family asked those who joined the movement to "forsake all"—to give up all of their worldly possessions—renounce materialism, live communally, devote their lives to personal worship and evangelism, and follow the teachings of an Endtime prophet. These teachings, in combination with unusual sexual beliefs and practices, led the media to classify The Family as a "cult," grouped with religions such as the Unification Church (the Moonies), and the Peoples Temple. Especially in its first decade, The Family attracted young, college-age adults, many of whom were involved in the 1960s counterculture movement. Despite extreme resistance from parents, members of the anticult movement, media, and even governments, members of the group led hundreds of thousands of people to Christ through evangelism. Over the course of the movement's lifetime, about thirty-five thousand people have spent at least some time within the group, though it has never numbered more than ten thousand members at one time. Recently, facing serious challenges to its long-term viability, The Family International moved away from its most distinct beliefs and practices, resulting in a contemporary movement that is far more similar to Christian evangelical groups. Despite these dramatic changes, the long-term survival of the movement is uncertain.

This new religion originated around a charismatic leader named David Berg (1919–1994), whose maternal grandfather, John Lincoln Brandt (1860–1946), was a preacher and author affiliated with the Methodists and later with the Disciples of Christ, and whose mother was the well-known radio evangelist Virginia Brandt Berg (1886–1968). By the time he was a young adult, Berg claimed spiritual gifts, including the gift of prophecy.[1] He obtained conscientious objector status in World War II and a disability discharge due to a heart ailment,[2] and later claimed that during his service he was miraculously healed from pneumonia. After the war he married Jane Miller (who would eventually be known as Mother Eve, 1922–2011), and together they had four children. Like his mother, Berg became a Christian and Missionary Alliance minister in the 1940s, but he was removed from his position a short time later over disagreements with group leaders. This and other conflicts with religious authorities appear to have contributed to Berg's rejection of established religions, which he came to call "Churchianity." In the 1950s Berg ministered with the evangelist Fred Jordan (d. 1988) at his Soul Clinic in Los Angeles, and went to Florida to begin his own Soul Clinic. Even in the 1950s Berg's religious style was unconventional: he encouraged followers to distribute literature in church parking lots, and to interrupt church services with their own gospel message.

In 1961 Berg received a revelation that he was appointed by God to destroy the "false System" of religion.[3] For several years he traveled throughout North America and Mexico with his three youngest children, all in their teens, in an old Dodge camper, proselytizing.[4] In 1967 his mother wrote to encourage him to return to California to witness to hippies. After moving with his family to his mother's home in Huntington Beach, Berg began to use the Light Club coffeehouse to evangelize counterculture teens and young adults, especially through music. His children and a small handful of followers would play guitar and sing, and after they began to dress and communicate like the hippies that they were trying to interest, they had some success attracting young people. Berg's anti-establishment talk about destroying the system appealed to hippies, and Berg invited some followers to live with him and his family in his mother's home (his mother died in 1968).

Berg, soon called a number of names by his young followers—such as Uncle Dave, Dad, Moses, Mo, King David, and Father David, among others—combined elements of Pentecostal Holiness religion with hippie culture. Followers were encouraged to read and trust the Bible, and to withdraw from "the System"—established churches and all social institutions. Former drug addicts and street people were attracted to the direct, personal experience with Jesus the movement offered. Originally Berg emphasized abstinence, encouraging followers to give up their worldly possessions, drugs, tobacco, most alcohol, and sex outside marriage, and by the spring of 1969, Berg had around fifty followers.[5] In April 1969 they split up into caravans and traveled around the United States and Canada engaging in a number of provocative protests, such as picketing churches. The press soon noticed. Traveling around the country in buses, camping, dressing as hippies, and employing enthusiastic singing as a tool for proselytism, the group attracted attention—especially when Berg's followers appeared at public events, such as the trial of the Chicago Seven.[6] Group members donned red robes, smeared ashes on their foreheads, and carried long staffs with which they would strike the ground while yelling "Woe!" The press dubbed the group the Children of God, and they adopted the name.[7]

The Children of God reconvened in the Laurentian Mountains in Quebec in the summer of 1969. In August of that year Berg received his "Old Church, New Church" prophecy, in which God said he would destroy the existing church and replace it with "*This little one, My infant church*"—the Children of God.[8] Not only did God instruct Berg that his movement was the New Church, but also that Jane, Berg's wife of more than thirty years, was to be supplanted. Around that time Berg began a sexual relationship with a young recent convert, Karen Zerby (later known as Maria, Queen Maria, or Mama Maria, b. 1946), as well as sexual liaisons with other female disciples. At first Berg's sexual experimentation was kept a closely held secret in his inner circle; it would be a few years before his more sexually explicit letters—such as "Scriptural, Revolutionary Love-Making"—were distributed more widely within the group.[9]

The group formed one caravan of about 120 people in forty vehicles and resumed traveling, camping, and staging vigils around the country, eventually settling at the Texas Soul Clinic just outside Thurber, Texas, where they worked, worshiped, and studied the Bible, and Berg participated in pastoral training.[10] By then Berg was called Moses or "Mo," Uncle Dave, or King David, and some of Berg's followers had begun to assume biblical names. He originally modeled the group on the Twelve Tribes of Israel, dividing his followers into tribes, and taught that God's covenant with Israel was intact.[11] After traveling to Israel in 1970 and finding Jews unreceptive to his message, however, Berg came to believe that the Children of God were God's covenant people and expressed anti-Semitism in some of his "Mo Letters" to his followers. Berg began to use the metaphor of gypsies rather than Jews to describe his followers, and soon began to receive messages from a medieval gypsy, Abrihim, whom he called a spirit guide.[12]

The early Children of God looked like hippies (though some men cut their hair short after joining the movement), and embraced Berg's Pentecostal style. Women wore their hair long, usually with a center part, and dressed in skirts. Followers were increasingly encouraged to accept Berg as the Endtime prophet (who predicted specific dates for the end of the world a few times, including in 1993), accept a literalist interpretation of the King James Bible, practice street proselytism, call themselves by biblical names, and embrace a communal lifestyle. Disciples were asked to forsake all—to turn over all that they owned to the movement when they joined—and embrace antimaterialism. The group attracted new followers, especially following media attention (such as a favorable NBC documentary, *First Tuesday*), and by the early 1970s the movement averaged fifteen to twenty recruits each week.[13]

Converts were mostly young—between the ages of eighteen and twenty-two—and from upper-middle-class backgrounds. Their parents, often distraught at their children's participation in the unfamiliar movement, labeled the group a "cult" and accused Berg of "brainwashing." Parents of teens and young adults who joined were so startled by what they perceived to be sudden dramatic changes in their children that they initiated the first anticult group in the United States, called FREECOG (Free the Children of God; originally the Parents' Committee to Free Our Children from the Children of God), which pioneered a variety of techniques to try to remove people from unconventional religions, even including kidnapping members and holding them hostage for days or weeks in an effort to "reverse-brainwash" them.

Nonetheless, the movement continued to grow. During his 1970 trip to Israel, Berg underwent a spiritual crisis and transformation of his prophetic role. He received a vision in 1970 in which he saw himself "seated at a table with a pen in hand . . . and, as I was writing on the table before me, from my pen there shot out rays of light in several directions."[14] Following this vision, Berg withdrew from public leadership and began to communicate with his followers almost exclusively via letters. Some of these—the Mo Letters—were written in King James English and others in a familiar, colloquial voice, and they provided followers with contact to Father David's leadership. The letters eventually numbered more than three thousand. Most important, Father David explicitly claimed a prophetic role through the letters, which were distributed to followers from the early 1970s until his death in 1994. The letters were divided into categories depending on for whom they were intended—some for the general public (GP), others for disciples and friends only (DFO), disciples only (DO), leadership trainees only (LTO), or leaders only (LO). Those for the general public were circulated for sale on the street as disciples engaged in "litnessing" (witnessing with literature) and thereby provided some revenue for the movement. Following his announcement that he would communicate as a prophet via the Mo Letters, Father David lived a secluded life with a select group of followers in a series of secret locations. He was rarely seen by most of his followers, and the Mo Letters provided primary contact and guidance for the movement.

As Father David withdrew from his public role, his children and a handful of trusted disciples participated more in the leadership of the movement. Fearing the anticult movement in the United States, his daughter Faith (b. 1951) led a group to Europe to establish the first colony there in the early 1970s.[15] The movement used pop music to attract followers with free concerts, and by the mid-1970s, hundreds of communal colonies had been established around the world, in Asia, Europe, Australia, the Middle East, the Pacific Islands, and Latin America. Teams of two to six members would be sent to a new city, where they would rent or lease a house. They took no secular jobs, instead spending their time studying scriptures and the Mo Letters and engaging in street witnessing and litnessing and, sometimes, bringing a potential convert home for an evening meal, followed by reading scripture and the Mo Letters. In addition to earning funds by litnessing, disciples formed relationships with new friends in the cities they moved to who were encouraged to make donations to support the group's evangelical work. Disciples supported themselves largely by provisioning, a practice in which members introduced themselves as missionaries and asked businesses or individuals for what they needed. The parents of some converts also sent financial support to the group.

By 1976 the Children of God claimed 4,500 full-time disciples (not including approximately 800 children of members) who lived communally in colonies, and by the mid-1970s, they claimed about six hundred colonies in more than seventy countries. Conversions were replaced, by the mid-1970s, by births as the primary source of new members. The young people attracted to the movement in the late 1960s and early 1970s began to have children by the mid-1970s, and increasingly became focused on concerns associated with parenting. As the movement grew, major strains emerged. Any new religion must develop an organizational structure to survive, and Father David received a revelation in 1975 that established such a structure. With Father David (King David) and Karen (now Mama Maria or Queen Maria) at the top, the Chain of Cooperation included shepherds as intermediaries overseeing disciples living in colonies, and a series of leadership positions—such as bishops, archbishops, ministers, and king and queen counselors (to King David and Queen Maria)—overseeing shepherds and each successive layer of the movement.

Though the leadership structure of The Family has changed often and significantly, it has tended to emphasize heterosexually paired leaders. Shepherds were usually married couples, and Father David talked with Maria while receiving revelations in a way that was explicitly included in the Mo Letters (where Maria's voice is recorded and her questions spark revelation). Father David also placed his daughters in leadership positions. For these reasons, the researchers Rex Davis and James T. Richardson argue that The Family was not as "male-dominated . . . as . . . most other fundamentalist-oriented sects."[16]

The Chain of Cooperation, with about three hundred leadership positions, was expensive, and by 1978, concerned that his leaders were not revealing the true content of Mo Letters to disciples, Father David disbanded the organizational structure, fired all leaders except the king and queen counselors, and reorganized the movement as The Family of Love.[17] This process, dubbed the Reorganization Nationalization Revolution (RNR), introduced a more democratic organizational structure, in which homes (formerly colonies) elected their own shepherds, and the number of people living in each home was reduced. Homes were now to answer directly to Father David. Concerned about possible negative reactions to new religions following the tragedy of Jonestown in 1978, Father David encouraged his followers to blend into the communities in which they lived. Without intermediary leaders to connect them, many homes lost contact with other homes, witnessing declined, and the movement lost members.[18] By 1979 The Family had declined 80 percent from its peak in 1977.[19]

Part of this decline is attributed to unusual sexual practices introduced in the mid-1970s. Although in the early years in colonies male and female disciples were separated, and were not even supposed to kiss until they were married, Father David and some of his inner circle had secretly experimented with sex since at least the 1969 "Old Church, New Church" revelation. By the early 1970s, Father David commenced sharing his revelations on sex with disciples in Mo Letters such as "One Wife," "Revolutionary Sex," "Revolutionary Love-Making," and "Revolutionary Marriage." "One Wife" outlined his evolving theology of sex, which held that disciples were to put their relationships to The Family before their connections to their spouses or children:

> The System proclaims and brags about the sanctity of the home and marriage, and marriage being the building block of the home and family, and yet the way they live belies the whole hypocrisy of their lying self-righteousness. They only promote marriage on the surface . . . but it's perfectly all right for them to have licenses and then still be running around with other people! God is the God of marriage, too, and the main thing is to be married to Him and His Work, and when a marriage is not according to His Will, He doesn't hesitate to break it up and form other unions to further His work! . . . He's breaking up private families! . . . He came not to bring peace, but a sword and the dividing asunder of families to make of them His Chosen, One larger happy Family![20]

It became clear in Mo Letters of the mid-1970s that not only was one's relationship to The Family to be prioritized, but that that relationship was to include sexual contact. Adapting elements of the sexual revolution of the 1960s and 1970s, especially emphasis on eradicating sexual restrictions, Mo Letters increasingly called for uninhibited expression of sexuality. Unlike in the larger culture, these admonitions to engage in more open sex were couched in terms of the theology of The Family. Father David indicated that "God will have no other Gods before him, not even the sanctity of the marriage God. . . . Partiality toward your own wife or husband or children strikes . . . against the unity and supremacy of God's family and its oneness and wholeness!" Members of The Family were told that they were married first to God, and that marital exclusivity undermined the "greater unit of The Family." Father David explained,

> We are not forsaking the marital unit.—We are adopting a greater and more important and far larger concept of marriage: The totality of the Bride and her marriage to the Bridegroom is The Family! We are adopting the larger Family as The Family unit: The Family of God and His Bride and Children![21]

Central to these Mo Letters was the idea that sex is created by God and natural, not sinful, and should not be discouraged more than other healthy practices. "So many children have grown up with the teaching that sex and masturbation and their sexual parts are sinful, when they're perfectly normal, healthful, physical activities just as much as hiking, swimming, exercising, eating, breathing," wrote Berg.[22] Though local custom or law might forbid it, sex was God-given and not to be suppressed.

> Therefore, although nudity and sexual activity are perfectly normal, lawful activities as far as God is concerned and as far as humanity is concerned, however, as far as the particular culture in which you live, particularly in the Western culture, it has been made a taboo. This has made public nudity or public sexual activity not only considered sinful, but they've passed laws to make it even illegal, when as far as God's laws are concerned, these things are not unlawful at all![23]

Filled with explicit sexual references and sometimes illustrations, these Mo Letters encouraged nudity, masturbation, and sexual experimentation, suggested that sexual limitations were imposed by "the System," and decried sexual prohibitions. Father David identified only four prohibitions on sex—"fornication, adultery, incest and sodomy"—but concluded, "He even makes a few exceptions to some of these under certain circumstances!"[24] Significantly, Father David forbade use of contraceptives. Disciples were informed that God would not allow them to become pregnant unless he wanted them to conceive.

A 1974 Mo Letter entitled "The Law of Love!" told disciples that as God's last church, The Family was being given "total freedom." Warning, "If you are weak in the flesh, full of selfish lust and play with it foolishly like a dangerous toy, it will only harm yourself and others and hinder the work of God,"[25] Mo encouraged his followers to embrace a new sexual ethos. In order to adhere to God's Law of Love, he explained, something needed to meet three criteria:

1. Is it good for God's work?
2. Is it good for His Body?
3. Is it good for you? Does it glorify God, His Body and edify your own soul? Does it help someone and harm no one? Does it help you or some-one else to do a better job for the Lord? Do you even need it for you[r] own good?[26]

Sex should have the "willing consent of all parties concerned or af-fected, including the approval of leadership and permission of the Body."[27] Father David eventually outlined a number of sexual practices, such as a Come-union (in which members of a group paired off for sexual intercourse), which might seem to outsiders like a violation of biblical proscriptions on adultery or fornication,[28] and ultimately held that all sex was permissible except sex between men (which was called "expressly, definitely and specifically forbidden and cursed").[29]

Married partners were encouraged to engage in "sexual sharing"—having sex with people in addition to one's spouse—as demonstrations of God's love. Framed as an extension of disciples holding "all things in common," Berg called sexual sharing "the ultimate ideal in total sharing, total giving, total forsaking all, total freedom, total living, total loving and total liberty in the total love of God!"[30] Father David's revelations called sex between unmarried people and/or people married to other people part of "creation" and asserted that it was fine, so long as it was loving, consensual, and undertaken to serve God.[31] God made bodies, God made sex, and these were to be "revealed and enjoyed to the full."[32] Those who resisted were "old bottles," unworthy of new truths. Female disciples were told that their bodies were "the love of God, your orgasm is the love of God . . . everything about you is His love," and that they shared God's love by sharing sex.[33] Women were more often admonished in the Mo Letters for not sharing or for being jealous, but both women and men were to "share" sex.

Some Mo Letters seem to indicate that women should not refuse to have sex with men. For example, "Love vs. Law!" asserts,

> Now if she is withholding herself or giving begrudgingly and he gets no real love out of it, then she's not satisfying his need for love by giving mere sex. If she's giving it begrudgingly or resentfully or even with abjection and she doesn't give it gladly, willingly, cheerfully and in love, then she is not supplying that need, and she is guilty of denying herself to that husband and she herself is causing him to seek it elsewhere.[34]

Mo Letters instructed wives to submit and be obedient to their husbands, and eventually came to blame independent women, or "women's libbers," for contention in couples. Berg equated the feminist movement with the Devil's work:

> God's law was that a woman's desire shall be unto her husband (Gen.3:16), & the Devil's been trying to overthrow that ever since, of which Women's Lib is a classic example. They don't desire to please their husbands, they desire to rule over them. They don't want equality, they want to enslave their husbands & to be the boss! It's rebellion against the plan & order of God. The Devil inspires women to rise up against it & rebel against it & hate it & fight it.[35]

Instead, Father David made it plain that women were to submit to men:

> The Lord didn't say that a man had to trust, honour & obey his wife, but that wives had to trust, honour & obey their husbands (Eph.5:22–24; 1Pet.3:1)[.] It's the wife's place to yield & trust & love, honour & obey, but the women probably feel it's unfair, especially if they are women libbers & willful & stubborn, not the yielding, clinging-vine types. I guess they feel it's unfair of God to expect them to trust a man & love, honour & obey & respect him.[36]

Expression of sexuality in The Family differed from that advocated by proponents of the sexual revolution, especially feminist proponents of sexual freedom, not only in the lack of emphasis on women's sexual autonomy from men, but in other ways as well. Sexual sharing was extended, by the 1970s, to a practice called "Flirty Fishing" (or FFing), whereby mostly female followers were encouraged to use loving sexual encounters to bring people to God.[37] The practice originated from Berg's experimentation, beginning in 1973, with asking Maria to dance with men and use sex in order to try to convert them. When Maria had some success, Father David secretly taught the practice to a small group of attractive, trusted female disciples. Flirty Fishing combined Berg's idea that sex was God-given and good with his emphasis on bringing people into The Family.

Flirty Fishing was outlined in a Mo Letter titled "Flirty Little Fishy!," which told female disciples that "if they have to fall in love with you first before they find it's the Lord, it's just God's bait to hook them! You have to love them Honey. You have to love them with all your heart and with all your soul and thy neighbor as thyself."[38] Men were initially involved, though less often, in FFing.[39] In either case, FFing was to entail the consent of all who participated, as outlined in the Law of Love.[40] The practice was not widely encouraged until the publication of the "King Arthur's Nights" series of Mo Letters in 1976, and it was widespread by 1978. The Family provided the sociologist William Sims Bainbridge data indicating that more than two hundred thousand people were "provided orgasms as well as Bible reading" by FFing.[41] Further, the sociologist James Chancellor suggests, "Almost all adult female disciples were involved in FFing to some degree."[42] FFing sometimes entailed acceptance of money or gifts for the movement, and female disciples at times worked for escort services (called ESing) to Flirty Fish, and so detractors criticized the practice as prostitution. The use of Flirty Fishing was accompanied by a shift in focus in evangelical efforts from the disenfranchised and marginal to those who were economically better off. According to Chancellor, "There is little question Father David envisioned Flirty Fishing not only as an outreach method, but also as a principal avenue for developing financial support and political protection."[43] Those engaged in FFing were told not to use contraceptives, including condoms, and children born from the practice were called Jesus Babies.

During the period when FFing was in practice, women were often portrayed in Family literature using sexualized religious imagery.[44] In one graphic from the "Flirty Little Fishy" comic that was widely broadcast in the media after FFing became public, a thin, white woman's mostly nude body is pierced by a fishhook, illustrating that she is the bait to catch a soul for the Lord. Numerous other images portray women who are scantily clad and/or engaged in sexual activities with men. Women, far more than men, were instructed by Father David to use sex to attract men to The Family's religious message, and to bring men to Jesus.

Even more controversially, Berg's writings on the Law of Love intermingled advice on child rearing with enthusiastic celebration of what Berg described as natural childhood exploration of sexuality. Though Father David never published explicit official sanction of sexual contact between adults and minors, Family publications, including Mo Letters, did celebrate childhood sexuality, including sexual contact between children and adults, in pictures of nude children or children and adults in sexual poses, and in written descriptions of childhood sexuality. These publications reached homes just as large numbers of disciples were confronting child rearing for the first time.[45] In "My Childhood Sex!—Doin' What Comes Naturally," Father David discussed ways his childhood exploration of sexuality had been suppressed, and encouraged adults to allow prepubescent children to explore their sexuality naturally and openly. In the same letter he recounted his nanny performing oral sex on him as a child to get him to take his nap, as well as a sexual experience with his cousin when he was seven.[46] This letter set the tone for later Mo Letters on the topic—that adults should encourage childhood sexuality.

Two books presenting child-rearing techniques in Father David's own home were distributed to Family homes around the world. One, *The Story of Davidito*, featured Maria's toddler son, Davidito (Ricky Rodriguez),[47] and the other, *Techi's Life Story*, featured Maria's daughter, Techi. These included depictions of childhood masturbation, adults having sex in front of children, children simulating sex with other children, children asking adults for sexual favors, adults performing oral sex on children, and other sexually explicit scenarios. A quote by Father David declared,

God made children able to enjoy sex, so he must have expected them to!
I did! All my life!—Thank God!—I love it!—And it didn't hurt me any!
Nearly all kids do anyhow, despite prohibitions!—And the only reason
the system frowns on it is that the churches have taught sex is evil!—
Which is contrary to the Bible![48]

Since these children were being raised in Father David's home, and since
he acted as a father to them, it would not be unreasonable for Family members to understand these books as instructive on child-rearing
practices. Numerous charges of child sexual abuse emerged stemming
from practices in the mid-1970s through the mid-1980s, including allegations of abuse made by Mama Maria's son, Ricky.[49]

After receiving a video made by members involved with Music With
Meaning (MWM) in Greece featuring female members (including female children) dancing erotically, Father David provided instructions
for female members to dance in erotic videos. In a Mo Letter he wrote,
"I've gotten so inspired by MWM's love tape that I've encouraged The
Family to make a Love Video with this tape as a musical background,
making beautiful dances!" He provided explicit instructions as to how
to make the videos, telling disciples how to use music "for a video dance
tape which our beautiful girls could dance in in a very artistic & soft &
loving way, what the World might call 'soft porn.'" Berg instructed disciples to shoot longer videos because, if videos were only half an hour
in length, they "kind of whet our appetites . . . and then boom, you're
gone—just when we're beginning to get excited."[50]

Still, by the 1980s, The Family began to revise its sexual practices.
The prevalence of HIV/AIDS and other sexually transmitted infections
(STIs) encouraged a move away from Flirty Fishing. In a 1983 Mo Letter titled "Ban the Bomb!," Maria expressed desire to restrict sex due to
"serious venereal diseases." She forbade sexual sharing at home Fellowship meetings and limited sexual sharing to Family members residing
in the same home.[51] By 1984, Maria prohibited sexual sharing with new
converts for the first six months after they joined The Family in order to
"avoid pressure on female converts."[52]

In 1986, at a summer training camp for young people, several girls,
asked to write private letters to Family leaders, described sexual abuse
by adults. Maria was at the camp, became aware of the accusations, and

requested the publication of "Liberty or Stumblingblock?," which reaf-
firmed that

> we of course believe in God's Love & the freedom & liberties of love, sex
> & nudity in its proper place & with the proper people, but the actual tes-
> timonies & personal opinions from the young people themselves seem to
> point to the fact that overall, older adult sex with young people has not
> borne good fruit.

Instead, for teenage girls, "sex has not been a good edifying experience
for them as children or young teens, & has left most of them stumbled
& fearful & overall very regretful of almost every experience they've
had with adults."[53] By 1989 Maria published another letter, "Flirty Little Teens, Beware!," which officially forbade adult sexual contact with
minors, making such contact an excommunicable offense.[54]

The Story of Davidito and Mo Letters on sex, as well as accusations of immoderate nudity, open display of sexuality in the presence
of children, and sexual contact between adults and minors in homes
became the backbone of former members' charges of sexual abuse in
the 1990s. Negative attention focused on the group after an ABC *20/20*
episode drew attention to FFing. Vivian Shillander, a former member, was featured taking her four oldest children from their father—a
Family member who had legal custody—with the assistance of two
"private detectives." Though the children cried and begged to stay
with their father on national television, the episode sparked investiga-
tions of child abuse in numerous countries. In Argentina, Australia,
Brazil, France, Italy, Japan, Norway, Peru, Spain, Sweden, the United
Kingdom, the United States, and Venezuela, allegations of child sexual
abuse were investigated, and at least six hundred children in Family
homes were removed by authorities, sometimes for months. Despite
extensive investigation of Family homes and materials, no criminal
charges of child abuse were ever legally substantiated, and all children were returned to their parents. By the time that children were
removed from Family homes, *The Story of Davidito* and other sexually explicit materials had been ordered destroyed, and the movement
had proscribed sexual contact with children. Still, those accused of
child abuse were sometimes subjected to invasive and illegal searches

and detention, and deprived of contact with their children for long periods.[55]

Apologies for former actions of The Family followed in the 1990s. At least one of these was offered in the context of a child custody dispute. In a United Kingdom child custody case in the 1990s, a woman raised in the movement testified that she had been instructed to dance erotically in a nude video for Father David at the age of six. The custody case did not directly involve this or other former members called to testify, but in determining the safety of the child in question (whose grandmother sought to gain custody of him from her daughter, a member of The Family), the judge delved into sexual practices of the movement in the 1980s. Other former members raised in the group also testified to having been subjected to sexual contact with adults. Among these was one of Father David's granddaughters, who testified that Father David sexually abused her as a child. Lord Justice Sir Alan Hylton Ward, who presided over the 1995 case, concluded that sexual abuse of children in The Family *had* been prevalent—at higher levels than in the wider society. He required that Maria's longtime partner, Peter Amsterdam (Steven Douglas Kelly, b. 1951), write a letter disavowing sexual contact between children and adults, and after Peter did, the case was resolved with the child's mother retaining custody of her son.

Father David died in 1994, after which Maria and Peter assumed leadership of the movement and introduced dramatic changes in The Family. Called The Family International (TFI) since 2004, The Family adopted the "Love Charter" (the "Charter of The Family International" or simply the charter), which codified members' rights and responsibilities. Distributed to Family homes beginning in 1995, the Love Charter emphasized long-standing core tenets of The Family, especially sharing God's love for the purpose of bringing people to Jesus, helping people, and improving people's personal relationships with Jesus.[56] Members' responsibilities were outlined, as were offenses for which a member would be excommunicated, the first of which was "sexually or physically abusive mistreatment of a child." The Love Charter explicated a "'zero-tolerance policy' for child sexual abuse whether physical, sexual, or educational," called such abuse "not only a crime, but a sin in the eyes of God," asked members to follow the laws of the country in which they resided and report abuse, and threatened to "expel any member who violates this policy."[57] The charter repeatedly and explicitly proscribed any adult sexual contact with children, including "behaving in a manner which could be construed as inappropriate or sexually provocative."[58] Strict limits were placed on sexual contact between minors, prohibiting it for those under sixteen and restricting it to between those of similar ages thereafter.

More changes followed. A document issued in 2000 called "The Shake-up 2000"—which criticized members for becoming more like the world in clothing, music, and in other ways, and gave them six months to decide whether they would accept the responsibilities of living in a home and sign a contract to that effect, or leave the movement—failed to shore up membership. Shortly thereafter, TFI moved away from attempting to reinforce difference from the world, instead allowing members to become more integrated into broader society.[59] In 2004 membership categories permitting lower levels of commitment were incorporated; these created new opportunities for people to be members of The Family without agreeing to abide by all of the rules included in the Love Charter. Those who accepted the highest level of commitment, called Family Disciples (FD), lived communally; forsook all; accepted Father David, Maria, and Peter as prophets; and agreed to abide by the charter. Missionary Members (MM) did not agree to abide by all aspects of the charter, and thus might be employed and educate their children in secular schools, and were not expected to forsake all or live communally. Fellow Members (FM) supported the doctrines of the group, but did not live according to the charter or actively engage in proselytism. Outside Members (OM) included a range of more nominal supporters of The Family. This inclusion of various levels of membership in The Family both diminished the distinctive character and lifestyle of the group as a whole, allowing large parts of the membership to be more like "the world," and resulted in an increase in the number of members worldwide, which was most pronounced at the levels of membership requiring less commitment.[60]

These membership changes also allowed much greater autonomy, especially for children born into the movement, who could exercise greater choice regarding how they would live their lives, yet remain members of the group (and maintain contact with their biological families). Also, the charter and recent membership rules replaced strict discipline targeting teens in the past (especially in the 1980s) with more permissiveness, as well as models of socialization into the movement that encouraged greater autonomy and leadership by young people. Some young adults who had been children and teens in the 1980s accused adults of employing abusive practices—including harsh corporal punishment, long periods of isolation, and meaning-less physical labor—in Teen Training Camps, Teen Combos, and Vic-tor Camps used successively by The Family primarily in the mid- and late 1980s. These practices contributed to the disillusionment of many teens with The Family, as did some of the sexual activities of adults of which they were aware, and most of the children born into the move-ment in the 1970s ended up leaving the movement.[61] Changes in the movement since the 1980s take significant steps to correct some of these abuses.

Under the Love Charter, sex continued to be an important aspect of the religion, and The Family continued to emphasize sexual sharing in a more limited way within the group. Online TFI publications currently indicate,

> The relationship between God and His people—Christ and His Church—is likened in the Bible to that of a bridegroom to his bride. The Bible tells us, "For your Maker is your husband, the Lord of hosts is His name" (Isaiah 54:5), and that we are "married to Him who was raised from the dead [Jesus], that we should bear fruit to God" (Romans 7:4).[62]

Called the "Loving Jesus Revolution," this revelation was introduced by Maria and Peter in 1996, and encouraged believers to imagine them-selves engaged sexually with Jesus during masturbation, intercourse, or other sexual encounters, and to verbally express love for Jesus. Accord-ing to the group's website, the "marital metaphor used in the Bible to describe the intimate spiritual relationship between Jesus and His Church is meant to represent the passionate union of heart, mind, and spirit that Jesus seeks with each of His followers."[63] The Family taught that "loving Jesus" included sexual love. Still, by the first decade of the twenty-first century, sexual sharing was much more restricted than in past decades—to those living within the same home, to private settings, and by age as per local law.

Most recently and dramatically, Maria and Peter instigated a "Reboot" of Family beliefs and practices, first relayed to followers in a series of communications beginning in 2009 and implemented shortly thereafter. Change has been a constant of the movement, but the sociologists Gary Shepherd and Gordon Shepherd, who have interviewed Maria and Peter, describe the Reboot as shifting TFI "thinking 180 degrees: from emphasis on subordination of individual preferences to collective needs to the primacy of individual choice."[64] The reboot was undertaken to allow TFI to be "more effective, inclusive, and universal in outreach" and to attempt to provide followers with "general life principles rather than . . . a lengthy list of specific organizational rules."[65] According to the religious studies scholar Sanja Nilsson, "The overarching change that the Reboot is aiming to institute is to relocate the ultimate responsibility over the members' lives from the leadership to the individual members. This means abolishing a major part of the rules and regulations that have served to sustain the Family as a high-tension movement."[66] Specifically, the Reboot lessens each of the most distinguishing aspects of The Family: communal living is a choice; levels of membership are abandoned—adults are either members or not, and one must be eighteen years old to qualify for membership; participation in secular education and employment is acceptable, as is interaction with nonmembers; members may pay tithing or donate monies to sustain the movement, but the amount of such gifts is not stipulated. The charter is revised, and is much shorter as it now omits rules pertaining to homes.[67]

Other modifications in belief include the following: the end of the world is presented as less imminent; individual prophecy has replaced prophecy directing the group as a whole; members are no longer encouraged to accept all of the Mo Letters as divinely inspired, and instead are told that they applied to the specific context in which they were originally given or are simply wrong; members are encouraged to prioritize teachings of the Bible and told that "God continues to speak to his people today" through prophecy;[68] evangelical efforts are voluntary, and have declined dramatically; and sex, including sexual sharing among members, is de-emphasized and has declined significantly.[69]

The Reboot also radically changed the organizational structure of the movement. The administrative arm known as World Services has been replaced with a more limited organizational structure—The Family International Services (TFIS), which includes Public Affairs and Mission Services—and most interactions between TFI and those outside the movement, as well as interactions within the movement, are electronic—online, via Skype, and via the group's webpage.

It would be difficult to overstate the dramatic departure that the Reboot represents for The Family International. Distinguishing characteristics of the movement are transformed, by the Reboot, into practices in many regards indistinguishable from those of evangelical Christians, especially Pentecostals.[70] Given that, and given all that long-term adherents invested in time, energy, commitment, and in other ways to the movement, it is not surprising that some followers are unhappy with the changes. Shepherd and Shepherd describe members' reactions to the Reboot as "mixed," and, though "reliable record keeping no longer exists," they note that based on self-reports and financial contributions, only 3,473 TFI members remained as of the fall of 2012, a 40 percent decline from the 6,000 members at the time that the Reboot was implemented in 2010.[71]

With a declining membership, falling revenues, and diminished distinction from other Christian evangelicals, the future of TFI is uncertain. Despite a highly publicized murder/suicide in 2005 involving Ricky Rodriguez (Davidito) and one of his several childhood nannies, which connected The Family once again in the public imagination to charges of child sexual abuse,[72] The Family has successfully survived the death of its charismatic founder, and undergone profound theological and organizational shifts. Before Berg's death in 1994, The Family had developed well-established publishing, proselytism, education, and humanitarian efforts, as well as an administrative organization—World Services. Today TFI is predominantly a "cyber service community" in which the most distinguishing features of the movement have been radically transformed.[73] The movement, now more loosely organized, emphasizes individual choice, and allows members' participation in the secular world. Gary Shepherd and Gordon Shepherd, based on extensive interviews with Maria, Peter, and others in the movement, describe changes implemented in TFI as contributing to "democratic expansion of decision-making procedures—including egalitarian participation of women and young people—at all levels of TFI."[74]

Gender in TFI

Gender and sexuality crosscut Family beliefs and practices, but not entirely as an outsider might expect. Women have long been central to the movement and its leadership in a way that is linked to movement organization and belief, especially beliefs and practices surrounding sexuality.[75] Locating leadership in heterosexual couples, even at the highest levels, The Family included women in positions of influence. From the very beginning of his prophetic career, Berg enacted a religious community modeled on a family, with himself as Father David, his then-wife Jane as Mother Eve, and followers living first with him, then communally. Members called one another "brother" and "sister," new converts were called "babes," and children born into the movement called adults "aunt" and "uncle." First-generation members called Father David informally "Dad" (while their children called him "Grandpa"), and Maria was often called "Mama Maria." Members led extremely mobile lives after Father David encouraged them to leave North America and Western Europe in the 1970s, and many children born into TFI consequently spent significant time apart from their biological family members. Many children raised in the movement spent years in a communal child care or educational setting, or in a home away from their "flesh" (biological) parents. As family was defined and constructed in this religious setting, women's influence extended from local homes, to Maria's participation in Mo Letters, and to her assumption of authority—with Peter—following Berg's death.

The Family was *family*. The Family has never maintained separate buildings for worship, and their religious rituals occurred mostly in homes or privately wherever disciples were. Disciples began the day with Fellowship Time, which included singing, usually accompanied by a guitar; reading Mo Letters or the Bible; and emotional, spontaneous prayer. Jesus was the focus of disciples' lives. Throughout the day, prayer was frequent, spontaneous, and informal, as disciples talked with Jesus about their lives and sought guidance. Disciples spent a large amount of time evangelizing, which often included some performance, such as singing (children especially might sing in a group for passersby—"busking"), dressing as a clown and tying balloons for a small donation, or performing with a guitar. The primary goal of witnessing was, and continues to be, to bring people to Jesus through prayer, and the movement claims that it has, in this way, saved hundreds of thousands of souls. Disciples also contributed to the work of cleaning and maintaining the homes in which they lived, as well as the work of TFI. Although some of this work was gendered—women were more often secretaries and men handymen—there was also overlap, as men washed dishes and cared for children and couples led together.[76] Evenings were filled with song and worship.

Emphasis on sexuality in The Family assumed a gender binary, and was significant to most members' experiences in the movement by the late 1970s. Women participated—and were encouraged to engage—far more extensively than men in FFing, and were more explicitly sexualized in Mo Letters. Still, women as well as men contributed to sexualization of children, including as depicted in *The Story of Davidito*. Sexualization of others within The Family was not simply a matter of women being sexualized or sexually exploited by men, but of those who had less power being sexualized by those with more power, at least when children were involved. There is no question that sexual sharing and FFing were often mutual and consensual. It is also clear that Father David discouraged disciples, especially female disciples, from withholding consent, telling them that it was their duty to submit sexually to their husbands. (Sexual sharing could never have been consensual with children, who are unable to offer consent.)

Clearly, dramatic evolution is one striking feature of TFI, which has undergone more changes in organization and practice than most new religions.[77] The movement openly acknowledges mistakes of the past, and works to prevent any mistreatment of children. Those who abuse children face excommunication, the single most serious sanction the group can impose, and group rules ask that abusers be turned in to law enforcement officials. Though sexual practices of the group continue to distinguish TFI, they are now strictly circumscribed, and The Family emphasizes commitment to humanitarian efforts around the world through TFIS. This emphasis in the movement is especially attractive to members of the second generation.[78]

With the Reboot, the distinct lifestyle of the group is a choice for members, and more and more members appear to be abandoning aspects of it. Fewer live communally, and members' evangelical efforts have declined dramatically. Many members now live with their nuclear families, work in secular employment, send their children to secular schools, and participate in their communities. The most distinguishing practices and beliefs of TFI are no longer prescribed in a way likely to imbue a strong sense of collective identity and distinction from those outside the movement. Many followers continue to recognize Berg as an Endtime prophet (though no longer as *the* Endtime prophet), but expectations of the Endtime are less defined and more distant. Berg's prophetic work continued through messages received by Maria and Peter after his death, and now members are encouraged to rely on individual prophecy for guidance in their personal lives. It is impossible to know the long-term outcome of the Reboot, or even whether or when it might be replaced by a new direction. Still, the Reboot implements changes that continue to reduce the tension between the movement and its social context.

While TFI continues to condone sexual sharing, with the dramatic turn from communal living since the Reboot, its actual expression is uncommon. TFI's current statement of beliefs continues to compare the relationship between bride and bridegroom to that between "Christ and His Church,"[79] but open expression of sexuality has declined. According to Shepherd and Shepherd, while "sexual sharing, for appropriate reasons under appropriate circumstances, continues as an acceptable individual choice . . . , its actual practice . . . has . . . diminished to a point of likely insignificance."[80]

Though uncommon, to the extent that the movement continues to allow sex between unmarried partners, that distinguishes TFI from evangelical Christians. Evangelical Christianity generally attempts to restrict sexual expression—most often to monogamous heterosexual marriage—and does not conceptualize the relationship between people and God as primarily sexual. Given the potency and import of sex, reproduction, and children's socialization for any group, and the subsequent social attention to control of sexuality, emphasis on freer, more "natural" expression of sexuality, including as part of one's expression of love for God, has in the past invited curiosity and much criticism. It is unclear to what extent decline in emphasis on sexuality in TFI will alter popular perceptions of the movement, as many media accounts of the movement note past practices.[81]

Nonetheless, especially since the Reboot, most aspects of belief shared by TFI are compatible with evangelical Christianity, such as belief in a triune God; adherence to the Bible; belief in a literal resurrection, a six-day creation, and the virgin birth; and belief that there is an ongoing battle between Satan and the angels, and that people will be judged after death. Other Family beliefs, particularly prior to the Reboot, while compatible with Christianity, suggested a difference in emphasis: Family beliefs call adherents to develop and sustain a close, personal, and emotional relationship with God via, in part, communication through prayer, and note that prophecy—the ability to receive direct messages from God—is available to all believers and "can play an active role in their daily lives."[82]

Prospects for The Family's future are unclear. Past religious sexuality contributed to a high birthrate in The Family. Conversions peaked in 1977, and the mean age of converts remains young, at 20.3 years. Eight-eight percent of converts are between the ages of sixteen and twenty-seven. Consequently, the combination of the age of converts, emphasis on the Law of Love, and prohibition of any use of contraceptives contributed to a high birthrate, especially in the 1970s and 1980s, so that by the 1990s, with an average of 5.4 children per family, those born into the movement far outnumbered converts.[83] Since Maria published "Go for the Gold" in 1996—which allowed that although those who endeavored for gold and silver (the best) would not use birth control, those who strove for bronze might—many younger disciples use birth control regularly.[84] As second-generation Family members use birth control, the group's birthrate falls. This, in combination with high rates of disaffection, leaves the movement's future in doubt.

Women have always played key roles in The Family. Heterosexual couples led the movement at every level, and Karen and Peter continue to provide guidance to the movement today. There was a gendering of work in homes (such as childcare, cleaning, and secretarial work), but this was not demanded by Family theology, and was not enforced. Many Family humanitarian efforts focus on helping women—incarcerated women, abused women and their children, and unwed mothers and children. Explicit sexualization of women is nowhere on the current Family International website, which features benign images of families, individuals, and couples. Though still distinct, The Family has shed those aspects of identity that created the greatest potential for serious tension with those outside the movement.

4

Wicca

Valuing the Divine Feminine

Origin of Wicca

Although some Wiccans claim that their religion has ancient roots, scholars and academically inclined practitioners trace its origin to Gerald B. Gardner (1884–1964), an Englishman who published claims that he had discovered a coven of witches at Christchurch, Hampshire, in England, into which he had been initiated. Gardner asserted that the coven had ties to ancient pagan fertility religions dating prior to the rise of Christianity, and he published descriptions of a midwinter Wiccan celebration, including casting a circle, purification ("scourging") of participants, and "Drawing Down the Moon"—invoking the Goddess into the priestess.[1]

Gardner claimed that the New Forest coven, theretofore secret, gave him permission to publish these and other rites, which he did in *Witchcraft Today* (1954) and *The Meaning of Witchcraft* (1959) following the English Parliament's repeal of the country's last laws banning witchcraft in 1951. Gardner provided many of the basic elements of rituals that came to inform contemporary Wicca. He described seasonal celebrations based around solstices (summer and winter) and equinoxes (spring and autumn) in which celebrants venerated a Goddess and God with secret names by dancing naked. He encouraged a ritual in which Wiccans draw a circle with a sword or knife to contain the magical power the ceremony would release, acknowledge the four cardinal points, participate in scourging participants, and dance frenetically. Gardner described covens with thirteen members led by a high priestess in concert with a high priest, cross-sex initiation into the coven to celebrate and promote polarity of the sexes, and a religion that viewed sex as sacred, and honored and celebrated fertility.

The high priestess Gardner claimed invited him into Wicca, and who later initiated him into her coven, was someone he called "Old Dorothy," whom he described as a local, wealthy, elderly woman who always wore a strand of pearls. The historian Ronald Hutton cast doubt on this claim, identifying "Old Dorothy" as Dorothy Clutterbuck (1880–1951), who did live in Christchurch, but whose diaries, dating to the time when Gardner claims to have known her (discovered on her lawyer's shelves in 1986), reveal what Hutton describes as a "simple, kindly, conventional, and pious woman." Dorothy Clutterbuck was an active Tory and dedicated Anglican, with no demonstrated historical relationship to Gerald Gardner, and no apparent interest in "paganism or the occult."[2]

While academics do not accept Gardner's claims of Wicca's historical connection to ancient religion, it is important to recall that new religions commonly claim ancient origins. Christianity tied its own texts to those of Judaism (pairing its own Bible with the Hebrew Bible and calling the Jewish scriptures "old" and its own scriptures "new"), Islam claimed connections to Jewish and Christian prophets, and Mormonism claims ties to Judaism. The veracity of these claims is of less interest, perhaps, than what they tell us about the religions that make them: what a religion projects as its past reflects something critical about its contemporary self-perception—its sense of its core beliefs, traditions, practices, history, and identity.

Nonetheless, a prophet initiates an original constellation of beliefs, and although Gardner made no claims to be a prophet, his influence on Wicca is undeniable. Gardner drew from a variety of sources in constructing his vision of Wicca. From the British anthropologist and Egyptologist Margaret Murray (1863–1963), who wrote the introduction to *Witchcraft Today*, Gardner adopted the idea of an ancient fertility religion that had been suppressed by patriarchal witch hunts. Murray popularized the idea of an ancient religion celebrating the Goddess of fertility and the God of the hunt, and Gardner adopted these ideas, as well as beliefs about celebration of seasonal cycles and magic.[3] Hutton traces other influences on Gardner as well, including secret Masonic societies, Theosophy's emphasis on mysticism and the occult, growing interest in Britain in folklore, the English practice of using folk magic to find lost objects or cast spells, and the Hermetic Order of the Golden Dawn.[4]

Through his publications Gardner began to attract initiates into Wicca in the mid-twentieth century. Press accounts describing Wiccan celebrations were sometimes condemnatory and sometimes more sympathetic, and both increased the notoriety of the movement and attracted more participants. Raymond Buckland (b. 1934) and Rosemary Buckland (b. 1936) were drawn to the movement after Raymond read some of Gardner's books in the United States in the early 1960s. The two are credited with bringing Wicca to the United States from the United Kingdom. Growth of Wicca in the United States commenced originally via word of mouth, and the movement became inextricably linked with the ideas of those who first embraced it. Most especially, the feminist spirituality and environmental movements profoundly influenced Wicca in the United States, as did the counterculture movement, beliefs in anti-authoritarianism, and American individualism.[5]

In 1968 WITCH (Women's International Terrorist Conspiracy From Hell), a New York–based group, published a manifesto asserting that witchcraft had dominated ancient Europe, but had been brutally repressed by witch hunters who opposed the sexual independence and boldness of female witches. The group repeated the claim first made by the German scholar Gottfried Christian Voigt (1740–1791), and later echoed by the nineteenth-century suffragist Matilda Joslyn Gage (1826–1889), that nine million people, mostly women, were killed as witches during the witch hunts in Europe from the fifteenth century through the mid-eighteenth century. WITCH called on women to become witches—sexually free, independent, and assertive—again. Even though WITCH disbanded the following year, the group's ideas about witches proved longer-lasting. The radical feminist Mary Daly (1928–2010) repeated assertions made in the manifesto in her writing, as did the feminist theorist and activist Andrea Dworkin (1946–2005), though Daly and Dworkin focused on the use of Wicca to oppose patriarchy rather than as a religion.[6]

These claims of early persecution of independent and sexually free women as witches were influential, especially among radical feminists, in supporting a vision of history in which powerful women had been suppressed as witches, and pointing to a way for strong women to re-emerge. The archaeologist Marija Gimbutas (1921–1994) bolstered a view of history in which pre-Christian Europe venerated a female Goddess in her publications *The Goddesses and Gods of Old Europe* (1974), *The Language of the Goddess* (1989), and *The Civilization of the Goddess* (1991), as well as in earlier articles. Gimbutas claimed that archaeological

evidence pointed to prehistoric European matriarchal culture and worship of a great Goddess, both of which she claimed were destroyed by
patriarchal Indo-European invaders. Gimbutas also repeated the assertion that the witch hunts primarily targeted wise women and healers, resulting in "eight million" of their deaths.[7] By the 1980s references to the
"Burning Times" (shorthand for the persecution of women as witches in
the European witch hunts) were common in radical feminist literature.[8]

At the same time that some radical feminists adopted the idea that ancient Europe was populated by matriarchal societies that worshipped a
Goddess, but that the religion had been virtually destroyed by the witch
hunts, Wicca was promoted as a form of authentic spirituality and a way
to reclaim access to the feminine divine. For most feminists (like Andrea
Dworkin), Wicca was merely symbolic of female resistance. Some feminist Wiccans incorporated a more literal interpretation.

Zsuzsanna (Z.) Budapest (b. 1940), a Hungarian immigrant, moved
to the United States in 1956, and in 1971 founded the Susan B. Anthony
Coven Number 1 in Hollywood, California. Budapest reinvigorated the
emerging radical feminist interpretation of Wicca (as connected to ancient matriarchal cultures, a Goddess, and suppression during the Burning Times) with explicitly religious rites and symbols—magic, chanting,
dancing, seasonal celebrations, and sacred objects. Budapest combined
Wicca with radical feminism, focusing on female empowerment and
embracing female separatism. Unlike other branches of Wicca—which
emphasize polarity of the sexes through such components as belief in
Goddess and God, celebration of heterosexual polarity, mixed-sex
covens, and leadership by a high priestess and high priest—Dianic
Witches, as these Wiccans are called, best typify the convergence of radical feminism and Wicca in feminist spirituality.

Budapest's influence has been significant, both through her publication in 1989 of The Holy Book of Women's Mysteries[9] and through
the effect that she had on another important figure in contemporary
Wicca, Miriam Simos (b. 1951). Simos was drawn to nature and a Pagan
view of the world in 1968 when camping along the California coast. She
explored Wicca with a friend by teaching a course on the topic in the
early 1970s, and Simos met Budapest after returning from a failed move
to New York to become a novelist.[10] Simos also studied with the Pre-
Gardnerians and in the Feri Tradition,[11] was initiated as a Feri, changed

her name to Starhawk, and in 1979 published one of the most influential books in Wicca, *The Spiral Dance: A Rebirth of the Ancient Religion of the Great Goddess.*[12] Indeed, taken together, Z. Budapest and Starhawk are the most widely read Wiccans in the world.

Starhawk's thinking evolves somewhat through her work. She published *Dreaming the Dark: Magic, Sex, and Politics* (1982); *Truth or Dare: Encounters with Power, Authority, and Mystery* (1987); *Webs of Power: Notes from the Global Uprising* (2002); *The Earth Path: Grounding Your Spirit in the Rhythms of Nature* (2004); and *The Empowerment Manual: A Guide for Collaborative Groups* (2011), as well as a number of coauthored works and works of fiction.[13] She combines Wicca with progressive politics, particularly environmentalism, feminism, and antimilitarism. Her inclusion of men in Wicca calls for a redefinition of gender premised on egalitarian relationships, and she emphasizes a form of self-empowerment that asks people to exercise "power-from-within" (self-empowerment) or "power-with" (working with), rather than "power-over" (domination of) others or nature. Starhawk advocates rethinking power and relationships to prioritize connectedness—to self, to the earth, to others—assuming a responsibility to each of these, and thereby transforming each and the connections between each to make all healthier. Although she does not clearly specify whether she understands the Goddess literally or metaphorically, and celebrates differences in specific beliefs (though within certain confines), the wide readership of Starhawk's works has contributed significantly to the spread of Wicca and has helped to shape contemporary Wicca.[14]

Despite charges of Satanism leveled against practitioners of Witchcraft made by conservative Christians—such as those made in the late 1990s and early 2000s by evangelical Christians against military personnel at Fort Hood who celebrate Wiccan rituals—Witches are in no way connected to Satanism.[15] Fear of Satanism and some charges of Satanic ritual abuse were made in the 1980s and 1990s, but careful investigation by sociologists,[16] journalists, and the Federal Bureau of Investigation failed to reveal any evidence supporting the claims, and by the early twenty-first century, academics and law enforcement concurred that such accusations were the result of a moral panic rather than indication of any actual abuse. Satanism, specifically the Church of Satan, is a very small religion founded by Anton LaVey (1930–1997) in San Francisco in the late 1960s, which encourages qualities including indulgence and self-interestedness, but does not promote belief in any supernatural entities, not even Satan.

Wicca is the largest Neopagan religious group,[17] though many who self-identify as Wiccans or Witches may have no formal training, may practice alone, and may continue ties with other religions, such as Judaism or Christianity.[18] Until at least the 1970s, Witches were most often portrayed as ugly older women in black dresses and pointy caps carrying brooms, or as young, attractive women who "covertly used their magical powers to 'catch' or keep a man or to maintain the peace (as well as traditional gender roles) within their homes."[19] A plethora of information about Witchcraft available via new technologies has dramatically changed those older stereotypes. Television shows such as *Charmed* (1998–2006), *Sabrina, the Teenage Witch* (1996–2003), and *Buffy the Vampire Slayer* (1997–2003), the *Harry Potter* novels and movies (1997–2011), and diverse other media representations of Witches have attracted unprecedented attention to "the Craft." It was originally spread via word of mouth in the 1970s and 1980s, but social networks, online publications, books, journals, newsletters, and other media now allow people to learn about Wicca without personal contact, and to develop their own covens or to practice alone as solitary practitioners. Older stereotypes have been replaced, at least in media representations, with Witches who are "often characterized as attractive, youthful, strong, and independent females who openly use their magical powers to fight against evil for the greater good."[20] It is important to note that Wicca lacks any centralized record-keeping, and so no one knows how many self-identify as Witches or Wiccans, but "there is a sense among researchers that all forms of magical religion are becoming more popular," largely as a result of increased media representations and access to information and resources via modern technologies.[21]

Becoming a Witch used to entail being trained in a coven, but now is often as simple as reading about Wicca online and declaring oneself a Witch, a phenomenon that some older Wiccans fear may diminish the rigor of training and practice within Wicca.[22] Most who become Wiccan report feeling like they have found something in Wicca that they were drawn to even before they knew that it existed, that finding Wicca is like "coming home."[23] The sociologist Helen A. Berger and her colleagues at West Chester University published a census of Neopagans in 2003, and estimate that there are more than 150,000 Neopagans in the United States, the majority of whom identify as Witches.[24] There is some risk to initiates in identifying with a religion that is so poorly understood, which complicates counting adherents, and the boundaries of Wicca are particularly porous, as there is no universal standard for joining or leaving. Moreover, Neopaganism incorporates a wide variety of movements, such as contemporary shamanism, Odinism, and Druidry, not to mention various forms of Wicca, such as Dianic Wicca, the Faery and Feri movements, and others. As Berger points out, contemporary Wicca is eclectic, and incorporates beliefs and practices from a variety of traditions, including shamanistic traditions and Native American and Asian religions. The focus here is the beliefs and practices of those who self-identify as Wiccans.

As Wiccans are averse to any form of authoritarianism, in Wicca each individual is the authority on her or his beliefs; each finds and follows a spiritual path, resulting in a highly individualized and privatized religion. Even those who are trained in covens practice mostly in homes, backyards, or parks. Although some individual groups own land, Wicca has no prophet, single sacred text, dogma, national structure, buildings that are available in communities across the country for worship, or paid ministry. Still, Gardnerian form and access to shared sources of information about belief and practice shape the infinite possibilities for belief and worship. Witches share information through a few online, degree-granting seminaries, such as Cherry Hill Seminary in South Carolina, and Woolston-Steen Theological Seminary in the state of Washington; via books, journals, and newsletters; at festivals; and in covens; and so practices that Gardner advocated—though the specific elements, such as the words of a chant, may vary—generally remain consistent, at least in basic form. The specifics of ritual and belief are open to personal creativity, and Wicca's emphasis on innovation, anti-authoritarianism, and personal responsibility for one's own spiritual development encourage diversity.[25]

Gardner embraced a gender binary, and wrote that Witches should be trained and initiated in covens—secret enclaves comprising thirteen members, including a high priestess and six women and six men. Initiates take an oath of secrecy (though many coven secrets are widely available today on the Internet and in books) and learn the rituals, beliefs, and practices of Wicca. In mixed-sex groups, which Gardner advocated, the high priestess is the leader of the coven, and works closely with the high priest in order to create balance between masculine and feminine energies. All of the other members of the coven are initiated into one of three levels of attainment, and all are also priestesses or priests.[26] Women-only feminist spirituality groups, in contrast, eschew hierarchy, and do not recognize priestesses or levels of attainment, though some initiates may serve as de facto leaders based on personal characteristics that suit them to the task. Although covens form and break apart, and initiates leave and join, they often provide close, emotional connections for their members, especially in a modern world of high geographic mobility, where relationships tend to be fragile. Berger notes that the metaphor Witches use to describe the relationships they form in their covens is family: like a family, a coven is "filled with caring and concern and also with internal tensions and power struggles."[27] This sense of closeness is strengthened by Witches' experience as co-participants in a marginalized group, by shared beliefs and practices, and often by shared participation in political action.

The number of Witches who practice not in covens but alone is growing. The Pagan Census finds that just over half of Witches (51 percent) are solitary practitioners.[28] Books, especially Scott Cunningham's *Wicca: A Guide for the Solitary Practitioner* (1988),[29] and modern technologies contribute to this trend, easing access to both media representations, which may spark interest, and materials that allow learning and self-initiation. Witches also may vary their participation, working with a coven at some times and alone at others. Data from the Pagan Census indicate that solitary practitioners tend to be younger than other Witches, are more likely to live in rural or isolated places, are less concerned about gender and sexuality equity issues, and are less politically active on average.[30]

Berger asserts that Wicca exemplifies late modern emphasis on the individual, self-inquiry, individual reflexivity, and individual transformation. These emphases, particularly among the young, allow Wicca to help form for practitioners a "personal myth,"[31] a cognitive framework that guides their social and environmental activism. At the same time, young Wiccans, though they generally support gender equality, are less likely than older practitioners to identify as feminists, or with particular political perspectives. For the young, Wicca is less connected to a specific political identity or physical community, and is more a privatized religious experience, with emphasis on the individual.[32]

Still, Wicca emphasizes connectedness—of selves to community and to nature, of life to death, of the seasons, of all life. Each individual is part of the web of life and has the power to both influence and be transformed by it. Veneration of nature is central to Wicca; the individual is *part* of nature, and all of nature is worthy of respect. Living and nonliving things have spirits, and each has energy, which can be focused, raised, and used to sway how things unfold. Magic is key. Everyone, Witches believe, has some capacity to use magic, though some may have better innate ability than others, and anyone can improve her proficiency through proper training. Rituals manifest veneration of nature, and allow coalescence of energy and magic. But all of life, even the mundane, is sacred. Nothing happens that is entirely random. Synchrony—the notion that nothing happens by chance, that events are connected—informs the interpretation of life.[33] Actions and thoughts have influence; Wicca helps one to understand and direct that influence, often in order to transform one's self and life.

Still, Wicca is incredibly diverse. With no central dogma and no overarching leadership, as well as the emphasis in Wicca on innovation, Sabbats, esbats, rites of passage, festivals, and personal rituals often incorporate new elements, and reflect the individual(s) involved. This is so often the case that exceptions exist for almost any generalization about Wiccan ritual or belief. Nonetheless, the tendency to follow the outline provided in Gardner's writings, as well as the more recent propensity to draw ideas from publications and Internet sources, both contribute to common patterns. Those are discussed here with the caveat that Wiccan belief and practice vary greatly.

Gender and Sexuality in Wicca

As a nature-based religion that celebrates the web of life, seasonal change, and fertility, Wicca sees mortality as part of the cycle of life. Different sects of Wicca understand Goddess(es) and God(s) differently, but all privilege the feminine, symbolized as Goddess(es). Wiccan groups that include men venerate the horned God along with the Goddess, though they too privilege the Goddess. Wiccans have tended to accept a gender binary, and both Goddess, associated with the moon and the divine feminine, and God, associated with the sun and the divine masculine, are necessary for sexual polarity, according to many Wiccan groups that include men.[34] Diversity of interpretation is common, however, and some Wiccans accept the Goddess and God as literal deities, while others view them as representations of the divine, or as metaphors for nature. Women-only groups celebrate only the Goddess, but here too there is variation in belief about whether she is a literal deity or a sacred symbol.

Despite great variation in understanding the divine feminine, it is most often represented as the triple Goddess whose aspects include maid, associated with the new moon; mother, associated with the full moon; and crone, as the moon wanes. The triple Goddess gives birth to the horned God (celebrated at Yule, 21 December), who later is her consort (Beltane, 1 May), and dies to ensure fertility of crops (Samhain, 31 October). Seasonal changes correspond with emblematic changes in the Goddess and horned God, and rituals celebrate these on eight Sabbats, spaced approximately every six weeks throughout the year as seasons begin and peak. Each aspect of the Goddess is associated with a life stage for women, recasting female bodies and their processes as divine, part of the eternal cycle, and to be celebrated. The feminine sacred is venerated above the masculine sacred, even in Wiccan groups that include men. Many male Wiccans identify with the Goddess, in whom they see a "representation of their female 'selves' or female energy."[35]

Wicca is a deeply experiential religion in which ritual celebrations—Sabbats, esbats, rites of passage, and personal rituals—play a critical part. Most Wiccan rituals follow the outline provided by Gardner, and unique, individual components—words, songs, symbols, dance—are easily inserted into this. Sabbat celebrations follow the wheel of the year and focus on the changing seasons. Before a Sabbat ritual begins, participants normally prepare themselves via meditation or breathing exercises in order to "center" themselves. The ritual begins with the creation of a sacred circle as the high priestess and high priest call the cardinal directions, using a ritual knife, or *athame*. Each direction is associated with certain elements and colors (East—air, yellow; North—

Figure 4.1. Handfasting ceremony in Avery, England, on Beltane, in the spring of 2005.
Photograph by ShahMai Network, http://www.shahmai.org.

earth, black; West—water, blue/aqua; and South—fire, red). As almost
all Wiccan rituals take place in mundane spaces—a backyard, a living
room—sacralizing the space by casting the sacred circle is important.[36]

After the circle is cast, participants enact the main part of the ritual.
Each Sabbat is associated with an aspect of the Goddess and celebrates
her relationship (in mixed-sex groups) with the horned God. The seasons are likened to the process of birth, fertility, aging, and death; each is
seen as connected to the others and necessary for the whole. Participants
may read something written for the ritual or participate in an enactment
in honor of the season—dance around the Maypole, or call back the
distant sun in winter. Goddess(es) and/or God(s) are often called into
the circle. Wiccans dance skyclad (nude), in street clothes, or in robes,
and dancing and chanting can allow participants to achieve an ecstatic
state and to raise energy. Sabbats sometimes involve more participants
than do esbats, though both are often celebrated by the coven, and Sab-

bats connect participants to seasonal change, assist them in transforming their lives, and nurture a sense of Wiccan community. When the symbolic enactment of the ritual is done, the Watchtowers or guardians of the cardinal directions are dismissed, the circle is opened, and participants share food in order to ground themselves.

While Sabbats are celebrated throughout the year and mark the movement of the sun and seasons, esbats are usually lunar rituals marking new and/or full moons. The phases of the moon are symbolic of the aspects of the Goddess—the new moon of youth, the maiden, menarche; the full moon of fertility and middle life; and the waning moon of age and wisdom—and each is essential, part of the cycle of life. At esbat, the high priestess and her coven draw down the power of the moon; the coven chants, sings, drums, and raises energy, and that energy may be directed toward magic. Energy raised at esbat is often focused on personal transformation—finding a lover, empowering oneself, physical healing, alleviating depression, or recovering from a traumatic experience.

Magic is central in Wiccan belief and practice, though the notion of connectedness applies here as well, as beliefs about magic are informed by ideas about the workings of the natural world and the Wiccan emphasis on the connections among things within it, such as thinking and energy. Common descriptions of magic emphasize that because things are interconnected, and because we are surrounded by energy, thoughts and actions have consequences, even if the person who initiates them is unaware.[37] Wiccans believe that the mind, especially the focused mind, can influence the physical world: they believe that "human consciousness is magick, that human consciousness has the ability to manifest change outside itself."[38] Magic relies upon focusing the mind, meditation, out-of-body experiences, and visualization. These—achieved with the aid of chanting, dance, drumming, and singing—may be used in rituals to "raise 'energy.'"[39] Energy can be directed—to an end, such as closing a polluting coal-burning power plant; to an object, which will then convey energy to its wearer; or to a person who is ill, to help heal her.

Even in nonritual settings, thoughts, actions, words, and energy can all be directed, more or less skillfully, to achieve a desired goal. Many Wiccans believe in the paranormal, and use Tarot readings and/or horoscopes to understand and help influence the path of life. Wiccans generally see magic not as something outside themselves, but as something via which they transform themselves, thus allowing them to realize their desired ends.[40] Most Wiccans also believe that one should have permission of any person on whose behalf one might direct magic, and many adhere to the notion that whatever energy one sends out will come back threefold, and so avoid using magic to harm unnecessarily (see discussion of the Wiccan Rede below).

One of the most common uses of magic is to heal. Wiccans, who have been profoundly influenced by the writings of Starhawk and others who portray Witches in medieval Europe as traditional healers, commonly employ folk health remedies, such as tinctures or herbal therapies, and other alternative medical approaches.[41] To heal, Wiccans may also raise and direct energy toward the malady, and/or use laying on of hands or massage. Wiccans also use magic to heal nonphysical maladies: the sociologist Janet Jacobs notes Wiccans' use of a feminist spirituality ritual to heal rape survivors, and concludes that the ritual allowed healing, solidarity among survivors, and political response.[42]

Wiccans have also developed various rites of passage to mark transitions from one stage of life to another, including initiation into Wicca, introduction of an infant by her parents into the community (Wiccaning), entry into puberty and later adulthood, marriage (handfasting), magical naming ceremonies, croning, and death. Though practitioners may draw from available sources in determining the specific elements of a rite, such as a personal Book of Shadows containing instructions for magical rituals (the earliest of which was used by Gerald Gardner, and which modern practitioners may keep, modify, and use), practitioners innovate and personalize rites of passage.

After initiation, Wiccans are encouraged to choose and adopt a magical, secret name—which may change as the individual undergoes transformation—to capture the person's essential self. This is the name by which the individual is called in Wiccan ceremonies. Handfasting ceremonies link people in adult relationships, but unlike marriage, connect people for life or so long as there is love, or as desired by participants. In keeping with the Wiccan view that sexuality is sacred and to be celebrated so long as it is not coercive, handfasting is available to lesbians, gay men, trans people, and bisexuals. Wiccans also allow for polyamory, and handfasting sometimes connects more than two partners, although the Pagan Census found more theoretical support than practice of group marriage in Wicca.[43]

Wiccan parents sometimes participate in a Wiccaning, a naming ceremony welcoming their child into the community after birth. Later, Wiccans may participate in a rite of passage for a child as she enters puberty—around the time of menarche for girls—and sometimes a rite of passage as the young person graduates from high school and prepares to leave his parent's home. Both puberty rites are normally unisex. Wiccans encourage the child to find her own spiritual path.[44] Witches borrow ideas about rituals from a variety of sources, especially available information about prehistoric practices, and see rites of passage filling a gap in modern culture, which lacks rites of passage, especially into adulthood.

In middle age, a woman may participate in a croning rite, which generally celebrates aging and the wisdom that comes with it. This can be commemorated in a coven, a larger group, or alone, and may occur more than once. In a society that overwhelmingly encourages women to retain their youth—or at least the appearance of youth—cronings celebrate old women. Wicca also sees death as part of the web of life, and Wiccans are more likely than those in the general population to believe in reincarnation.[45] The specific contours of belief in reincarnation vary, though Wiccans commonly reference a place of rest and reconciliation first mentioned in the Spiritualist movement—Summerland—where the essential self prepares for its next time of life. Wiccans tend to focus more on living in the present than on death, and Starhawk's *Pagan Book of Living and Dying* (1997) presents death as part of the cycle of life; contains chants, meditations, prayers, rituals, and songs for dealing with death; and provides practical ideas for preparing for death, including information about grieving and such things as a durable power of attorney and living will.

Larger celebrations are likely to occur at annual festivals, most of which attract dozens to a few hundred participants.[46] For a weekend or as much as a week, Wiccans (and often other Pagans) gather to camp, share meals, attend workshops, and dance, chant, and drum around a ritual fire that is kept burning in the center of the camp. Festivals are a time to build community and "come out of the broom closet" for Witches, many of whom hide their connection to Wicca from friends, coworkers, and family members. Festivals have the atmosphere of a summer camp as participants wear ritual robes, go skyclad, or wear street clothes to participate in two or three rituals each day, attend workshops, purchase materials from vendors, and help with the work of the camp. For a religion with amorphous boundaries, festivals provide an opportunity to connect with others, create a sense of community, share resources, and live openly as a Witch.

Solitary practitioners now probably constitute more than half of all Wiccans, and their growth is thought to have increased use of personal ritual. Just as a circle is cast at coven rituals, the individual practitioner is encouraged in instructive writings to create a sacred space (temple), usually with an altar. Personal rituals are innovative; Wiccan training materials encourage creativity and customization of the ritual to allow it to better accomplish healing or whatever ends the practitioner seeks.[47] An altar usually is cloth-draped, and displays a pentacle, a wine-filled chalice, candles of symbolic colors, and incense. It aids the practitioner in focusing her attention and centering the ritual. Altars are also often used in coven rituals, where they serve a similar purpose.

Wicca is not, for most practitioners, a religion of withdrawal from the world, but a religion that encourages participation and responsibility. Moreover, informed by second-wave feminism, Wicca is a religion that values the feminine in the divine and mundane. Women's bodies and bodily processes are not sexualized or impure, but celebrated; sex itself is not sinful, but joyful and integral to life. The individual is encouraged in much Wiccan literature to see her self as whole and connected to the divine, and to see her self and actions both transformed by the web of life and creating transformation in the world.

Many Wiccans adhere to the Wiccan Rede, an ethical guideline that, although quoted differently in different sources, is some version of "An ye harm none, do what ye will." Here too, Wicca varies and there is no universal understanding of the Rede, but most interpret it as a guideline, not a commandment, and a common understanding is not unlike the golden rule, that what a Witch does will come back to him three times as strongly. Called the Law of Return, the Rule of Three, or the Three-Fold Law, as its name suggests, the Rede advises that whatever energy one puts out into the universe, positive or negative, will be returned three times.

Given this, it is not hard to understand why Wiccans tend to be politically engaged. The Pagan Census found that Wiccans are better educated, more politically liberal, and more politically active than the general public. Women make up just less than 60 percent (58.9 percent) of those who identify as Witches.[48] Since Wicca emerged in concert with the modern feminist movement, from which it adopted the notion that *the personal is political*—that personal problems and issues are connected to larger social forces such as policies, laws, and institutional practices—politics are integral to Wicca.

All Wiccan rituals potentially include the possibility of both personal and community/social transformation, and these are seen as connected. Energy is raised in order to direct it to magical ends, and those ends, though they are sometimes as personal as finding a new lover, are often about helping to reconcile relationships, protect the earth, or heal the self and community. Still, not every Wiccan is politically active. Berger suggests that solitary practitioners are drawn to Wicca more out of interest in self than community or social transformation, have less personal connection to the feminist movement, and are unlikely to be trained by older Witches, all of which make their political participation less likely. Berger asserts also that the growth of solitary practitioners may change the direction of Wicca in the future, making it a religion more focused on self-transformation, though she notes that most who join new religions leave, and that some who join will be trained by older Witches.[49] It is important to note that even though they are less politically active, solitary practitioners are politically and demographically more like other Wiccans; both are more politically liberal, are more likely to be white, and have a higher average educational attainment, for example, than the general public in the United States.[50]

Women in Wicca do not have to translate their experiences as embodied selves to their religious beliefs: the language, symbols, rituals, and leadership of Wicca incorporate the feminine in an immediate, valued way. In Wicca, as in all of the other new religions examined in this volume and religions examined in this series, "the self that is developed . . . is a gendered self."[51] The sociologist of religion Meredith McGuire asserts that the increased fluidity of gender that emerged in response to the modern feminist movement has forced religions to respond to social constructs of gender, by either reinforcing traditional gender norms or challenging them.[52] In response both to changing social definitions of appropriate gender and to expanded social acceptance of formerly sanctioned expressions of sexuality, religions position themselves vis-à-vis the secular world.

Wicca, which draws heavily from the second-wave feminist movement, primarily challenges traditional gender constructs, but often does so in a way that reinforces a gender binary, the idea that there are basic differences between female and male, femininity and masculinity. Wicca posits a cosmology that affirms women and challenges male dominance, encouraging connection to the feminine and feminist spirituality for both women and men. Female power, expressed in the symbol of the Goddess, promotes individual and group empowerment and healing for participants, and by participants, in the world. Second-wave feminism celebrated the feminine, which the movement saw as systematically culturally devalued, and in doing so some second-wave feminist theorists reified the notion of the feminine. Writings such as Starhawk's suggest that there are fundamental differences between men and women. In contrast, some other feminists are more likely to see gender as socially constructed, as something that people do (Candace West and Don Zimmerman),[53] or perform (Judith Butler),[54] and as created at the macro level through social systems (laws, policies), at the mezzo level through institutions and organizations (regulations, rules), and at the micro level through interactions (Lynn Weber).[55]

Most paths of Wicca view the divine as both feminine and masculine, and suggest that the two are different. Elements of essentialism (the notion that men and women have inherent, unchanging "essential" behavioral and other qualities) appear in some Wiccan writings. But many contemporary Wiccans also have modified ritual in order to allow women and men to choose which role they play in mixed-sex rituals, and so even though masculine and feminine are distinguished, neither is always and necessarily linked to one sex. Instead, it is more common for Wiccans to describe themselves as having both masculine and feminine facets.

In Wicca, people are encouraged to perform gender in nonnormative ways, to rewrite gender scripts. At festivals, men wear skirts and participate in providing childcare; trans people are almost always welcomed; everyone is expected to help prepare and serve community meals. Many male-identified Wiccans are critical of patriarchy and seek to develop a new type of masculinity, one that values feminine qualities and their own femininity. Most Wiccans believe that, as all people may have masculine and feminine energy, men may celebrate the Goddess to get in touch with their feminine energy, and women in mixed groups may celebrate the God to access and develop their masculinity. The sociologist Wendy Griffin argues that women and men are encouraged in Wicca to reimagine aspects of the feminine in ways that value aspects of bodies and experience devalued in the wider society.[56] In Wicca, menstruation is not dirty or shameful, but powerful and linked to fertility; the pregnant body is beautiful, even divine; age is equated with wisdom rather than the decline of sexuality and beauty. All of these elements of Wicca suggest some recognition that gender may be at least partially constructed through social processes, as the rituals themselves seek to construct gender differently.

This thealogy (preferred over "theology"—thea, Goddess; theo, God) in its celebration of the feminine also reifies the feminine in order to suggest that it is different from the masculine and worthy of celebration. Dianic Wicca explicitly advocates gender essentialism. Women-only groups are most likely to suggest that prehistoric matriarchal societies worshiped a Goddess, and that these were overthrown by patriarchal monotheistic religions. Dianic Wicca idealizes these groups as peaceful, egalitarian communities, in balance with nature, and sees in them a model to emulate, at least in one's own life. Dianic Wiccans are more likely than Wiccans in mixed-sex groups to worship the Goddess (rather than Goddess[es]) as a literal deity, though in every group there is diversity of belief. Feminists in mainline religions incorporate aspects of criticism and practice from women-only groups without adopting beliefs whole-scale in most instances, but women-only groups have rethought religion in a manner that has far-reaching implications even for mainstream religions.[57]

The feminine is privileged over the masculine *because* it is thought to incorporate qualities valued in this earth-based religion such as nurturing, connectedness, and caring. As Berger notes, "Elements of essentialism . . . coexist with attempts to create a community of equity between men and women within Wicca." Masculinity is valued in mixed-sex Wiccan groups as a necessary pole to create sexual polarity, and Wiccan men often embrace the role of protector in their communities. But as

Berger points out, essentialism exists in tension with attempts to "create a community of equity between men and women within Wicca."[58]

Wicca celebrates the earth and all of the natural world, bodies, fertility, and the divine feminine; for Wiccans the mundane is imbued with the spiritual. This is true of sexuality as well. For Wiccans, sexuality is sacred, including same-sex sexuality and polyamorous sexuality. Wiccans, influenced by second-wave feminism, see adult, consensual sexuality as positive. Wiccans incorporate celebration of sexuality into many rituals, including Sabbats associated with fertility and renewal, such as Beltane. Sexual symbolism and skyclad or seminude dancing at esbats or Sabbats are not uncommon. Nonheterosexual, nonmonogamous families are accepted and supported at Wiccan events.

As in other aspects of human relationships, in sex "power-over" is discouraged. Sexuality is unrestricted as per sexual orientation or number of sexual partners, but Wiccan authors almost universally encourage sexual partners to communicate openly and honestly, and to establish clear consent (which precludes sex with anyone who is too young to consent or who is intoxicated, and therefore cannot legally consent).[59] In keeping with the emphasis on power-with and power-from-within sexual expression, condoms are available at Wiccan festivals, where it is not uncommon for partners to hook up, and their use is encouraged in order to reduce transmission of STIs.

This is not to say that there is no sexual abuse in Wicca. Lacking a mechanism to enforce rules or expel those who behave in a way at variance with practices generally accepted by self-identified Wiccans, or even ability to establish dogma against which practices could be measured, some Wiccans have encouraged sexual practices that violate the elements of consent more generally advocated in Wiccan materials. In their 1972 book *The Witch's Bible* (retitled *The Good Witch's Bible* in its 1976 and subsequent publications), Gavin Frost (b. 1930) and Yvonne Frost (b. 1931) advocate sexual initiation of children into Wicca—that the "physical attributes of male and female virginity are destroyed at the youngest possible age, either by the mother or by a doctor."[60] In later editions of the book the Frosts expunge practices other Wiccans criticized as most offensive, but they continue to advocate surgically breaking the hymen for female initiates, and cutting the membrane of the male initiate's penis, as well as sexual instruction prior to initiation:

In the female case, the hymen is painlessly broken surgically. In the male case, the mother makes absolutely sure that the foreskin can be drawn fully back by cutting the underside attachment membrane. At the last sabbat or eshbat before the initiation, the female novice is given the sacred phallus and the instruction sheet in Table 5 so that she can learn to insert and remove the phallus quickly and comfortably. She is also taught how she should lie and what she should do during the initiation ceremony.[61]

Others who self-identify as Wiccans have been charged with sexual crimes, including an Illinois man in 2010 and an Ohio couple in the spring of 2012.[62] Each was accused of sexually assaulting a minor, and in each case the defendant is reported to have cited Wiccan practice in police interrogation.

Although these charges may be consistent with misconceptions of Wicca that link it to Satanism or ritual abuse, they are antithetical to the bulk of Wiccan belief and practice as outlined in books, websites, and other materials. In fact, Wiccans have historically taken a strong stand against sexism and sexual exploitation. When Gerald Gardner asserted that an aging priestess should step down because a younger, more attractive woman would better symbolize the Goddess, Doreen Valiente (1922–1999), an influential member of Gardner's original coven, protested. Contemporary Wicca, heavily influenced by modern feminism, explicitly challenges as sexist any double standard of sexuality or beauty. The notion of emulating youth and beauty in high priestesses has today been replaced by accenting age and wisdom, as in celebrations of croning. According to Berger, North American Witches have worked to eliminate what they perceived as sexism in Gardnerian Wicca.[63] For example, several researchers have observed that when men respond with sexual aggression or harassment to nude or seminude dancing at rituals, it is not tolerated.[64] Though not without inequalities, Wicca celebrates the divine feminine, affords women equal access to leadership (at least as that exists in a nonhierarchical religion, as priestesses are discouraged from practicing power-over) or at least autonomy in worship, and supports social changes in the direction of gender and LGBT equality.

Conclusion

New religions provide an indispensable site for examining gender in religions. They generally claim in their early years that they have unique access to the truth, and so emerge in tension with their sociocultural context. New religions provide us the opportunity to examine Max Weber's assertion that new religions tend to allot equality to women. The religions we have examined here are diverse, but examination of them supports this assertion. One must avoid overgeneralizing from four examples, and use caution in drawing any definitive conclusions about new religions, which are both innumerable and incredibly varied. Nonetheless, we can see interesting patterns of gender construction in at least some new religions. To the extent that the religions examined here emerged in social contexts that limited opportunities for women, each provided some greater access to leadership than was common in dominant institutions at the time. In those religions that became institutionalized (unlike Wicca), restriction of opportunities for women followed institutionalization. For each, the sociocultural context changed over the life of the movement, complicating the movement's relationship to that context in a way that continues to affect definitions of gender and opportunities for women within it.

Catherine A. Brekus suggests that the practical concerns a new religion faces often give rise to a willingness to allow women's greater participation in activities normally reserved for men. Just as Ellen White insisted that "not a hand should be bound, not a soul discouraged, not a voice should be hushed" in order "to help forward this grand work,"[1] Brekus asserts that the real-world requirements of a new religion make women's contributions less dispensable. This—in combination with the break from tradition that charismatic leadership provides, emphasis on lay leadership and direct connection to the divine, and heightened emotionalism, all of which frequently characterize new religions—contributes to a context in which all believers are more likely to be encouraged to participate.[2] Still, new religions frequently define themselves through distinction from the world—the larger secular context—and so that context is important in defining women's role in new religions.

Jackson W. Carroll, Barbara Hargrove, and Adair T. Lummis provide a useful conceptual framework for understanding gender and religious change. They suggest a first phase, the "'charismatic' stage," in which there is "dissatisfaction with the patterns of the old system," and "a new movement which sees itself in direct contact with the divine" "transcend[s] established role definitions" to provide women greater opportunities.[3] The emphasis on charismatic leadership and a break from tradition, as well as the excitement, immediacy, and sometimes—as with an Endtime prophecy—urgency of new truth encourage a religion in which women's contributions are important. The argument here is that the new religion provides opportunities to those not privileged in the wider society—especially women—and to do so amplifies the distinctiveness of the movement. The movement may consent to women speaking in tongues, training to become pastors, healing by the laying on of hands, serving as prophets, contacting the divine, speaking to congregations, or publishing religious journals because *to the degree that the social context restricts women*, each of these sets the movement apart. As a religion matures—as it recognizes that the world will not end as quickly as anticipated; as members of the second and subsequent generations take positions of leadership, especially if children of founders participate in secular educational institutions; as it develops a system to recruit and train new followers; as it attempts to build and pursue secular accreditation for its own institutions, such as hospitals and colleges; as members become more participant in the secular world and more concerned with the way that outsiders view their movement—it is likely to seek some alignment with the larger sociocultural context. To the extent that this occurs, *if the social context restricts women's access to authority*, the religion is likely to do so as well. Women's earlier religious participation may come to be seen as embarrassing, and it may be downplayed for a time. The third stage is "maturity," when a religion's "boundaries blur into the general social structure."[4] The religion, now far more integrated into its social context, becomes more comfortable and tolerant of diverse views, sometimes even going so far as to tolerate "mildly prophetic" expressions of conscience. Modern examples of this may be found in the ordination of women by numerous denominations—including the Evangelical Covenant Church, the Mennonite Church USA, and others—in the 1970s, or the election of Gene Robinson, an openly gay man in a committed relationship, as an Episcopalian bishop in 2003.[5]

Carroll, Hargrove, and Lummis's description of the first two stages of religious development fits Mormonism and Seventh-day Adventism well. Mormon women, with complete propriety, participated through the early nineteenth century in gifts of the Spirit that were later restricted to male priesthood holders. Brigham Young and religious periodicals encouraged their endeavors both inside and outside the home, in education and in professions then reserved for men. They led an autonomous Relief Society until 1971, yet by the 1970s not only did the Relief Society come under greater control of male priesthood leaders, but women were more explicitly encouraged to engage with priesthood power in a supportive role—and earlier Mormon women's participation in religious rituals such as healing was largely forgotten. Seventh-day Adventism emerged under the leadership of Ellen White, and in the first decades of the movement's history the *Review* often published articles defending the propriety of women's public preaching and religious leadership. Ellen White called for women to be set apart by the laying on of hands, and to receive equal pay for their ministerial efforts, and withheld her tithes in order to establish a fund from which to pay them when that call was not heeded. By the middle of the nineteenth century, though, Adventism too had redefined gender in a way that limited women's participation in religious leadership. By 1950, women had disappeared from leadership in every Adventist department. Calls for a broader contemporary role for women in both movements face resistance from movement leaders. Adventism's more than four-decades-long ordination debate continues. Mormon leaders have made some changes in policy as they confront (especially online) debate about gender roles among active members, but they have excommunicated feminist scholars and recently excommunicated a prominent advocate of women's ordination.

It is important to note that Mormonism and Seventh-day Adventism do not currently retain a collective (institutional) memory of women's access to authority in their early decades, and in each many believers embrace more recent, more restricted gender ideology and concomitant limitation of opportunities as normative and historically consistent. Certainly historical resources lay these expanded opportunities bare, and some adherents within each movement expound upon these early opportunities for women, even citing them as examples. Even religious leaders may quote female leaders or earlier male leaders in their support of women, but current leaders couch these in a larger narrative in which men are in control and men (with the possible exclusion of an *exceptional* woman, like Ellen White) are understood to have always been in control of the movement.[6] This is not to say that individuals and groups do not either remember or uncover history explicating women's wider roles, but they may be censured for doing so, and even if that history is widely recovered from relative obscurity, it is *re-covered*.

The Family International and Wicca emerged in the same decades as the modern feminist movement, but while feminism informed Wicca in a profound way, The Family rejected elements of second-wave feminism. Mo was critical of feminists; still he created a leadership structure that, though it changed over time, tended to emphasize heterosexual *couples* in leadership, effectively placing women in even the highest positions in the movement. In the decades of their origins these religious movements faced a social context in which gender ideology and roles were more overtly contested. In recent decades, gender ideology has changed dramatically, and so movements—facing contested constructions of gender—confronted divergent definitions, more feminist or reactionary. Today, The Family International is still a relatively young religion and continues its tradition of leadership via partners, as Karen Zerby (Maria Fontaine) and Steve Kelly (Peter Amsterdam) serve as primary leaders. Moreover, Zerby's leadership has been accompanied by her efforts to attempt to align the movement more with dominant social norms, especially by proscribing practices—such as child sexual abuse—deemed most offensive within the larger social context. Nonetheless, the movement faces an uncertain future. Wicca lacks any movement-wide leader, but women have always played at least as important roles as leaders as men within the movement.

The gender ideology that is articulated by a religious movement appears to be profoundly affected by that movement's social context, and the fact that the social context changes—or may, especially in the modern world, contain contradictory strains of dominant thinking about gender and sexuality—tremendously complicates the evolution of religious constructions of gender. Mormonism and Adventism both restricted women's access to religious opportunities most explicitly in the middle of the twentieth century, in the decades around the end of the Second World War, when media, psychologists, educators, political leaders, and others called for women to leave the workplace and return to the home. (White) men were to again have access to employment in (especially) highly paid and prestigious fields with little competition from members of other groups. Women, especially more affluent women, were told to marry early, to have children, and perhaps to work for money for minor expenditures. If they attended college, they should find a husband there. If they worked, it should be as a secretary, a teacher, a nurse, a librarian—something consistent with then-prominent ideas about women's role and their relationship to men. As contemporary Mormonism and Adventism face internal debates about the role of women, it is unclear when they will embrace women's full participation in religious leadership, authority, and opportunities, but Adventism— with a more democratic leadership structure, policy changes in recent decades to accommodate women's participation in ministry, and facing unions and conferences that ordain (and recently elect) women even when told not to—is poised to ordain women before Mormonism.

Wiccans present a very different and interesting case. With their diverse beliefs and practices, lack of buildings of worship or overarching hierarchy, and emphasis on individual innovation and responsibility, they have created an amorphous community with porous boundaries. Not only is there no one leader or hierarchy to enforce rules, there is no universal consensus about what the rules are. Some Wiccans express strong resistance to the development of a hierarchy, which is sometimes interpreted as entailing development of power-over. Even though the 2003 Pagan Census found that a majority of Neopagans supports development of some structures, such as a paid clergy, and 80 percent of respondents agreed that Witches should meet high standards of training, there was no consensus regarding what those standards should be.[7]

Though Wicca has yet avoided the development of typical religious hierarchy, some standardization is expanding in the movement via new technologies. Helen A. Berger argues that leaders are emerging in Wicca based not on religious qualifications and "purity," but on technical expertise to oversee Wicca's burgeoning websites, newsletters, journals, training manuals, and proliferation of other materials. Wicca today is less a religion of face-to-face contact, and increasingly a religion growing via the Internet. This sharing of information by way of new technologies nevertheless increases the degree of homogenization of belief and practice, as initiates draw from similar materials.[8]

What does this version of routinization mean in a religion that was so deeply influenced by second-wave feminism, that centralizes the feminine and Goddess(es), and that gives women indispensable roles in ritual? Many new religions, including Mormonism and Seventh-day Adventism, have provided women access to opportunities during their initial decades that are unavailable in the wider society, only to redefine gender in a way that restricts women's access to religious leadership as they have matured. This seems unlikely, at least on a large scale, in Wicca given not only the centrality of the feminine in conceptions of earth, fertility, Goddess, and other central tenets of thealogy, but also that as some homogeneity expands around new technologies, women show every indication of contributing to the creation of those materials.

Meredith McGuire asserts that modern fluidity regarding gender forces religious movements to take sides—to align themselves either with those who promote traditional gender ideology or with feminists in their challenge to traditional gender constructs. Of the movements examined here, only Wicca sometimes explicitly rejects the gender binary. To embrace women's leadership may establish a degree of tension with the wider social context; to move beyond the gender binary may pose a more fundamental break with gender constructions and norms, depending on the social context. Recall that if a religion is *too different*, it faces difficulty recruiting or retaining members. Additionally, there is evidence that—in response to increased social acceptance of marginalized sexualities and gender identities (such as lesbian, gay, bisexual, genderqueer, gender-nonconforming, or trans)—religions sometimes link their construction of gender ideology to definitions of acceptable gender identity or sexuality. Examples abound. The LDS church's proclamation on the family calls gender an "essential characteristic . . . of eternal identity," which is linked to dichotomized gender duality and heterosexual marriage and reproduction ("fathers" "protect" while "mothers" "nurture").[9] Seventh-day Adventism calls "homosexual practices" an "obvious [perversion] of God's original plan."[10] Wiccans not only promote valuation of the feminine and feminism, but also embrace trans people and non-heteronormative sexual expressions and relationships.

There is also evidence that the personality of a religious leader, most especially of a charismatic founder, is important in framing the initial thinking about gender and sexuality in a religion. The founder's ideas, desires, and experiences may influence a movement in specific ways. We see this with Joseph Smith's institution of plural marriage and with the expression of sexuality in The Family. In each of these cases, the religious founder's sexual experimentation was initially kept secret, and when revealed contributed to a degree of tension with the larger society so high that some disaffiliation followed. Ellen White, on the other hand, embraced sexual norms that were at least as restrictive as those of the society at large, strongly discouraging masturbation, for example.[11] Both male and female charismatic leaders can potentially offer novel definitions of gender or sexuality. Moreover, here too the social context in which a leader emerges interacts in dynamic ways to influence the leader's thinking, and the expression, articulation, and justification of ideas. The important point is that the *individual* charismatic leader contributes to this process.

Individual contributions, though, are overlaid with larger patterns. In all of the new religions examined here, Weber's prediction that new religions will generally allot equality to women is supported. Though specific manifestations vary in each religion, each provided women opportunities for leadership in its early decades. And in the oldest of the religions discussed in this book—Mormonism and Seventh-day Adventism—the religions limited those opportunities as they matured with the development of religious bureaucracy. Each movement responded to its historical context in ways that allowed it to create and emphasize its difference from the world most especially in its emergence, and each has continued to be influenced by its sociohistorical context in restricting opportunities for women, if and when it did. Gender has been constructed in each movement in a way that helped the movement to define its boundaries and thereby to define itself.[12]

Religions seek to answer questions of ultimate meaning, and those answers both emerge from and reinforce ideas about gender. Religions develop and perpetuate notions of what it means to be not only *human* but also *gendered*, what it means within a gender binary to be *male*, to be *female*, or to fall outside the binary.[13] Religions imbue most aspects of life with gendered meaning and connect those to the cosmos—through creation stories, sacred texts, access to religious authority, notions of appropriate sexuality, forms of socialization, or models of marriage and divorce. Gender is critical to religions as they construct identity, both of individuals and of the religious community, in substantive and symbolic ways. To the extent that gender is connected to ideas about the sacred, gender markers can become emblematic of personal and group religious identity. As such, debate about gender takes on added significance: To challenge gender roles can call into question a group's sense of its collective self. This is why debate about gender in religions is often so contentious.

To the extent that a religion's conception of ultimate meaning is gendered, adherents may embody and enact it in their religious attire, participation in ritual, prayer, recitations, worship, and in other ways. Chanting, interpreting text, discussing the afterlife, relating to the divine, wearing sacred attire, participating in rites of passage, completing religious work, performing rituals (or being prevented from doing so), or doing anything that emerges from shared religious belief may also entail doing gender. At the larger group and corporate levels, gender may be incorporated and established in policies, patterns of authority, collective rituals, symbolic representations, and a plethora of other ways. This gendered religious enactment, to the extent that it is patterned, reinforced, and habituated over time, helps to both define and perpetuate individual and group identity. Moreover, if an adherent who contests the religious group's gender arrangements is expelled from the group for doing so, this can reinforce the group's sense of boundary and identity, at least for a time. Publicly punishing rule-breakers, after all, clarifies the rules.

Consequently, examination of gender is indispensable for those who would understand religions. Religions—those examined here and others—gender the sacred in ways that are connected to their origins, leaders, sociohistorical contexts, and identities. All of these may change over time, and are especially complex in modern pluralistic societies. Though numerous and greatly varied, new religions do the following: construct gender ideology and norms vis-à-vis their larger social and historical contexts; sacralize their gender ideology and norms; and present their current gender ideology as historically consistent. Religions, especially new religions, attempt to provide truth, not just a perspective; endeavor to settle questions, not just to offer an opinion. Gender, connected to virtually every aspect of religious meaning and action, is likely to be reified in new religions. Notions of gender, linked to the sacred and to members' collective identity, take on significance far beyond whether women should be ordained or wear pants to church, or whether men should connect with the feminine divine or share leadership with female partners; gender helps new religions to demarcate religious boundaries, understand group history and identity, and comprehend the divine.

QUESTIONS FOR DISCUSSION

1. How do most religions begin? Why is it important to study beliefs and practices pertaining to gender in new religions, according to the author? Do you agree that new religions offer an indispensable site for the study of gender? Why or why not?

2. The author claims that gender varies, and that this variation demonstrates that gender is malleable. Does gender vary over history, across cultures, or within a culture? Discuss, using examples to support your position.

3. The author asserts that individuals are socialized in institutions, but may also respond to and shape institutions. Provide examples of both and discuss. Is religion a "site of ultimate meaning," as the author asserts? If so, how might that affect the importance of religious socialization for the individual, or the importance of religious socialization for social patterns of gender?

4. A religion's response to its social context changes over time, and is critical in making sense of gender in religions, according to the author. Explain. How do new religions tend to respond to the world—the social context—in their early decades? How does that response shift generally?

5. Compare the origins of Mormonism and Seventh-day Adventism. How are they similar, and in what ways do they differ? Did charismatic leadership play a parallel role in each movement? Did the gender of the charismatic leader shape the way the charismatic leader was accepted in each movement?

6. What is the Mormon priesthood? What authority does it convey? Contemporary Latter-day Saint scholars disagree about whether Mormon women ever held the priesthood, but generally agree that there is historical evidence that nineteenth-century women in the church performed some rituals that are today reserved for priesthood holders. How could Mormon women's religious participation

be limited during the same decades in which opportunities for women in the wider society were widened? Explain.

7. How would you characterize women's position in late nineteenth-century Mormonism compared to the position of women in the wider society at that time? How would you characterize their position vis-à-vis that of women in the wider society by the 1950s? In the 1970s? Today?

8. Contemporary LDS feminists pursue online efforts to encourage Mormon women to "wear pants to church" (and encourage Mormon men to wear purple ties to show their support), as well as ask Latter-day Saints to post personal profiles explaining why they support women's ordination to the priesthood (at Ordainwomen. org). The founder of Ordainwomen.org was excommunicated for apostasy based on her work with the organization. Will her excommunication deter online debate about gender in Mormonism? Do you think that the Internet fundamentally changes the debate about women's roles in Mormonism? Why or why not?

9. Seventh-day Adventism emerged from the failed expectations of the Millerite millennial movement. What was Ellen (Harmon) White's role in the emergence of Seventh-day Adventism? Did Ellen White display characteristics of charismatic leadership as sociologists of religion have defined those? What responsibilities did Ellen White advocate for women in Seventh-day Adventism? What responsibilities did she advocate for Adventist men?

10. Seventh-day Adventist leaders first formally considered extending ordination to women in 1881, but the resolution was tabled and never voted on. The issue emerged again in the 1950s and 1960s, and remained contentious for more than four decades in the modern movement. In the 1880s Seventh-day Adventism was more encouraging of women's religious participation than most then-contemporary American religions. A century later, Adventism's position on women's ordination was more conservative than that of many American religions. How does the author explain this shift? Discuss. What are the major arguments and events of the women's ordination debate in contemporary Adventism?

11. The Children of God/The Family International has been an especially controversial new religion. Who was David Berg? Did he

display characteristics of charismatic leadership as sociologists of religion have defined those? In your opinion, why has this movement garnered so much media attention? It is, after all, much smaller than the other religions discussed in this book.

12. The Family International has undergone more institutional restructuring than most new religions. What are the major changes that we see in TFI, both in terms of beliefs and in terms of organizational structure? What roles have women played in the movement over the course of its history?

13. There are many misconceptions and stereotypes about Wicca. What are some of these? Why might they persist? Do you think that the proliferation of media depictions of Wicca affects popular perceptions of Wicca? In what ways?

14. Is Gerald Gardner a "charismatic leader" in the sociological sense? How does the origin of Wicca compare to the origins of other new religions discussed in the book? In what ways is Wicca's origin different?

15. All religions are diverse, but Wiccan beliefs and practices are especially varied, according to the author. Why? Even given this diversity, are there common patterns of belief and practice pertaining to gender or to women's participation in the movement? If so, what are they? In what ways is Wicca different from other religions discussed in the book? Are there ways it is similar?

16. Does gender intersect with "virtually every aspect of religion," as the author suggests? Discuss, providing examples from each of the religions examined in the book.

17. The author argues that new religions are especially well suited to examination of religious ideas and rules about gender. Do you agree? Do you think differently about women in these four religions after reading this book? In what ways?

18. The author asserts that "to the extent that gender is connected to ideas about the sacred, gender markers can become emblematic of personal and group religious identity. As such, debate about gender takes on added significance: To challenge gender roles can call into question a group's sense of its collective self. This is why debate about gender in new religions is often so contentious." Is the sacred gendered in each of the religions discussed? How? Does this lead to the "added significance" of gender that the author asserts?

NOTES

INTRODUCTION

1. Elaine Pagels, *The Gnostic Gospels* (New York: Vintage, 1989), chaps. 2 and 3.
2. Martin Luther, *First Principles of the Reformation, or The Ninety-Five Theses and Three Primary Works of Dr. Martin Luther*, ed. Henry Wace and C. A. Buchheim (1883; reprint, Grand Rapids, MI: Christian Classics Ethereal Library, n.d.), available at http://www.ccel.org/ccel/luther/first_prin.pdf.
3. John Calvin, *The Institutes of the Christian Religion* (1536; reprint, Grand Rapids, MI: Christian Classics Ethereal Library, n.d.), available at http://www.ccel.org/ccel/calvin/institutes.pdf, accessed 8 July 2014.
4. Meredith B. McGuire, *Religion: The Social Context*, 5th ed. (Long Grove, IL: Waveland, 2002), 187.
5. Douglas E. Cowan and David G. Bromley, *Cults and New Religions: A Brief History* (Malden, MA: Blackwell, 2009), 8.
6. Ann Braude, "Women's History *Is* American Religious History," in *Retelling U.S. Religious History*, ed. Thomas A. Tweed (Berkeley: University of California Press, 1997), 87.
7. Candace West and Don H. Zimmerman, "Doing Gender," *Gender and Society* 1, no. 2 (June 1987): 125.
8. Francine M. Deutsch, "Undoing Gender," *Gender and Society* 21, no. 1 (February 2007): 106–27.
9. Judith Butler, *Gender Trouble: Feminism and the Subversion of Identity* (1990; reprint, New York: Routledge, 1999), 122–23.
10. Lynn Weber, *Understanding Race, Class, Gender, and Sexuality: A Conceptual Framework*, 2nd ed. (New York: Oxford University Press, 2009).
11. In complex information-age societies, ideas about gender within the society are diverse, and so there is never universal consensus about gender norms. Still, more commonly shared ideas and expectations emerge and evolve, and some of these prevail, at least for a time, so that those who assert public variance from them may be considered unusual, or in extreme cases, punished. For example, people disagree about whether women should work outside the home for pay in America today, but a national politician would be unlikely to express the view that they should not, as to do so would limit his or her electability; and while at one time the state supreme court of North Carolina held that a husband could physically chastise his wife, today domestic violence is illegal. While it is impossible to

present every nuance of gender ideals in a complex society, this work aims to consider major patterns of gender norms. As Lynn Weber asserts, while gender patterns (and patterns of race, class, and sexuality) are always changing, they are also pervasive—they influence various social domains, including family, work, and religion—and persistent. Weber, *Understanding Race, Class, Gender, and Sexuality*, 17–23.

12. McGuire, *Religion*, 128.
13. Peter L. Berger, *The Sacred Canopy: Elements of a Sociological Theory of Religion* (1967; reprint, New York: Anchor Books, Doubleday, 1990), 4–9.
14. Some religious studies scholars and sociologists have observed this tendency of religions less integrated into the dominant social order to provide a greater range of opportunities to women. Catherine Wessinger, for example, notes opportunities for women to "function in important leadership roles" in some American Buddhist and Hindu groups, particularly those "in which the male divine is de-emphasized." The sociologist Hans Baer finds some evidence of empowerment of women in black spiritual churches, and Thomas Robbins and David Bromley suggest that new or marginal religions provide an opportunity for experimentation, including experimentation with gender. Moreover, scholars who have examined specific marginal or new religious traditions often find within those evidence of expanded opportunities for women, at least in their formative years. Catherine Wessinger, "Woman Guru, Woman Roshi: The Legitimation of Female Religious Leadership in Hindu and Buddhist Groups in America," in *Women's Leadership in Marginal Religions: Explorations outside the Mainstream*, ed. Catherine Wessinger (Urbana: University of Illinois Press, 1993), 125; Hans Baer, "The Limited Empowerment of Women in Black Spiritual Churches: An Alternative Vehicle to Religious Leadership," *Sociology of Religion* 54, no. 1 (Spring 1993): 65–82; Thomas Robbins and David G. Bromley, "Social Experimentation and the Significance of American New Religions: A Focused Review Essay," in *Research in the Social Scientific Study of New Religion*, ed. Monty Lynn and David Moberg (Greenwich, CT: JAI, 1992), 1–28.
15. Max Weber, *On Charisma and Institution Building* (Chicago: University of Chicago Press, 1968), 48.
16. Weber distinguishes charismatic from other types of leaders, such as those whose authority is based in tradition (traditional authority), or those whose authority is based in law and rules (legal-rational authority). See Weber, *On Charisma and Institution Building*, 46.
17. This claim to new truth is articulated explicitly in some religious texts, such as the Gospel of Matthew, which portrays Jesus repeatedly instructing followers with a message that incorporates phrases that begin "ye have heard that it hath been said," followed by phrases commencing with "but I say unto you." See, for example, the version of Matthew 5 available at https://www.lds.org/scriptures/nt/matt/5?lang=eng, accessed 7 January 2013.
18. McGuire, *Religion*, 252.

19. Catherine Wessinger, "Charismatic Leaders in New Religions," in *The Cambridge Companion to New Religious Movements*, ed. Olav Hammer and Mikael Rothstein (Cambridge: Cambridge University Press, 2012), 82.

20. Bryan Wilson, *The Noble Savages: The Primitive Origins of Charisma and Its Contemporary Survival* (Berkeley: University of California Press, 1978), 7.

21. Gordon Shepherd and Gary Shepherd, *Talking with the Children of God: Prophecy and Transformation in a Radical Religious Group* (Urbana: University of Illinois Press, 2010), 1.

22. Wessinger, "Charismatic Leaders in New Religions," 80.

23. See David G. Bromley and J. Gordon Melton, "Reconceptualizing Types of Religious Organization: Dominant, Sectarian, Alternative, and Emergent Tradition Groups," *Nova Religio* 15, no. 3 (February 2012): 20.

24. Benton Johnson, "Church and Sect Revisited," *Journal for the Scientific Study of Religion* 10, no. 2 (Summer 1971): 124–37. The sociologist Bryan Wilson incorporates this idea in his later work, *Magic and the Millennium* (New York: Harper, 1973).

25. William Sims Bainbridge and Rodney Stark, "Sectarian Tension," *Review of Religious Research* 22, no. 2 (December 1980): 105–24. See also William H. Swatos, "Church-Sect and Cult: Bringing Mysticism Back In," *Sociological Analysis* 42, no. 1 (Spring 1981): 17–26.

26. Bromley and Melton, "Reconceptualizing Types of Religious Organization," 4.

27. The four major categories of religious traditions that Bromley and Melton propose include dominant religious traditions (which have "most completely aligned with one another and with other dominant institutions"); sectarian religious traditions (which "share a claim to the dominant religious tradition but . . . have broken organizational ranks and created new organizational auspices to represent the tradition"); alternative religious traditions (which "lay claim to legitimacy as authentic representatives of non-dominant religious traditions [both indigenous and transplant]"); and emergent religious traditions (which are "located outside of recognized and accepted traditions" and "originate from two sources: those whose claim to dominant or alternative tradition legitimacy has been rejected . . . and those who have made no such claim"). Bromley and Melton provide a framework for conceptualizing religions based not on strict categories but on making sense of religious difference by focusing on the cultural (symbolic) and social (behavioral) alignment or disalignment of religious traditions with dominant institutions. Bromley and Melton, "Reconceptualizing Types of Religious Organization," 6–7.

28. Bromley and Melton, "Reconceptualizing Types of Religious Organization," 20.

29. Max Weber, *The Sociology of Religion* (1920; reprint, Boston: Beacon, 1991), 104.

30. McGuire, *Religion*, 145.

31. McGuire, *Religion*, 145.

32. Janet Liebman Jacobs, "Hidden Truths and Cultures of Secrecy: Reflections on Gender and Ethnicity in the Study of Religion," *Sociology of Religion* 61, no. 4 (2000): 434.

33. Puttick describes Osho valuing what he described as feminine qualities, as he saw in those qualities of a good disciple, and placing women in positions of leadership. Nonetheless, women's leadership sometimes embodied submission to Osho, a male charismatic leader. Elizabeth Puttick, *Women in New Religions: In Search of Community, Sexuality, and Spiritual Power* (New York: St. Martin's, 1997), 3, 162–63, 172–73.

34. Max Weber, *Economy and Society* (1922; reprint, Berkeley: University of California Press, 1978), 247.

35. Thomas F. O'Dea and J. Milton Yinger, "Five Dilemmas in the Institutionalization of Religion," *Journal for the Scientific Study of Religion* 1, no. 1 (October 1961): 31, 30–39.

36. Weber, *The Sociology of Religion*, 104.

37. McGuire, *Religion*, 145.

38. Jackson W. Carroll, Barbara Hargrove, and Adair T. Lummis, *Women of the Cloth: A New Opportunity for the Churches* (San Francisco: Harper and Row, 1983), 23.

39. McGuire, *Religion*, 146. See also Carroll, Hargrove, and Lummis, *Women of the Cloth*, 22; and Margaret M. Poloma, *The Assemblies of God at the Crossroads: Charisma and Institutional Dilemmas* (Knoxville: University of Tennessee Press, 1989), 119–21.

40. J. Milton Yinger, *Religion in the Struggle for Power* (1946; reprint, New York: Russell and Russell, 1961), 22.

41. Rodney Stark and William Sims Bainbridge, *The Future of Religion: Secularization, Revival and Cult Formation* (Berkeley: University of California Press, 1985), 49, 23.

42. Bryan Wilson, "An Analysis of Sect Development," *American Sociological Review* 24, no. 1 (1959): 3–15.

43. Bromley and Melton, "Reconceptualizing Types of Religious Organization," 6, emphasis in original.

44. Carroll, Hargrove, and Lummis, *Women of the Cloth*, 23.

45. Carroll, Hargrove, and Lummis, *Women of the Cloth*, 22.

46. Audre Lorde, *Sister Outsider* (1984; reprint, Berkeley: Crossing, 2007), 116.

47. Simone de Beauvoir, *The Second Sex* (1949; reprint, New York: Vintage, 2011), 283.

48. McGuire, *Religion*, 130–31.

CHAPTER 1. MORMONISM

1. Seventh-day Adventism currently claims approximately 18 million members worldwide, while the Church of Jesus Christ of Latter-day Saints claims just over 15 million members. See Seventh-day Adventist Church, "Seventh-day Adventist World Church Statistics 2012," http://www.adventist.org/information/statistics/article/go/0/seventh-day-adventist-world-church-statistics-2012/; and Church of Jesus Christ of Latter-day Saints, "Facts and Statistics: The Church of Jesus Christ of Latter-day Saints," http://www.mormonnewsroom.org/facts-and-stats, accessed 7 July 2014.

2. Leonard J. Arrington and Davis Bitton, *The Mormon Experience: A History of the Latter-day Saints* (New York: Knopf, 1992), 4.

3. Church of Jesus Christ of Latter-day Saints, "LDS Church History: LDS History, 1818 Fall," http://lds-church-history.blogspot.com/2009/01/lds-history-1818-fall. html, accessed 23 July 2012.

4. Richard L. Bushman, *Joseph Smith: Rough Stone Rolling, A Cultural Biography of Mormonism's Founder* (New York: Vintage, 2005), 42; hereafter cited as *Rough Stone Rolling*.

5. Arrington and Bitton, *The Mormon Experience*, 3.

6. Richard Bushman describes religious revivals that "touched one town after another in the early decades of the nineteenth century," while Fawn Brodie points to "religious excitement that periodically swept through Palmyra." Bushman, *Rough Stone Rolling*, 36; Fawn M. Brodie, *No Man Knows My History: The Life of Joseph Smith, the Mormon Prophet* (1945; reprint, New York: Vintage, 1995), 25.

7. See Brodie, *No Man Knows My History*, 24–25; Bushman, *Rough Stone Rolling*, 39; and Letterbook 1, 1832–1835, Joseph Smith Papers, Church History Department, Church of Jesus Christ of Latter-day Saints, http://josephsmithpapers.org/ paperSummary/letterbook-1-1832%E2%80%931835#9, accessed 23 July 2012.

8. Institute for Religious Research, "Mormons in Transition: 1838 First Vision Account by Joseph Smith," https://irr.org/mit/first-vision/1838-account.html, accessed 23 July 2012.

9. In the first written account of his first vision, written in the winter of 1831–32 when Smith was twenty-seven, Smith wrote, "I saw the Lord and he spake unto me," saying, in part, "Behold I am the Lord of glory[;] I was crucifyed for the world that all those who believe on my name may have Eternal life[.] [Behold] the world lieth in sin and at this time and none doeth good." Letterbook 1, 1832–1835, Joseph Smith Papers. See also Arrington and Bitton, *The Mormon Experience*, 7.

10. Arrington and Bitton, *The Mormon Experience*, 9.

11. After three visits by Moroni during one night in 1838, Joseph continued to have visions for the rest of his life.

12. Bushman, *Rough Stone Rolling*, 49.

13. Mark Roscoe Ashurst-McGee, "Zion Rising: Joseph Smith's Early Social and Political Thought" (Ph.D. diss., Arizona State University, 2008), 96.

14. Joseph Smith described the plates as containing a language like ancient Egyptian hieroglyphics, which he translated with the help of the Urim and Thummim, two stones attached to a breastplate. He sometimes also translated by placing his seer stone into a hat into which he would look while cupping his hands around the gap between his hat and his face to block any light.

15. The actual composition of the Nephites and Lamanites is more complicated than this, and there are two more minor groups included in the Book of Mormon, the Jaredites and the Mulekites.

16. Brigham Young University Book of Abraham Project, "Oliver Cowdery, 1806–1850," http://www.boap.org/LDS/Early-Saints/OCowd-AP.html, accessed 23 July 2012.

17. Claudia L. Bushman and Richard L. Bushman, *Mormons in America* (New York: Oxford University Press, 1999), 15.

18. Dale A. Whitman, "Extermination Order," n.d., Brigham Young University Studies, http://web.archive.org/web/20061020144758/http://ldsfaq.byu.edu/emmain.asp?number=74, accessed 29 December 2012.

19. Bushman, *Rough Stone Rolling*, 323–24. See also Brodie, *No Man Knows My History*, 181–82.

20. Bushman, *Rough Stone Rolling*, 443.

21. Fawn Brodie asserts that Smith had at least eleven wives who were teenagers, and at least a dozen who were married to other men before (and while) they were married to Joseph. The historian Todd Compton suggests ways Joseph Smith's plural marriages combined "spiritual attraction, sexual attraction, and desired dynastic links" in complex ways, and explores how at least some of the marriages created important connections between Smith and other leaders in the early Mormon community. Todd Compton, *In Sacred Loneliness: The Plural Wives of Joseph Smith* (Salt Lake City: Signature, 1997), 4–6, 637.

22. At the time of this writing, there is no DNA evidence that Joseph Smith fathered children with any of his wives other than Emma, though not all of Smith's potential offspring, as suggested in historical documents, have been genetically excluded as his descendants via DNA testing. Carrie A. Moore, "DNA Tests Rule Out Two as Smith Descendants," *Deseret News*, 10 November 2007, http://www.deseretnews.com/article/695226318/DNA-tests-rule-out-2-as-Smith-descendants.html, accessed 29 December 2012.

23. Brian C. Hales, "Emma Smith, Eliza R. Snow, and the Reported Incident on the Stairs," *Mormon Historical Studies* 10, no. 2 (2009): 63–75, http://mormonhistoric-sites.org/wp-content/uploads/2013/04/Emma-Smith-Eliza-R.-Snow-and-the-Reported-Incident-on-the-Stairs.pdf, accessed 5 August 2013.

24. Joseph Smith, *The Doctrine and Covenants* 132:61, http://www.lds.org/scriptures/dc-testament/dc/132?lang=eng, accessed 29 September 2012.

25. Smith, *Doctrine and Covenants*, 54.

26. Brodie, *No Man Knows My History*, 341–42.

27. Bushman, *Rough Stone Rolling*, 446.

28. Bushman, *Rough Stone Rolling*, 447. See also Carol Cornwall Madsen, "Mormon Women and the Temple: Toward a New Understanding," in *Sisters in Spirit: Mormon Women in Historical and Cultural Perspective*, ed. Maureen Ursenbach Beecher and Lavina Fielding Anderson (Urbana: University of Illinois Press, 1992), 80.

29. Maxine Hanks, ed., *Women and Authority: Re-emerging Mormon Feminism* (Salt Lake City: Signature Books, 1992), esp. chap. 2.

30. Beecher and Anderson, *Sisters in Spirit*.

31. Though not uncommon in the early decades of the Church of Jesus Christ of Latter-day Saints, glossolalia was discouraged by the 1870s and "relatively infrequent" by 1900. Dan Vogel and Scott C. Dunn, "'The Tongue of Angels': Glossolalia among Mormonism's Founders," *Journal of Mormon History* 19, no. 2

(1993): 25, http://digitalcommons.usu.edu/cgi/viewcontent.cgi?article=1021&conte
xt=mormonhistory, accessed 8 July 2014.

32. Linda King Newell, "The Historical Relationship of Mormon Women and
    Priesthood," in Hanks, *Women and Authority*, 25.

33. Madsen, "Mormon Women and the Temple," 84.

34. Madsen, "Mormon Women and the Temple," 91.

35. Seventy is a Melchizedek priesthood office that has varied over the course of LDS
    history, but generally is associated with spreading the gospel under the direction
    of the Quorum of the Twelve Apostles. Newell, "The Historical Relationship of
    Mormon Women and Priesthood," 35; see also 23–25 and 50.

36. D. Michael Quinn, "Mormon Women Have Had the Priesthood since 1843," in
    Hanks, *Women and Authority*, 378.

37. Bushman, *Rough Stone Rolling*, 446–47.

38. Bushman, *Rough Stone Rolling*, 443.

39. Brodie, *No Man Knows My History*, 375.

40. Brodie, *No Man Knows My History*, 377.

41. Martha Sonntag Bradley, *Pedestals and Podiums: Utah Women, Religious Authority
    and Equal Rights* (Salt Lake City: Signature Books, 2005), 12.

42. Jean Bickmore White, "Women's Suffrage in Utah," Utah.Gov Services: Utah
    History to Go, http://historytogo.utah.gov/utah_chapters/statehood_and_the_
    progressive_era/womenssuffrageinutah.html, accessed 12 November 2013.
    Non-Mormon women in the Utah Territory sometimes opposed suffrage in Utah,
    fearing that it would strengthen the power of the church.

43. Leaders of the church and the Relief Society, however, provided different
    justifications for extending the vote to women; see Bradley, *Pedestals and
    Podiums*, 16–18.

44. White, "Women's Suffrage in Utah." The historian D. Michael Quinn presented
    evidence that in testimony before the U.S. Congress, Mormon leaders denied
    the post-1890 practice of polygamy at the same time that they continued to
    allow polygamous marriages. See D. Michael Quinn, "LDS Church Authority
    and New Plural Marriages, 1890–1904," *Dialogue: A Journal of Mormon Thought*
    18, no. 1 (Spring 1985): 56–59, 61, 65, 81, 93, 96–98. https://www.dialoguejournal.
    com/wp-content/uploads/sbi/articles/Dialogue_V18No1_11.pdf, accessed 8 July
    2014.

45. The *Woman's Exponent* was founded in 1872 and published by Mormon women
    for the next twenty-seven years. For more than twenty years of its publication the
    Exponent was published under a masthead reading, "The Rights of women of
    Zion and the rights of women of all nations." Only under the leadership of
    Emmeline B. Wells did the journal engage controversial issues, such as suffrage.

46. Second-wave feminism is a period of feminist movement that began in the United
    States in the 1960s and focused on legal equality for women and men, including
    the failed attempt to secure ratification of the Equal Rights Amendment.

47. Bradley, *Pedestals and Podiums*, 18–19.

48. Jay M. Todd, "Improvement Era," in *Encyclopedia of Mormonism* (New York: Macmillan, 1992), http://eom.byu.edu/index.php/Improvement_Era, accessed 23 May 2012.

49. Emphasis on women's work in the home, and the necessity of that work for the well-being of society, did not prevent women from working outside the home, but it did help to limit the fields in which it was acceptable for women to work, and even the kinds of paid work that women were allowed to do. For example, the 1873 *Bradwell* decision by the U.S. Supreme Court held that the state of Illinois could restrict Myra Bradwell from the state bar. Justice Bradley, in his concurring opinion, held that the "natural and proper timidity and delicacy which belongs to the female sex evidently unfits it for many of the occupations of civil life." *Bradwell v. State*, 83 U.S. 130 (16 Wall. 130, 21 L.Ed. 442), available from Legal Information Institute, Cornell University School of Law, http://www.law.cornell.edu/supremecourt/text/83/130#writing-type-1-MILLER, accessed 19 November 2013.

50. Barbara Welter, "The Cult of True Womanhood, 1820–1860," *American Quarterly* 18, no. 2 (Summer 1966): 152.

51. Christine E. Bose, "Dual Spheres," in *Analyzing Gender: A Handbook of Social Science Research*, ed. Beth B. Hess and Myra Marx Ferree (Newbury Park, CA: Sage, 1987), 278–79.

52. Lynn D. Gordon, ed., *Gender and Higher Education in the Progressive Era* (New Haven: Yale University Press, 1990), esp. chap. 1.

53. B. H. Roberts, "The Church of Jesus Christ of Latter-day Saints at the Parliament of Religions," *Improvement Era* 2, no. 12 (October 1899): 901.

54. Susa Young Gates (1856–1933) was an active Mormon periodical editor and writer, and a promoter of women's rights and suffrage, serving as a delegate and speaker to five congresses of the International Council of Women as well as an officer of the National Council of Women.

55. Susa Young Gates, "A Message from a Woman of the Latter-day Saints to the Women in All the World," *Improvement Era* 10, no. 6 (April 1907): 449. Gates goes on to make specific reference to the independence of Mormon auxiliaries led by women—the Relief Society, the Mutual Improvement Association, and the children's Primary Association—"officered by women and directed entirely by them" (450). This independence would change, as many other aspects of idealized roles for Mormon women did, in the 1970s. See Bradley, *Pedestals and Podiums*, 111–13.

56. Gates attributed the valuation of women's participation in education to Mormon leaders, including Joseph Smith, and traced it back to the founding of Mormon institutions of learning, including Nauvoo University and the University of Utah. "The contention of the present president of the Church," she wrote, "is that if but one sex can receive higher education, let it be the girl." Gates, "A Message from a Woman of the Latter-day Saints," 448, 450, 451.

57. David O. McKay, "Safeguards against the Delinquency of Youth," *Conference Report*, October 1946, 111–17, http://scriptures.byu.edu/gettalk. php?ID=264&era=yes, accessed 30 September 2012.

58. This was perhaps most explicitly illustrated with the publication of the pink issue of *Dialogue: A Journal of Mormon Thought*, in which Mormon historians and feminists, including Claudia Lauper Bushman, Laurel Thatcher Ulrich, Leonard J. Arrington, and others published examinations of Mormon women's historically more expansive roles.

59. Thomas S. Monson, "The Women's Movement: Liberation or Deception?," *Ensign*, January 1971, http://www.lds.org/ensign/1971/01/the-womens-movement-liberation-or-deception?lang=eng, accessed 8 July 2014.

60. N. Eldon Tanner, "No Greater Honor: The Woman's Role," address delivered at the General Conference, 7 October 1973, http://www.lds.org/general-conference/print/1973/10/no-greater-honor-the-womans-role?lang=eng, accessed 8 July 2014.

61. Ezra Taft Benson, "To the Mothers in Zion," address delivered at the Fireside for Parents, 22 February 1987, http://fc.byu.edu/jpages/ee/w_etb87.htm, accessed 8 July 2014.

62. Lavina Fielding, "Problems, Solutions: Being a Latter-day Saint Woman Today," *Ensign*, March 1976, http://www.lds.org/ensign/1976/03/problems-solutions-being-a-latter-day-saint-woman-today?lang=eng, accessed 8 July 2014.

63. Susan Faludi, *Backlash: The Undeclared War against American Women* (New York: Crown, 1991), 9–10.

64. Laura Vance, "Evolution of Ideals for Women in Mormon Periodicals, 1897–1999," *Sociology of Religion* 63, no. 1 (2002): 97–102. See also Susanna Morrill, *White Roses on the Floor of Heaven: Mormon Women's Popular Theology, 1880–1920* (New York: Routledge, 2006), 63–66.

65. All publications, curricula, materials, and programs must be approved through the correlation process before being implemented. See Frank O. May, "Correlation of the Church Administration," in *Encyclopedia of Mormonism* (New York: Macmillan, 1992), 323.

66. Ronald W. Walker, David J. Whittaker, and James B. Allen, *Mormon History* (Urbana: University of Illinois Press, 2001), 177–78.

67. Robert Gottlieb and Peter Wiley, *America's Saints: The Rise of Mormon Power* (New York: Harcourt Brace Jovanovich, 1986), 57–58.

68. Marie Cornwall, "The Institutional Role of Mormon Women," in *Contemporary Mormonism*, ed. Marie Cornwall, Tim B. Heaton, and Lawrence Young (Urbana: University of Illinois Press, 1994), 239–64. See also Bradley, *Pedestals and Podiums*, 112.

69. Bradley, *Pedestals and Podiums*, 113–14.

70. Claudia Lauper Bushman, "Introduction," *Dialogue: A Journal of Mormon Thought* 6, no. 2 (Summer 1971): 5, 6, https://www.dialoguejournal.com/wp-content/uploads/sbi/articles/Dialogue_V06N02_7.pdf, accessed 8 July 2014.

71. Leonard J. Arrington, "Blessed Damozels: Women in Mormon History," *Dialogue: A Journal of Mormon Thought* 6, no. 2 (Summer 1971): 23, https://www.dialogue-journal.com/wp-content/uploads/sbi/articles/Dialogue_V06N02_24.pdf, accessed 8 July 2014.

72. Laurel Thatcher Ulrich, "Mormon Women in the History of Second-Wave Feminism," *Dialogue: A Journal of Mormon Thought* 43, no. 2 (2010): 45–63, http://www.dialoguejournal.com/wp-content/uploads/sbi/articles/Dialogue_V43N02_53_2.pdf, accessed 8 July 2014.

73. Bradley, *Pedestals and Podiums*, esp. chaps. 9 and 10.

74. Boyd K. Packer, "Talk to the All-Church Coordinating Council," 18 May 1993, http://www.zionsbest.com/face.html, accessed 8 July 2014. In his 1993 address to the All-Church Coordinating Council, Boyd K. Packer said, "The dangers I speak of come from the gay-lesbian movement, the feminist movement (both of which are relatively new), and the ever-present challenge from the so-called scholars or intellectuals."

75. First Presidency and Council of the Twelve Apostles of the Church of Jesus Christ of Latter-day Saints, "The Family: A Proclamation to the World," 23 September 1995, http://www.lds.org/family/proclamation, accessed 8 July 2014.

76. The proclamation goes on to claim that the "disintegration of the family will bring upon individuals, communities, and nations the calamities foretold by ancient and modern prophets." First Presidency, "The Family: A Proclamation." The Mormon church toned down its rhetoric against same-sex marriage after playing an influential role in support of Proposition 8 (a 2008 California ballot proposition and constitutional amendment that defined marriage as between one man and one woman), though the church did file an amicus brief against marriage equality in *United States v. Windsor*. See Stephanie Mencimer, "Mormon Church Abandons Its Crusade against Gay Marriage," *Mother Jones*, 12 April 2013, http://www.motherjones.com/politics/2013/04/prop-8-mormons-gay-marriage-shift, accessed 8 July 2014.

77. Timothy Pratt, "Mormon Women Set Out to Take a Stand, in Pants," *New York Times*, 19 December 2012, http://www.nytimes.com/2012/12/20/us/19mormon.html, accessed 8 July 2014. See also Jessica Finnigan and Nancy Ross, "'I'm a Mormon Feminist': How Social Media Revitalized and Energized a Movement," *Interdisciplinary Journal of Research on Religion* 9, article 12 (2013), http://www.religjournal.com/articles/article_view.php?id=80, accessed 16 July 2014.

78. See the Wear Pants to Church Day Facebook page, https://www.facebook.com/WearPantsToChurchDay, accessed 31 July 2013.

79. Peggy Fletcher Stack, "Menstruating Mormon Women Barred from Temple Proxy Baptisms?," *Salt Lake Tribune*, 5 March 2012, http://www.sltrib.com/sltrib/blogsfaithblog/53650972–180/temple-women-baptisms-mormon.html.csp, accessed 8 July 2014.

80. See http://ordainwomen.org/, accessed 8 July 2014.

81. Ordain Women: Mormon Women Seeking Equality and Ordination to the Priesthood, "Frequently Asked Questions," http://ordainwomen.org/faq/, accessed 1 August 2013.

82. Church of Jesus Christ of Latter-day Saints, "Handbook 2: Administering the Church," 2010, http://www.lds.org/manual/handbook?lang=eng, accessed 31 July 2013.

83. Peggy Fletcher Stack, "Mormons Launch Online Push to Ordain Women to the Priesthood," *Salt Lake Tribune*, 4 April 2013, http://www.sltrib.com/sltrib/news/56096212-78/women-priesthood-church-lds.html.csp, accessed 8 July 2014.

84. Laurie Goldstein, "Mormons Say Critical Online Comments Draw Threats from Church," *New York Times*, 18 June 2014, http://www.nytimes.com/2014/06/19/us/critical-online-comments-put-church-status-at-risk-mormons-say.html, accessed 15 July 2014.

85. For an engaging volume focusing on contemporary LDS women's voices and experiences, see Claudia L. Bushman and Caroline Kline, eds., *Mormon Women Have Their Say: Essays from the Claremont Oral History Collection* (Salt Lake City: Greg Kofford Books, 2013).

86. See Douglas J. Davies, *An Introduction to Mormonism* (Cambridge: Cambridge University Press, 2003), 3–4.

87. Latter-day Saints accept the Bible as divinely inspired, according to the thirteen "Articles of Faith" written by Joseph Smith and memorized by young Mormons, "as far as it is translated correctly." "The Articles of Faith of the Church of Jesus Christ of Latter-day Saints," http://www.lds.org/scriptures/pgp/a-of-f/1?lang=eng, accessed 1 October 2012.

88. LDS Church, *Gospel Principles*, "Chapter 6: The Fall of Adam and Eve," 26–30, https://www.lds.org/manual/gospel-principles/chapter-6-the-fall-of-adam-and-eve?lang=eng, accessed 22 October 2012.

89. Smith, *Doctrine and Covenants*, 76:103.

90. The LDS concept of a mother or mothers in heaven is referenced in a number of LDS hymns, including "O My Father," and "Oh, What Songs of the Heart," and in other LDS publications. Still, as the anthropologist Bradley Kramer observes, Mormon culture explicitly discourages open discussion of Heavenly Mother, and so members rarely talk about her openly in the modern church. Indeed, Mormons "do not really talk about her so much as talk about talking about and not talking about her." As Kramer notes, "structured silences" around certain gendered aspects of rituals (such as in temple ceremonies) or beliefs (such as a Mother in Heaven) help to "[shape] the experience of Mormon women and [cultivate] a distinctly Mormon model of femininity." Bradley H. Kramer, "Keeping the Sacred: Structured Silence in the Enactment of Priesthood Authority, Gendered Worship, and Sacramental Kinship in Mormonism" (Ph.D. diss., University of Michigan, 2014), 85, 4.

91. This doctrine was articulated in Joseph Smith's King Follet Discourse, delivered in Nauvoo on 7 April 1844, which stated that humans could become gods. Lorenzo

Snow is quoted on the LDS webpage: "As man now is, God once was; as God is now man may be"; see http://www.lds.org/churchhistory/presidents/controllers/ potcController.jsp?leader=5&topic=quotes, accessed 8 July 2014. The divine potential of humans was reiterated as recently as 1994 by Gordon B. Hinckley, "Don't Drop the Ball," *Ensign*, November 1994, http://www.lds.org/ensign/1994/11/ dont-drop-the-ball?lang=eng&query=king+follet, accessed 8 July 2014: "On the other hand, the whole design of the gospel is to lead us onward and upward to greater achievement, even, eventually, to godhood." In a 1997 *Time* interview, Hinckley seemed to distance LDS doctrine from the idea, stating,

> I don't know that we teach it. I don't know that we emphasize it. I haven't heard it discussed for a long time in public discourse. I don't know. I don't know all the circumstances under which that statement was made. I understand the philosophical background behind it. But I don't know a lot about it and I don't know that others know a lot about it.

David Van Biema, "Kingdom Come," *Time*, 4 August 1997, http://www.time. com/time/magazine/article/0,9171,986794,00.html, accessed 8 July 2014.

92. In her historical overview of Mormon women's missionary service, Sarah Elizabeth Jensen notes that women were involved in missionary service "since the Church was organized." She finds evidence that between 1830 and 1898 women received blessings, and later were set apart as missionaries, though their service was uncommon. She finds that between 1898 and 1945, the number of women serving missions increased, and they were "granted 'official' status" as missionaries. In 1951, however, the "Church decided to postpone calling sister missionaries until they reached the age of twenty-three to facilitate marriage and 'to keep the number going relatively small.'" Moreover, "articles in Church magazines throughout the 1970s—at the height of the women's liberation movement— contained iterations of the Church's longstanding position on female missionary service: female missionaries have much to offer in the mission field, but their primary responsibility is marriage." Sarah Elizabeth Jensen, "Women Proclaiming the Gospel on Missions: An Historical Overview," *Segullah* 2, no. 1 (2006), http:// segullah.org/spring2006/sisterhistory.html, accessed 8 July 2014.

93. Within one year of the change, the number of LDS women serving missions had increased by eleven thousand, and women made up 24 percent of all LDS missionaries, up from 15 percent at the time the change was announced. Barbara Bradley Hagerty, "Shift in Mormon Age Policy Widens Women's Options," *National Public Radio*, 13 October 2012, http://www.npr. org/2012/10/31/163631875/mormon-church-women-missionariesch, accessed 8 July 2014. Stina Sieg, "At a Younger Age, Mormon Women Are Eager to Share Their Faith," *National Public Radio*, 21 October 2013, http://www.npr. org/2013/10/21/236960006/at-a-younger-age-mormon-women-are-eager-to- share-their-faith, accessed 8 July 2014.

94. Deborah Laake, *Secret Ceremonies: A Mormon Woman's Intimate Diary of Marriage and Beyond* (New York: William Morrow, 1993).

95. Temples were built as grand architectural structures for the first century and a half of LDS history, and as a consequence, they were fewer in number and more geographically remote. Now they are usually built as smaller-scale structures adjacent to stake centers, and are more easily accessible to LDS church members.
96. Although the Mormon church leaders agreed to stop baptizing Holocaust victims in 1995, the 2012 discovery that the Holocaust survivor and Jewish activist Simon Wiesenthal's parents had been posthumously baptized resulted in an apology, church discipline of the church member involved, and church-wide instruction to cease such baptisms. "Utah: Mormons Apologize for Baptism," *New York Times*, 14 February 2012, http://www.nytimes.com/2012/02/15/us/utah-mormons-apologize-for-baptism.html?_r=0, accessed 8 July 2014.
97. After 1990, Mormon women were no longer asked to pledge obedience to their husbands as part of their temple marriage vows.
98. The Aaronic priesthood is conferred upon Mormon boys who are deemed worthy at the age of twelve, and the Melchizedek priesthood may be conferred on any worthy Mormon man who is at least eighteen years of age.
99. Spencer W. Kimball, "President Kimball Speaks Out on Morality," *Ensign*, November 1980, 97, http://www.lds.org/general-conference/1980/10/president-kimball-speaks-out-on-morality?lang=eng&query=%22president+kimball+speaks+out+on+morality%22, accessed 8 July 2014. Boyd K. Packer, "To Young Men Only," Church of Jesus Christ of Latter-day Saints General Conference priesthood session, 2 October 1976, http://www.mormonstudies.net/html/packer/youngmen.html, accessed 8 July 2014.
100. Gordon B. Hinckley, "Stand Strong against the Wiles of the World," *Ensign*, November 1995, 99, http://www.lds.org/general-conference/1995/10/stand-strong-against-the-wiles-of-the-world?lang=eng, accessed 8 July 2014.
101. Laura L. Vance, "Converging on the Heterosexual Dyad: Changing Mormon and Adventist Sexual Norms and Implications for Gay and Lesbian Adherents," *Nova Religio* 11, no. 4 (May 2008): 61–62. See also John Dehlin, "9/12 PFLAG Presentation on Preliminary Findings for LDS/Mormon SSA Study," Understanding LDS Homosexuality, 17 September 2012, 22, http://ldshomosexuality.com/?p=355, accessed 6 July 2014.
102. Church of Jesus Christ of Latter-day Saints, "Church Handbook of Instructions: Book 1, Stake Presidencies and Bishoprics," 1998, http://www.wikileaks.org/wiki/Mormon_Church_Handbook_of_Instructions,_full,_2006, accessed 8 July 2014.
103. Church of Jesus Christ, "Church Handbook of Instructions."
104. Church of Jesus Christ of Latter-day Saints, "God Loveth His Children," 2007, http://www.lds.org/ldsorg/v/index.jsp?locale=0&sourceId=3e05c8322e1b3110VgnVCM100000176f620a____&vgnextoid=e1fa5f74db46c010VgnVCM1000004d82620aRCRD, accessed 8 July 2014.
105. Church of Jesus Christ of Latter-day Saints, "Handbook 1: Stake Presidents and Bishops," 2010, http://ge.tt/5OcBdKQ/v/0, accessed 22 July 2013.
106. See http://www.mormonsandgays.org/, accessed 8 July 2014.

107. Church of Jesus Christ, "God Loveth His Children."
108. Church of Jesus Christ, "God Loveth His Children."
109. Church of Jesus Christ, "Handbook 1," 57, 28.
110. Scott Taylor, "Mormon Church Backs Protection of Gay Rights in Salt Lake City," *Deseret News*, 10 November 2009, http://www.deseretnews.com/article/705343558/Mormon-Church-backs-protection-of-gay-rights-in-Salt-Lake-City.html, accessed 8 July 2014.
111. See, for example, "Visiting Teaching Message: Gender Is an Essential Characteristic of Eternal Identity and Purpose," *Ensign*, October 2008, http://www.mormonchannel.org/magazines/ensign/2008/10/gender-is-an-essential-characteristic-of-eternal-identity-and-purpose, accessed 8 July 2014. Taylor G. Petrey argues that this is not necessarily so, and asserts that Mormonism could build on and expand existing doctrines, and recognize the social basis of gender, in order to broaden its beliefs regarding kinship and reproduction to create a "post-heterosexual theology." Taylor G. Petrey, "Toward a Post-Heterosexual Mormon Theology," *Dialogue: A Journal of Mormon Thought* 44, no. 4 (Winter 2011): 106–44.
112. First Presidency, "The Family: A Proclamation."
113. Mary N. Cook, "Seek Learning: You Have a Work to Do," Church of Jesus Christ of Latter-day Saints General Conference session, 24 March 2012, http://www.lds.org/broadcasts/article/general-young-women-meeting/2012/03/seek-learning-you-have-a-work-to-do?lang=eng&query=%E2%80%9Clearn+marketable+skill,%E2%80%9D, accessed 24 July 2012.
114. Julie B. Beck, "What Latter-day Saint Women Do Best: Stand Strong and Immovable," Church of Jesus Christ of Latter-day Saints General Relief Society session, 7 October 2007, https://www.lds.org/general-conference/2007/10/what-latter-day-saint-women-do-best-stand-strong-and-immovable?lang=eng, accessed 23 July 2013, emphasis in original.
115. D. Todd Christofferson, "The Moral Force of Women," Church of Jesus Christ of Latter-day Saints General Conference session, 5 October 2013, http://www.lds.org/general-conference/2013/10/the-moral-force-of-women, accessed 8 July 2014.
116. Church leaders have acknowledged domestic violence and sexual abuse more frequently since the 1980s, including in the proclamation, which "warns . . . individuals . . . who abuse spouse or offspring, or who fail to fulfill family responsibilities [that they] will one day stand accountable before God." First Presidency, "The Family: A Proclamation."

CHAPTER 2. SEVENTH-DAY ADVENTISM

1. Ellen Gould Harmon White, *Life Sketches of Ellen G. White* (Mountain View, CA: Pacific Press Publishing Association, 1915), 20.
2. Ronald L. Numbers, *Prophetess of Health: A Study of Ellen G. White*, 3rd ed. (Grand Rapids, MI: Eerdmans, 2008), 43–47.

3. Ingemar Lindén, *The Last Trump: An Historico-Genetical Study of Some Important Chapters in the Making and Development of the Seventh-day Adventist Church* (Frankfurt: Peter Lang, 1978), 149.

4. Wayne R. Judd, "William Miller: Disappointed Prophet," in *The Disappointed: Millerism and Millennialism in the Nineteenth Century*, ed. Jonathan M. Butler and Ronald L. Numbers, 2nd ed. (Knoxville: University of Tennessee Press, 1993), 18.

5. Lindén, *The Last Trump*, 28.

6. Judd, "William Miller," 27.

7. David T. Arthur, "Joshua V. Himes and the Cause of Adventism," in Butler and Numbers, *The Disappointed*, 37. See also Judd, "William Miller," 42–44.

8. Judd, "William Miller," 7.

9. Catherine A. Brekus, "Female Preaching in Early Nineteenth-Century America," Center for Christian Ethics at Baylor University, 2009, 22, www.baylor.edu/content/services/document.php/98759.pdf, accessed 8 July 2014.

10. Brekus, "Female Preaching," 22–23.

11. White, *Life Sketches*, chap. 5.

12. Numbers, *Prophetess of Health*, 54. See also Ann Taves, "Visions," in *Ellen Harmon White: American Prophet*, ed. Terrie Dopp Aamodt, Gary Land, and Ronald L. Numbers (New York: Oxford University Press, 2014), 33.

13. Arthur, "Joshua V. Himes," 51. See also Jon R. Stone, "Nineteenth- and Twentieth-Century American Millennialisms," in *The Oxford Handbook of Millennialism*, ed. Catherine Wessinger (New York: Oxford University Press, 2011), 501.

14. Ellen G. White, *A Sketch of the Christian Experience and Views of Ellen G. White* (Saratoga Springs, NY: James White, 1851), 5, http://www.anym.org/SOP/en_ExV.pdf, accessed 8 July 2014.

15. Numbers, *Prophetess of Health*, 65–67.

16. Numbers, *Prophetess of Health*, 61.

17. Numbers, *Prophetess of Health*, 62.

18. Ellen G. White, *The Great Controversy between Christ and Satan: The Conflict of the Ages in the Christian Dispensation* (1888; reprint, Washington, DC: Review and Herald Publishing Association, 1911), 482, http://www.whiteestate.org/books/gc/gc.asp, accessed 8 July 2014

19. Ellen G. White, "Satan's Rebellion," *Signs of the Times*, 23 July 1902, http://text.egwwritings.org/publication.php?pubtype=Periodical&bookCode=ST&lang=en&year=1902&month=July&day=23, accessed 8 July 2014

20. White, *The Great Controversy*, 498.

21. Butler, "Introduction," 12. See also Gary Land, "Coping with Change, 1961–1980," in *Adventism in America: A History*, ed. Gary Land (1986; reprint, Grand Rapids, MI: Eerdmans, 1998), 218–19.

22. Numbers, *Prophetess of Health*, 83–84, 95–126.

23. Numbers, *Prophetess of Health*, 217–18.

24. Today, with hundreds of health care institutions, Seventh-day Adventism is the largest nonprofit Protestant health care provider in the United States, and one of the largest in the world. See Adventist Health System, "About Us," https://www.adventisthealthsystem.com/page.php?section=about, accessed 8 July 2014

25. Still, the highly educated workforce necessary to maintain this complex system of institutions created a need to educate some Adventists in secular graduate programs, and the critical analysis those Adventists were encouraged to employ in their scholarship was focused, especially beginning in the 1970s, on their religious tradition, sometimes with serious consequences, especially charges of plagiarism in Ellen White's writings (see Numbers, *Prophetess of Health*, 134–55), debate about the relative necessity of sanctification (works) and justification (grace) for salvation, the theory of evolution versus creationism, and others. Tension regarding some of these issues was more pronounced in the last three decades of the twentieth century, and now is more subdued. See Laura L. Vance, *Seventh-day Adventism in Crisis: Gender and Sectarian Change in an Emerging Religion* (Urbana: University of Illinois Press, 1999), 75–94.

26. Harriet Sigerman, "An Unfinished Battle, 1848–1865," in *No Small Courage: A History of Women in the United States*, ed. Nancy Cott (New York: Oxford University Press, 2000), 239.

27. B. F. Robbins, "To the Female Disciples in the Third Angel's Message," *Advent Review and Sabbath Herald* 15, no. 3 (8 December 1859): 21–22.

28. S. C. Welcome supported women's equality, claiming the "authority of divine revelation that male and female are one in Christ Jesus." S. C. Welcome, "Shall the Women Keep Silence in the Churches?" *Advent Review and Sabbath Herald* 16, no. 14 (23 February 1860): 109–10.

29. Welcome, "Shall the Women Keep Silence?," 110.

30. Steven Daily, "The Irony of Adventism: The Role of Ellen G. White and Other Adventist Women in Nineteenth Century America" (Ph.D. diss., School of Theology at Claremont, 1985).

31. Nineteenth-century Adventist ministers were itinerant, traveling between several congregations, and sometimes served in husband-wife ministerial teams. Bert Haloviak, "Route to the Ordination of Women in the Seventh-day Adventist Church: Two Paths," March 1985, 3–5, http://www.adventistarchives.org/docs/AST/Ast1985.pdf, accessed 8 July 2014; Kit Watts, "An Outline of the History of Seventh-day Adventists and the Ordination of Women," SDAnet, April 1995, http://www.sdanet.org/atissue/wo/appendix5.htm#*, accessed 8 July 2014.

32. Watts, "An Outline of the History of Seventh-day Adventists."

33. Alexander Carpenter, "Sabbath Sermon: The Historic Role of Women in Ministry in the Adventist Church," *Spectrum*, blog post, 2 June 2012, http://spectrummagazine.org/blog/2012/06/02/sabbath-sermon-historic-role-women-ministry-adventist-church%E2%80%94stan-hickerson, accessed 8 July 2014.

34. Ellen G. White, "Address and Appeal, Setting Forth the Importance of Missionary Work," *Advent Review and Sabbath Herald*, 19 December 1878, http://egwtext.

whiteestate.org/publication.php?pubtype=Periodical&bookCode=RH&lang=en&
collection=2&section=all&QUERY=%22Nothing+will+deter+this+class+from+th
eir+duty.+Nothing+will+discourage+them+in+the+work.+%22&resultId=3&isLa
stResult=1&year=1878&month=December&day=19, accessed 19 November 2013.
In the summer of 2012 and again in the fall of 2013, the Ellen White Estate
revamped the electronic tools that the estate provides, and in so doing changed
URL strings for some publications to which the estate provides electronic access. I
provide here the most current URL for estate sources. If a reader is unable in the
future to locate an electronic source from the Ellen White Estate, go to http://
www.whiteestate.org/, click on "search writings of Ellen G. White," and type into
the search engine a portion of the quote or title provided.

35. Ellen G. White, "Women as Missionaries," *Advent Review and Sabbath Herald*, 10
December 1914, http://egwtext.whiteestate.org/publication.php?pubtype=Periodic
al&bookCode=RH&lang=en&year=1914&month=December&day=10, accessed
22 November 2013.

36. Ellen G. White, "Words to Lay Members," *Advent Review and Sabbath Herald*, 26
August 1902, http://egwtext.whiteestate.org/publication.php?pubtype=Periodical
&bookCode=RH&lang=en&year=1902&month=August&day=26, accessed 19
November 2013.

37. Ellen G. White, *Daughters of God* (Hagerstown, MD: Review and Herald
Publishing Association, 1998), 97, para. 3, http://egwtext.whiteestate.org/
publication.php?pubtype=Book&bookCode=DG&lang=en&collection=2&sectio
n=all&pagenumber=97&QUERY=%22lines+of+work+just+as+thoroughly+as+th
e+men+are+educated%22&resultId=1&isLastResult=1, accessed 19 November
2013. In addition to completing Endtime work, Ellen White saw women's work as
apropos to certain contexts. She especially encouraged women to be trained as
physicians in order to allow women and men to be treated by doctors of the same
sex. White wrote, "in Bible times the women always took charge of the
women. . . . [Women and men are] not to mix and mingle right together." White,
Daughters of God, 97.

38. Ellen G. White, "The Duty of the Minister and the People," *Advent Review and
Sabbath Herald*, 9 July 1895, 443–44, http://docs.adventistarchives.org/docs/RH/
RH18950709-V72-28__B.pdf#view=fit, accessed 19 November 2013.

39. Bert Haloviak, "Longing for the Pastorate: Ministry in 19th Century Adventism,"
unpublished paper, 1988, 23, http://www.adventistarchives.org/docs/AST/
Pastorate.pdf, accessed 8 July 2014.

40. Though women's religious work in Christianity is referenced as early as the
Pauline Epistles (Rom. 16:1), the responsibilities of deaconesses varied in different
Christian religious, cultural, and historical contexts, and the institutional
responsibilities of the role generally declined following Constantine's institutionalization of the ministry in the fourth century. In Protestant traditions the
position was revived in Germany in 1836, when the Lutheran pastor Theodore
Fliedner (1800–1864) established the first Protestant order of deaconesses to train

women for service. The movement grew quickly and by the 1880s had spread to the United States among groups including the Evangelical Lutheran Church in America and the United Methodist Church. Adventist writers mention deaconesses as early as 1856, and records indicate ordination of some Adventist women as deaconesses in the late 1800s and early 1900s. By 1932, however, the first published *Adventist Church Manual* cites "no record" of ordination of women as deaconesses as evidence that "the practice is not followed by our denomination." Nineteenth- and early twentieth-century Adventist deaconesses, ordained or nonordained, looked after the welfare of members, including by administering funds for the poor, and cared for church buildings and materials. See Jeannine E. Olsen, *One Ministry Many Roles: Deacons and Deaconesses through the Centuries* (St Louis: Concordia, 1992), 22–29, 41–70; Charles W. Deweese, *Women Deacons and Deaconesses: 400 Years of Baptist Service* (Macon, GA: Mercer University Press, 2005), 85; Nancy Vyhmeister, "Deaconesses in the Church," pt. 2, *Ministry: International Journal for Pastors*, September 2008, https://www.ministrymagazine. org/archive/2008/September/deaconesses-in-the-church.html, accessed 31 December 2012.

41. Daily, "The Irony of Adventism," 228.

42. Michael Pearson, *Millennial Dreams and Moral Dilemmas: Seventh-day Adventists and Contemporary Ethics* (Cambridge: Cambridge University Press, 1990), 140.

43. Ellen G. White, *Evangelism* (Washington, DC: Review and Herald Publishing Association, 1946), 469, http://egwtext.whiteestate.org/publication.php?pubtype= Book&bookCode=Ev&lang=en&collection=2&section=all&pagenumber=469&Q UERY=%22women+to+do+this+work%2C+and+it+will+feel+the+loss+if+the+ta lents+of+both+are+not+combined%22&resultId=1, accessed 19 November 2013. For a more extensive treatment of Ellen White's writings on women, see Laura Vance, "Gender," in Aamodt, Land, and Numbers, *Ellen Harmon White*, 279–94.

44. Bert Haloviak, "Ellen White Endorsed Adventist Women Ministers," *Spectrum* 19, no. 5 (1989): 34.

45. The Society of Friends (Quakers) allowed women to minister in the early nineteenth century. Mark Chaves, *Ordaining Women: Culture and Conflict in Religious Organizations* (Cambridge: Harvard University Press, 1997), 16–17.

46. White, *Daughters of God*, 202, para. 3.

47. White, "The Duty of the Minister and the People," para. 8.

48. Ellen G. White, "The Need of Trained Workers," *Advent Review and Sabbath Herald* 70, no. 7 (14 February 1893): 98. See Lynn D. Gordon, ed., *Gender and Higher Education in the Progressive Era* (New Haven: Yale University Press, 1990), chap. 1.

49. She taught that women should be trained as physicians to avoid the impropriety of anyone having to depend on a physician of the opposite sex, for example.

50. White, "Address and Appeal," para. 15.

51. Ellen G. White, *Christian Education* (1894), 21, para. 2, https://egwwritings.org/.

52. White, *Daughters of God*, 111, para.1.

53. Ellen G. White, Manuscript Releases, vol. 12 (1990), 160, http://egwtext.whiteestate.org/publicationtoc.php?bookCode=12MR&lang=en&collection=2&section=all, accessed 8 July 2014.

54. Ellen G. White, Testimonies for the Church, vol. 4 (1881), 612, https://egwwritings.org/.

55. T., "The Man of the House," Advent Review and Sabbath Herald 72, no. 17 (1895): 261, emphasis added.

56. "The Sensible Girl," Advent Review and Sabbath Herald 66, no. 32 (1889): 501.

57. Caroline Abbott Stanley, "Homemaking: A Vocation," Advent Review and Sabbath Herald 77, no. 25 (1900): 390; "Her Husband Also, He Praiseth Her," Advent Review and Sabbath Herald 82, no. 2 (1905): 13.

58. Luella B. Priddy, "Women and the Message," Advent Review and Sabbath Herald 87, no. 2 (1910): 11.

59. Carpenter, "Sabbath Sermon."

60. Vance, Seventh-day Adventism in Crisis, 115–16.

61. A. L. Bietz, "Why Homes Crumble," Advent Review and Sabbath Herald 132, no. 8 (1955): 13.

62. Ernest Lloyd, "I Want My Mother," Advent Review and Sabbath Herald 127, no. 12 (1950): 14.

63. D. H. Kress, "The Influence of a Godly Mother," Advent Review and Sabbath Herald 127, no. 19 (1950): 15.

64. Ida M. Johnson, "The Far-Reaching Influence of Christian Women," Advent Review and Sabbath Herald 132, no. 4 (1955): 12.

65. Helen K. Oswald, "Happier Homes in 1955," Advent Review and Sabbath Herald 132, no. 1 (1955): 12.

66. Ella M. Robinson, "Little and Unimportant?," Advent Review and Sabbath Herald 137, no. 6 (1960): 12.

67. Bietz, "Why Homes Crumble," 12.

68. Berneice Lunday, "Please Stay Home with Me!," Advent Review and Sabbath Herald 137, no. 21 (1960): 12.

69. Bertha Dasher, "Leadership Positions: A Declining Opportunity?," Spectrum 15, no. 4 (1984): 36, 37.

70. Rose Otis, "Take Time to Be a Mother," Review and Herald 147, no. 8 (1970): 9.

71. June Strong, "A New Kind of Women's Lib," Advent Review and Sabbath Herald 152, no. 15 (1975): 15.

72. Kenneth H. Wood, "The Home Is in Big Trouble," Adventist Review 157, no. 2 (1980): 3.

73. Marvin Moore, "Happy Homes Require Equal Effort," Adventist Review 167, no. 26 (1990): 18.

74. Credentialed ordained ministers perform ordination services by prayer and the laying on of hands in the presence of the church. General Conference of Seventh-day Adventists, Seventh-day Adventist Church Manual, 17th ed. (Hagerstown, MD: Review and Herald Publishing Association, 2005), 50.

75. North American Division of the General Conference of Seventh-day Adventists, "Theology of Ordination and the Ordination Study Committee Report," November 2013, http://www.adventistarchives.org/north-american-division-brc-report.pdf., 5, accessed 8 July 2014.

76. Watts, "An Outline of the History of Seventh-day Adventists."

77. Watts, "An Outline of the History of Seventh-day Adventists."

78. Camp Mohaven documents are available from the Seventh-day Adventist Church Office of Archives, Statistics, and Research, "1973 Role of Women in the Church Committee: Mohaven Documents," http://www.adventistarchives.org/1973-5-mohaven#.Un054401Zr6, accessed 8 November 2013.

79. Carpenter, "Sabbath Sermon."

80. Watts, "An Outline of the History of Seventh-day Adventists."

81. Patricia A. Habada and Beverly J. Rumble, "Women in Seventh-day Adventist Educational Administration," in *A Woman's Place: Seventh-day Adventist Women in Church and Society*, ed. Rosa Taylor Banks (Hagerstown, MD: Review and Herald Publishing Association, 1992), 101.

82. Watts, "An Outline of the History of Seventh-day Adventists."

83. Beverly G. Beem, "Equality in Ministry: From 1881 to Now," n.d., http://aaw.cc/PDF_files/AAW%20Equality%20in%20Ministry%20Beem%201.pdf, accessed 3 January 2013.

84. These included a February 1988 *Adventist Review* focusing on women's expansive roles in early Adventism, including reprints of articles by *Review* editors James White and J. N. Andrews.

85. "Presidents' Document, Cohutta Springs, July 16, 1989," *Adventist Woman* 8, no. 5 (August/September 1989): 2, http://www.aaw.cc/PDF_files/TAW_Vol_8_No_5_Aug-Sep_1989.pdf, accessed 8 July 2014.

86. In Adventism, elders and deacons/deaconesses are lay ministers, and pastors/ministers constitute a single level of ordained clergy.

87. Carpenter, "Sabbath Sermon."

88. Jared Wright, "Southeastern California Conference Executive Committee Votes to Ordain Women," *Spectrum*, 22 March 2012, http://spectrummagazine.org/blog/2012/03/22/southeastern-california-conference-executive-committee-votes-ordain-women, accessed 8 July 2014. Adventist leaders in Denmark voted in 2013 to halt all ordinations—of women or men—until the summer 2015 session of the General Conference, when delegates will vote whether to take action on the recommendations of the Theology of Ordination Study Committee, a group tasked with studying the issue of women's ordination in 2014. See ANN Staff, "Danish Union Suspends All Ministerial Ordination until 2015," *Adventist News Network*, 14 May 2013, http://news.adventist.org/en/archive/articles/2013/05/14/danish-union-suspends-all-ministerial-ordination-until-2015, accessed 8 July 2014.

89. Mark A. Kellner, "World Church President Appeals for Unity in Television Interview," *Adventist News*, 9 August 2012, http://www.adventistreview.org/

article/5600/archives/issue-2012–1522/22-cn-world-church-president-appeals-for-unity-in-television-interview, accessed 8 July 2014.

90. Ted N. C. Wilson, G. T. Ng, and Robert E. Lemon, "A Response to the Action of the Pacific Union Conference Constituency Meeting on Sunday, August 19, 2012," *Adventist Review*, 19 August 2012, http://www.adventistreview.org/article/5625/archives/issue-2012–1523/a-response-to-the-pacific-union-conference-constituency-vote, accessed 8 July 2014; Adelle M. Banks, "Adventists Call Actions to Allow Women's Ordinations 'Mistakes,'" *Washington Post*, 18 October 2012, http://www.washingtonpost.com/national/on-faith/adventists-call-actions-to-allow-womens-ordinations-mistakes/2012/10/18/5e2aeb96–1961–11e2-ad4a-e5a958b60a1e_story.html, accessed 8 July 2014.

91. David Olson, "Corona's Sandra Roberts Makes Adventist History," *Riverside (CA) Press-Enterprise*, 28 October 2013, http://blog.pe.com/multicultural-empire/2013/10/27/religion-coronas-sandra-roberts-makes-adventist-history/, accessed 8 July 2014.

92. General Conference Executive Officers, "Adventist Officers Release Statement regarding a Local Conference's Recent Election of President," *Adventist News Network*, 31 October 2013, http://news.adventist.org/all-news/news/go/2013–10–31/adventist-officers-release-statement-regarding-a-local-conferences-recent-election-of-president-1/, accessed 8 July 2014.

93. In his address, Wilson said, "God has given to the Seventh-day Adventist Church a divinely inspired church organization and mutual agreements, called church policies, which, under the guidance of the Holy Spirit, are part of what helps to hold us together as a worldwide family. To discard or ignore these mutual agreements violates a sacred trust and creates unnecessary discord." Ted N. C. Wilson, "State of the Church," 14 November 2013, http://vimeo.com/79438041, accessed 15 November 2013.

94. Information on the Inter-European Division decision is at *EUD News*, "Inter-European Division Will Recommend That There Is 'Room for Women's Ordination,'" 12 November 2013, http://eud.adventist.org/news/detail/date/2013/11/12/inter-european-division-will-recommend-that-there-is-room-for-womens-ordination/, accessed 8 July 2014. Details of the South Pacific Division decision are provided by Kent Kingston, "SPD Recommends Women's Ordination," *Record*, 13 November 2013, http://spectrummagazine.org/blog/2013/11/13/south-pacific-division-recommends-womens-ordination?quicktabs_2=2, accessed 15 July 2014. An explanation of the Trans-European Division vote is at TED News Staff, "TED Executive Committee Recommends Inclusive Ministry without Gender Distinctions," 18 November 2013, http://www.ted-adventist.org/news/ted-executive-committee-recommends-inclusive-ministry-without-gender-distinctions, accessed 8 July 2014.

95. Indeed, by the time the Northern Asia-Pacific Division released its report, more than three thousand women were already serving as pastors in China, and the

division indicated that 38 percent of its membership was being served by female pastors. The report noted that "women in pastoral ministry are leading many of our large and effective churches within our Division." See Northern Asia-Pacific Division of the General Conference of Seventh-day Adventists, "Biblical Research Committee Report and Recommendations: Theology of Ordination and the Ordination of Women to Gospel Ministry," 17 December 2013, https://mail.warren-wilson.edu/service/home/~/?id=171836&part=2&auth=co&view=html, accessed 8 July 2014.

96. Bonnie Dwyer, "October Annual Council Next Step for TOSC Findings," *Spectrum*, 25 June 2014, http://spectrummagazine.org/blog/2014/06/25/october-annual-council-next-step-tosc-findings, accessed 8 July 2014.

97. Chaves, *Ordaining Women*, 66.

98. Samuel Koranteng-Pipim, "Does the Bible Support Ordaining Women as Elders or Pastors?," pt. 1, http://www.adventistsaffirm.org/article/157/women-s-ordination-faqs/2-does-the-bible-support-women-s-ordination, accessed 3 September 2012, emphasis added.

99. Martha Sonntag Bradley, *Pedestals and Podiums: Utah Women, Religious Authority and Equal Rights* (Salt Lake City: Signature Books, 2005), 281–329.

100. Chaves, *Ordaining Women*, 128.

101. Chaves, *Ordaining Women*, 128.

102. Ron Lawson, "Geopolitics within Seventh-day Adventism," *Christian Century* 107, no. 37 (1990): 1197.

103. Vance, *Seventh-day Adventism in Crisis*, 209–14.

104. "American Denominational Administrators Visit Women Serving as Ordained Ministers in the Adventist Church in China," *Adventist Today*, 2 June 2012, http://www.atoday.org/article/1214/news/2012/june-headlines/american-denominational-administrators-visit-women-serving-as-ordained-ministers-in-the-adventist-church-in-china, accessed 19 November 2013.

CHAPTER 3. THE FAMILY INTERNATIONAL

1. Douglas E. Cowan and David G. Bromley, *Cults and New Religions: A Brief History* (Malden, MA: Blackwell, 2009), 121.

2. Don Lattin, *Jesus Freaks: A True Story of Murder and Madness on the Evangelical Edge* (New York: HarperOne, 2007), 19.

3. Cowan and Bromley, *Cults and New Religions*, 122.

4. Deborah Davis and Bill Davis, *The Children of God: The Inside Story* (Grand Rapids, MI: Zondervan, 1984), 48.

5. James D. Chancellor, *Life in The Family: An Oral History of the Children of God* (Syracuse: Syracuse University Press, 2000), 2.

6. The Chicago Seven were anti–Vietnam War activists charged with conspiracy and inciting to riot in conjunction with the 1968 Democratic National Convention in Chicago.

7. David E. Van Zandt, *Living in the Children of God* (Princeton: Princeton University Press, 1991), 35.

8. Moses David [David Brandt Berg], "The Old Church and the New Church," Mo Letter no. A (26 August 1969), http://www.exfamily.org/pubs/ml/mlA.html, accessed 8 July 2014, emphasis in original. Whenever possible, I checked electronic copies of Mo Letters against hard copies housed in volumes of Letters of Moses David, Graduate Theological Union Special Collections, University of California at Berkeley. The collection does not include all letters, and so that was not possible in every case.

9. Moses David [David Brandt Berg], "Scriptural, Revolutionary Love-Making," Mo Letter no. N (August 1969), http://www.exfamily.org/pubs/ml/b4/mlo000N.shtml, accessed 8 July 2014.

10. Rex Davis and James T. Richardson, "The Organization and Functioning of the Children of God," *Sociological Analysis* 37, no. 4 (1976): 323.

11. Roy Wallis, "Yesterday's Children: Cultural and Structural Change in a New Religious Movement," in *The Social Impact of New Religious Movements*, ed. Bryan Wilson (New York: Rose of Sharon Press, 1981), 101.

12. Davis and Davis, *The Children of God*, 86.

13. Van Zandt, *Living in the Children of God*, 37.

14. Moses David [David Brandt Berg], "I Gotta Split," pt. 1, Mo Letter no. 28 (22 December 1970), in *The Mo Letters*, vol. 1, 231–36 (Geneva: Children of God, 1976), Graduate Theological Union Special Collections, 232.

15. Berg's four oldest children—Deborah (Linda), Aaron (Paul), Hosea (Jonathan), and Faith—and some of their spouses were involved in leadership in the movement, though Aaron died in 1973 and Deborah and her husband fell out of favor with her father. Moses David [David Brandt Berg], "The Bloodless Coup" ("The New Revolution," pt. 4), Mo Letter no. 329a (18 February 1975), http://www.exfamily.org/pubs/ml/b4/mlo329A.shtml, accessed 8 July 2014.

16. Davis and Richardson, "The Organization and Functioning," 328.

17. Chancellor, *Life in The Family*, 8.

18. Cowan and Bromley, *Cults and New Religions*, 129.

19. The lack of an intermediary structure between Berg and his followers was amended in 1981 with the "Fellowship Revolution." Several other dramatic reorganizations followed, including the recent adoption of the charter. Chancellor, *Life in The Family*, 11.

20. Moses David [David Brandt Berg], "One Wife," Mo Letter no. 249 (28 October 1972), in *The Mo Letters*, vol. 2, 1911–15 (Geneva: Children of God, 1976), Graduate Theological Union Special Collections, 1911.

21. David, "One Wife," 1911.

22. Moses David [David Brandt Berg], "Revolutionary Sex," Mo Letter no. 258 (27 March 1973), in *The Mo Letters*, vol. 2, 1988–2015 (Geneva: Children of God, 1976), Graduate Theological Union Special Collections, 1988.

23. David, "Revolutionary Sex," 1988.

24. Berg did not include sex outside marriage with other Family members in his definitions of fornication or adultery. In "One Wife," for example, he called on Family members to be "unselfish" by putting God "and His family first": Family members must, Berg wrote, "forsake" their "private families" and embrace God's family, "composed of many members, all of whom are . . . One Bride" of Christ. David, "One Wife"; David, "Revolutionary Sex."

25. Moses David [David Brandt Berg], "The Law of Love!," Mo Letter no. 302c (21 March 1974), in *The Mo Letters*, vol. 3, 2413–15 (Geneva: Children of God, 1976), Graduate Theological Union Special Collections, 2413.

26. David, "The Law of Love!," 2414.

27. David, "The Law of Love!," 2414.

28. Chancellor, *Life in The Family*, 112.

29. Berg references "Sodom" numerous times in his condemnation of male homosexuality, and so seems to refer to Jude 1:7, at least indirectly, in rejecting male homosexuality. Although Berg called lesbianism a "perversion," he allowed that women could have sex with other women so long as they also had sex with men. Moses David [David Brandt Berg], "Women in Love," Mo Letter no. 292 (20 December 1973), http://www.exfamily.org/pubs/ml/b4/mlo292.shtml, accessed 8 July 2014; for an example of Berg's references to male homosexuality, see Moses David [David Brandt Berg], "Sex Jewels," Mo Letter no. 919 (May 1980), http://pubs.xfamily.org/text.php?t=919, accessed 8 July 2014.

30. David, "The Law of Love!," 2415.

31. Although the first Love Charter restricted sexual sharing within homes, it was subsequently encouraged across homes, before later being restricted again. William Sims Bainbridge, *The Endtime Family: Children of God* (Albany: State University of New York Press, 2002), 138.

32. Moses David [David Brandt Berg], "Come on Ma!—Burn Your Bra!," Mo Letter no. 286 (22 December 1973), http://www.exfamily.org/pubs/ml/b4/mlo286.shtml, accessed 8 July 2014.

33. See Matt. 9:17. Moses David [David Brandt Berg], "You Are the Love of God!," Mo Letter no. 699 (5 June 1978), in *The Mo Letters*, vol. 5, 5409–13 (Geneva: Children of God, 1976), Graduate Theological Union Special Collections, 5409.

34. Moses David [David Brandt Berg], "Love vs. Law!," Mo Letter no. 647 (23 July 1977), in *The Mo Letters*, vol. 5, 5006–13 (Geneva: Children of God, 1976), Graduate Theological Union Special Collections, 5010.

35. Moses David [David Brandt Berg], "Trust the Lord!—On Husband/Wife Relationships," Mo Letter no. 2135 (29 November 1983), http://www.exfamily.org/pubs/ml/b5/ml2135.shtml, accessed 8 July 2014.

36. David, "Trust the Lord!"

37. In his letter initiating the RNR, Mo justified his decision to fire shepherds in part because "FAMILY MEMBERS WERE FORBIDDEN TO SUPPLY EACH

OTHER'S SEXUAL NEEDS, FFing was in many instances prohibited or at least discouraged, permission to even help out Family members sexually had to come from leaders far up the Chain, and decision-making and obedience to the FF Letters was frowned upon." Moses David [David Brandt Berg], "The Re-Organization Nationalisation Revolution!," Mo Letter no. 650 (January 1978), in *The Mo Letters*, vol. 5, 5031–37 (Geneva: Children of God, 1976), Graduate Theological Union Special Collections, 5031.

38. Moses David [David Brandt Berg], "Flirty Little Fishy!," Mo Letter no. 293 (3 January 1974), http://www.exfamily.org/pubs/ml/ml293.html, accessed 8 July 2014.

39. "In some places . . . we are hooking the girls through the boys. So either way, it works!" Moses David [David Brandt Berg], "FFing and Jealousy!," Mo Letter no. 603 (2 July 1977), in *The Mo Letters*, vol. 5, 4661–69 (Geneva: Children of God, 1976), Graduate Theological Union Special Collections, 4668.

40. Father David explicitly discouraged physical abuse by husbands in a letter addressing spousal jealousy in the face of sexual sharing and FFing:

So husbands who use actual physical violence on their wives must be out of their minds!—They need disciplining themselves!—And if they don't repent and desist, the beasts should be thrown out of the Family!—And let the wives stay with us if they want to!—Then they can FF all they want!—Ha! Praise God!—Amen? God bless you! I love you!

But Father David also indicated that women may provoke their husbands' violence because they "like it!": "Some women actually *like* masochism, flagellation, etc.!—Maybe because of a guilt complex, and it eases their conscience because they feel like they deserve it!—It's a strange perversion!" David, "FFing and Jealousy!," 4668.

41. Bainbridge, *The Endtime Family*, 123.

42. Chancellor, *Life in The Family*, 114.

43. Chancellor, *Life in The Family*, 120.

44. Family literature often resembled graphic comic books with sexualized illustrations of scantily clad or nude women and girls. An instructional series for children, *Heaven's Girl*, provides an example. The comic, for which Berg's granddaughter posed when she was in her mid-teens, depicts the Great Tribulation. Heaven's Girl is a superhero who navigates the Great Tribulation saving souls. In one scene, threatened with gang rape by a band of soldiers, Heaven's Girl willingly offers to have sex with the soldiers in an attempt to convince them of God's love and save them. Two soldiers eventually are saved through this action. The comic also depicts Heaven's Girl engaged in erotic dance to glorify God. Family literature from the 1970s, 1980s, and 1990s is replete with these kinds of sexualized images.

45. According to Chancellor, "most disciples were aware that sexual contact between adults and children was occurring in the King's [Father David's] household." *Life in The Family*, 111.

46. Moses David [David Brandt Berg], "My Childhood Sex! Doin' What Comes Naturally," Mo Letter no. 779 (28 June 1977 and 11 August 1978), http://www.exfamily.org/pubs/ml/ml779.shtml, accessed 8 July 2014.

47. Davidito, later Ricky Rodriguez, was a Jesus Baby born to Maria (Karen Zerby) as a result of her FFing with a waiter in Tenerife.

48. Father David wrote a number of other letters discussing childhood sexuality, including "Child Brides!," Mo Letter no. 902 (4 April 1977), http://www.exfamily.org/pubs/ml/b6/ml902.shtml, accessed 8 July 2014. In several places in his writings on sex, Berg cautions followers to hide what they are doing from those outside the movement, or to avoid being obvious to outsiders about their sexual activities. This section in *The Story of Davidito*, for example, is followed by the warning, "'let not your good be evil spoken of'! So take it easy!" *The Story of Davidito*, chap. 45, "Bed Bugs!," quoted in http://www.xfamily.org/index.php/Story_of_Davidito#Advocating_sex_with_children, accessed 5 October 2012.

49. The Family was banned from France as a result of charges of child sexual abuse and brainwashing recruits.

50. Moses David [David Brandt Berg], "Nudes Can Be Beautiful!—Movement with Meaning!," Mo Letter no. 1006 (compiled March 1981), http://www.exfamily.org/pubs/ml/b5/ml1006.shtml, accessed 8 July 2014.

51. Moses David [David Brandt Berg], "Ban the Bomb!," Mo Letter no. 1434 (March 1983), http://www.exfamily.org/pubs/ml/b5/ml1434.shtml, accessed 8 July 2014.

52. Cowan and Bromley, *Cults and New Religions*, 141. This followed another movement reorganization, the "Fellowship Revolution" in 1981, which organized communal homes into "local fellowship areas." Believers in each area met weekly, and leaders in several local fellowship areas met in districts monthly. District fellowships met with other districts in a national fellowship area. Most importantly, leaders at each level were elected. This new, more democratic leadership system probably contributed to an emphasis on reforming abuses, including sexual abuse of children.

53. Sara, "Liberty or Stumblingblock?," http://www.exfamily.org/pubs/misc/liberty_or_stumblingblock.shtml, accessed 5 October 2012.

54. Maria Zerby, "Flirty Little Teens, Beware!," Mo Letter no. 2590 (October 1989), http://www.exfamily.org/pubs/ml/b5/ml2590.shtml, accessed 8 July 2014. Chancellor suggests that prohibitions against sexual contact with children may have been in response to charges of childhood sexual abuse by those outside the movement, specifically a 1984 law enforcement raid on the Northeast Kingdom Community Church (part of the Twelve Tribes) at Island Pond, Vermont, initiated by those in the anticult movement charging that child abuse was occurring in the movement. Chancellor, *Life in The Family*, 195.

55. Scholars were invited to spend time with and study The Family when charges of child sexual abuse emerged in the 1990s. Susan Palmer visited The Family for a week in 1993 and concluded that there was no evidence of child abuse. See Susan Palmer, "'Heaven's Children': The Children of God's Second Generation," in *Sex*,

Slander, and Salvation: Investigating The Family/Children of God, ed. James R. Lewis and J. Gordon Melton (Stanford, CA: Center for Academic Publication, 1994), 1–26. Gary Shepherd and Lawrence Lilliston, based on psychological assessment of thirty-two children and observation in Family homes, found it unlikely that "systematic abuses [were] occurring throughout the Family as a matter of policy, custom, theology, or isolation." See Gary Shepherd and Lawrence Lilliston, "Field Observation of Young People's Experience and Role in The Family," in Lewis and Melton, *Sex, Slander, and Salvation*, 57–70. Later in the same decade, following court release of illegally obtained Family videos of prepubescent girls dancing erotically, as well as Lord Justice Ward's request that The Family write a letter disavowing adult sexual contact with children (which Peter did), and The Family's later more open discussion of possible misconduct by some movement members, some sociologists of religion have revised this earlier assessment. Based on interviews with members, observation in Family homes, reading Family literature, and other study, Chancellor concluded that sexual sharing was, in some cases, personally traumatic, especially when the rules of the Law of Love were ignored. Moreover, he determined that child abuse was, by 2000, "less frequent in The Family than in society at large." "However," Chancellor writes, "this has not always been the case." "The Family has come full face to the reality that literature such as 'Heaven's Girl' . . . and 'The Story of Davidito' did sanction adult sexual contact with minors." Chancellor, *Life in The Family*, 133, 138.

56. "Charter of The Family International, 4th ed.," June 2010, http://tficharter.com, accessed 8 July 2014.

57. "Charter," Article 11. Chancellor writes that

> at one level, the unique sexual ethos virtually defines the community. It shapes personal and community identity, communal values, and group loyalty. Sharply in the past and to a lesser degree in the present, it places a strain on fundamental human relationships. Sexuality continues to play a significant role in defining the nature of discipleship, and continues strongly to inform theology, mission, and worship.

Chancellor, *Life in The Family*, 149.

58. "Standard for the Care of Children at Events and Mission Works of The Family International," http://tficharter.com/en/standard-care-children/, accessed 18 June 2012.

59. Sanja Nilsson, "Rebooting The Family: Organizational Change within The Family International," *International Journal for the Study of New Religions* 2, no. 2 (2011): 163.

60. Gary Shepherd and Gordon Shepherd, "Accommodation and Reformation in The Family/Children of God," *Nova Religio* 9, no. 1 (August 2005): 74.

61. Chancellor, *Life in The Family*, 242.

62. The Family International, "The Bride of Christ," http://www.thefamilyinternational.org/en/about/our-beliefs/bride-christ/, accessed 12 November 2014.

63. The Family International, "The Bride of Christ."

64. Gary Shepherd and Gordon Shepherd, "Reboot of The Family International,"
    Nova Religio 17, no. 2 (November 2013): 80.

65. Shepherd and Shepherd, "Reboot of The Family International," 80.

66. Nilsson, "Rebooting The Family," 164.

67. Nilsson, "Rebooting The Family," 174.

68. The Family International, "The Word of God," http://www.thefamilyinternational.
    org/en/about/our-beliefs/word-god/, accessed 12 November 2013.

69. Shepherd and Shepherd, "Reboot of The Family International," 82, 87.

70. Shepherd and Shepherd, "Reboot of The Family International," 88–90.

71. Shepherd and Shepherd, "Reboot of The Family International," 83, 84.

72. Maria's (Karen Zerby's) son, Ricky Rodriguez (also called Davidito), left The
    Family in 2001 and shortly thereafter published an article on the Movingon.org
    website alleging sexual misconduct by David Berg (Mo, Father David) with
    women and children. In 2005, after filming a video of himself detailing allegations
    of child sexual abuse by David Berg and Maria, Rodriguez arranged a meeting
    with Angela Smith (1953–2005)—his childhood nanny, pictured in sexualized
    situations with him as a toddler in *The Story of Davidito*—at her apartment.
    Rodriguez stabbed Smith to death in her apartment, and then drove to California,
    where he committed suicide.

73. Shepherd and Shepherd, "Reboot of The Family International," 93. One important
    example of transformation of the movement is the creation of procedures for
    eventually replacing Maria and Peter when they become incapacitated or die. For
    a discussion of rational-legal authority, see Max Weber, *The Theory of Social and
    Economic Organization*, ed. Talcott Parsons (1947; reprint, New York: Free Press,
    1964), 328–29.

74. Shepherd and Shepherd, "Reboot of The Family International," 91. See also
    Gordon Shepherd and Gary Shepherd, *Talking with the Children of God: Prophecy
    and Transformation in a Radical Religious Group* (Urbana: University of Illinois
    Press, 2010), 209, and chap. 3.

75. Chancellor argues that "FFing moved many women into the center of Family life
    and offered them extraordinary opportunity and status." Chancellor, *Life in The
    Family*, 115–16.

76. Chancellor, *Life in The Family*, 171.

77. Cowan and Bromley, *Cults and New Religions*, 128.

78. Chancellor, *Life in The Family*, 172.

79. The Family International, "The Bride of Christ."

80. Shepherd and Shepherd, "Reboot of The Family International," 82.

81. See Christopher Kelly, "An Unorthodox Life Yields a Novelist of Promise," *New
    York Times*, 12 March 2011, http://www.nytimes.com/2011/03/13/us/13ttstevens.
    html, accessed 8 July 2014.

82. The Family International, "Communicating with God," http://www.thefamilyin-
    ternational.org/en/about/our-beliefs/communicating-god/, accessed 18 July 2013.

83. Bainbridge, *The Endtime Family*, 25.

84. Chancellor, *Life in The Family*, 230.

CHAPTER 4. WICCA

1. Helen A. Berger, "Witchcraft and Neopaganism," in *Witchcraft and Magic: Contemporary North America*, ed. Helen A. Berger (Philadelphia: University of Pennsylvania Press, 2005), 31.

2. Ronald Hutton, *The Triumph of the Moon: A History of Modern Pagan Witchcraft* (New York: Oxford University Press, 1999), 211.

3. Margaret Murray, introduction to *Witchcraft Today*, by Gerald B. Gardner (New York: Citadel, 2006), 15–16.

4. Hutton also finds Aleister Crowley to be a significant influence on Gardner. Crowley thought that magic was the "art or science of causing change in conformity with will," and asserted that one could perform magic by "understanding oneself" and "applying that understanding in action." Hutton, *Triumph of the Moon*, 174.

5. Helen A. Berger, Evan A. Leach, and Leigh S. Shaffer, *Voices from the Pagan Census: A National Survey of Witches and Neo-Pagans in the United States* (Columbia: University of South Carolina Press, 2003), 12.

6. In the context of an antipornography ordinance campaign in Bellingham, Washington, in 1988, the author attended a presentation by Dworkin. At the gathering, a local practitioner of Wicca requested Dworkin's permission to perform a magic ritual to dilute the power of pornographers, but Dworkin asked her not to do so, and expressed support for legal rather than religious solutions to social problems.

7. Marija Gimbutas, *The Language of the Goddess* (New York: Norton, 1989), 319.

8. See, for example, Mary Daly, *Gyn/Ecology: The Metaphysics of Radical Feminism* (Boston: Beacon, 1978), 178–222.

9. Zsuzsanna Emese Budapest, *The Holy Book of Women's Mysteries* (1980; reprint, San Francisco: Red Wheel/Weiser, 2007).

10. Rosemary Radford Ruether, *Goddesses and the Divine Feminine* (Berkeley: University of California Press, 2006), 280.

11. Feri is an initiatory tradition that has roots in the work and thinking of Victor Anderson (1917–2001) and Cora Anderson (1915–2008), and claims ties to ancient Celtic traditions. Practitioners seek to respect the natural world, and employ ritual magic, ecstatic experience, and attention to energy to transform themselves and their relationships.

12. Starhawk, *The Spiral Dance: A Rebirth of the Ancient Religion of the Great Goddess* (1979; reprint, New York: HarperCollins, 1999).

13. Starhawk, *Dreaming the Dark: Magic, Sex, and Politics* (1982; reprint, Boston: Beacon, 1997); Starhawk, *Truth or Dare: Encounters with Power, Authority, and Mystery* (San Francisco: HarperSanFrancisco, 1987); Starhawk, *Webs of Power: Notes from the Global Uprising* (Gabriola Island, British Columbia: New Society

Publishers, 2002); Starhawk, *The Earth Path: Grounding Your Spirit in the Rhythms of Nature* (New York: HarperCollins, 2004); Starhawk, *The Empowerment Manual: A Guide for Collaborative Groups* (Gabriola Island, British Columbia: New Society Publishers, 2011).

14. Hutton, *The Triumph of the Moon*, 349.

15. Chas S. Clifton, "Fort Hood's Wiccans and the Problem of Pacifism," paper presented to the New Religious Movements Group at the annual meeting of the American Academy of Religion, 20 November 2000, Nashville, Tennessee, http://www.chasclifton.com/papers/hood.html, accessed 8 July 2014.

16. For example, see James T. Richardson, Joel Best, and David G. Bromley, eds., *The Satanism Scare* (New York: Walter D. Gruyter, 1991); and Jeffrey S. Victor, *Satanic Panic: The Creation of a Contemporary Legend* (Peru, IL: Open Court, 1993).

17. Contemporary Pagan groups include a diverse array of traditions that are generally associated with pantheism, and claim to be derived from premodern European Pagan traditions. Some scholars point out that "pagan" is derived from the Latin *paganus*, which means "rural" or "of the country," and took on connotations of "unbelief" only when early Christians commenced using it to refer to those who were not Christians. See Elaine Pagels, *On the Origin of Satan: How Christians Demonized Jews, Pagans, and Heretics* (New York: Random House, 1995), chap. 5; see also Starhawk, *The Pagan Book of Living and Dying: Practical Rituals, Prayers, Blessings, and Meditations on Crossing Over* (New York: HarperCollins, 1997), 6.

18. Berger, "Witchcraft and Neopaganism," 29.

19. Tanice G. Foltz, "The Commodification of Witchcraft," in Berger, *Witchcraft and Magic*, 137.

20. Foltz, "The Commodification of Witchcraft," 137.

21. Helen A. Berger, introduction to Berger, *Witchcraft and Magic*, 5.

22. Berger, Leach, and Shaffer, *Voices from the Pagan Census*, 191.

23. Helen A. Berger, *A Community of Witches: Contemporary Neo-Paganism and Witchcraft in the United States* (Columbia: University of South Carolina Press, 1999), 79.

24. Berger, Leach, and Shaffer, *Voices from the Pagan Census*, 9.

25. Berger, *A Community of Witches*, 4.

26. Berger, Leach, and Shaffer, *Voices from the Pagan Census*, 155.

27. Berger, *A Community of Witches*, 62.

28. Berger, Leach, and Shaffer, *Voices from the Pagan Census*, 12.

29. Scott Cunningham, *Wicca: A Guide for the Solitary Practitioner* (St. Paul, MN: Llewellyn, 2004).

30. Berger, Leach, and Shaffer, *Voices from the Pagan Census*, 120, 230.

31. Helen A. Berger and Douglas Ezzy, *Teenage Witches: Magical Youth and the Search for the Self* (New Brunswick, NJ: Rutgers University Press, 2007), 231.

32. Berger and Ezzy, *Teenage Witches*, esp. chaps. 5 and 6. For a discussion of privatized religion, or individual religiosity, see Thomas Luckman, *The Invisible*

Religion: The Problem of Religion in Modern Society (New York: Macmillan, 1967), esp. 91–99.

33. Berger explains that belief in synchrony—the notion that events are connected and meaningful, not random and unconnected—leads "what might otherwise be interpreted as coincidence [to be] viewed . . . as magic or as an element of the Web of Life." *Witchcraft and Magic*, 35.

34. Some—especially LGBT—contemporary Witches challenge the notion of polarity between the sexes as reinforcing the heterosexual dyad and as excluding their experiences in ritual and belief, and some Wiccan groups have responded by eliminating elements of ritual that incorporated polarity (by allowing people to choose which part of the ritual they participate in instead of dividing ritual participation by gender, for example). Berger, *A Community of Witches*, 43–45.

35. Berger, *A Community of Witches*, 41.

36. Berger, Leach, and Shaffer, *Voices from the Pagan Census*, 6.

37. Berger, *A Community of Witches*, 19. Wiccans define magic differently, but most see it as incorporating the use of energy to effect change. Cunningham defines magic as the "projection of natural energies to produce needed effects." *Wicca*, 21.

38. A. J. Drew, *A Wiccan Bible: Exploring the Mysteries of the Craft from Birth to Summerland* (Franklin Lakes, NJ: New Page Books, 2003), 36.

39. Berger, "Witchcraft and Neopaganism," 34.

40. Berger, "Witchcraft and Neopaganism," 35.

41. Cynthia Eller, *Living in the Lap of the Goddess: The Feminist Spirituality Movement in America* (New York: Crossroad, 1995), 109–11.

42. Janet L. Jacobs, "Woman-Centered Healing Rites: A Study of Alienation and Reintegration," in *In Gods We Trust: New Patterns of Religious Pluralism in America*, ed. Thomas Robbins and Dick Anthony (New Brunswick, NJ: Transaction, 2009), 373, 382–83.

43. Berger, Leach, and Shaffer, *Voices from the Pagan Census*, 29.

44. Margot Adler, *Drawing Down the Moon* (Boston: Beacon, 1986), 23.

45. Berger, Leach, and Shaffer, *Voices from the Pagan Census*, 47–49.

46. Sarah M. Pike, *New Age and Neopagan Religions in America* (New York: Columbia University Press, 2004), 172.

47. Ruth Barrett, *Women's Rites, Women's Mysteries: Intuitive Ritual Creation* (Woodbury, MN: Llewellyn, 2007), 266.

48. The Pagan Census found that Neopagans, of which Wiccans constitute the largest single group, are more likely than the general public to support politically liberal positions on government spending, such as spending on the environment and education, and less likely to support spending for the military. They also reported higher support for the Equal Rights Amendment (ERA), LGBT rights, and same-sex marriage than those in the general public. Berger, Leach, and Shaffer, *Voices from the Pagan Census*, 28, chap. 2, 67–77.

49. Berger, *Witchcraft and Magic*, 40.

50. Berger, Leach, and Shaffer, *Voices from the Pagan Census*, 121.

51. Berger, *A Community of Witches*, 36.
52. Meredith B. McGuire, *Religion: The Social Context*, 5th ed. (Long Grove, IL: Waveland, 2002), 134–35.
53. Candace West and Don H. Zimmerman, "Doing Gender," *Gender and Society* 1, no. 2 (June 1987): 125.
54. Judith Butler, *Gender Trouble: Feminism and the Subversion of Identity* (1990; reprint, New York: Routledge, 1999).
55. Lynn Weber, *Understanding Race, Class, Gender, and Sexuality: A Conceptual Framework*, 2nd ed. (New York: Oxford University Press, 2009).
56. Wendy Griffin, "Webs of Women: Feminist Spiritualities," in Berger, *Witchcraft and Magic*, 64.
57. For a discussion of Dianic Wicca, see Kristy S. Coleman, *Re-Riting Woman: Dianic Wicca and the Feminine Divine* (New York: Altamira, 2009).
58. Berger, *A Community of Witches*, 45; see also 43.
59. Drew, *A Wiccan Bible*, 38.
60. Gavin Frost and Yvonne Frost, *The Witch's Bible* (Los Angeles: Nash, 1972), 84.
61. Gavin Frost and Yvonne Frost, *The Good Witch's Bible*, 7th ed. (New Bern, NC: Godolphin House, 1999), 66.
62. Huey Freeman, "Man Faces Sexual Assault Charges in Wake of Cleansing Ritual," *Decatur (IL) Herald-Review*, 20 April 2010, http://herald-review.com/news/local/article_ca11a396–60b3–5ebd-8bd7-ac539d5c2030.html, accessed 2 January 2013; Kevin Pierson, "Sexual Assault Suspects Cite Their Religion," *Marietta (OH) Times*, 29 March 2012, http://www.mariettatimes.com/page/content.detail/id/543116/Sexual-assault-suspects-cite-their-religion.html?nav=5002, accessed 2 January 2013.
63. Berger, *Witchcraft and Magic*, 32.
64. Berger, *A Community of Witches*, 46.

CONCLUSION

1. Ellen G. White, "The Duty of the Minister and the People," *Advent Review and Sabbath Herald*, 9 July 1895, http://docs.adventistarchives.org/docs/RH/RH18950709-V72–28__B.pdf#view=fit, accessed 8 July 2014.
2. Catherine A. Brekus, "Female Preaching in Early Nineteenth-Century America," Center for Christian Ethics at Baylor University, 2009, 22–23, www.baylor.edu/content/services/document.php/98759.pdf, accessed 8 July 2014.
3. Jackson W. Carroll, Barbara Hargrove, and Adair T. Lummis, *Women of the Cloth: A New Opportunity for the Churches* (San Francisco: Harper and Row, 1983), 20, 21.
4. Carroll, Hargrove, and Lummis, *Women of the Cloth*, 23.
5. Mark Chaves, *Ordaining Women: Culture and Conflict in Religious Organizations* (Cambridge: Harvard University Press, 1997), 17.
6. As Wessinger observes, "in highly patriarchal contexts where it is required that women maintain silent and uncomplaining roles within the home, access to

charismatic authority is an important means by which women gain voice and status." Catherine Wessinger, "Charismatic Leaders in New Religions," in *The Cambridge Companion to New Religious Movements*, ed. Olav Hammer and Mikael Rothstein (Cambridge: Cambridge University Press, 2012), 89.

7. Helen A. Berger, Evan A. Leach, and Leigh S. Shaffer, *Voices from the Pagan Census: A National Survey of Witches and Neo-Pagans in the United States* (Columbia: University of South Carolina Press, 2003), 201, 183.

8. Berger, Leach, and Shaffer, *Voices from the Pagan Census*, xiv.

9. First Presidency and Council of the Twelve Apostles of the Church of Jesus Christ of Latter-day Saints, "The Family: A Proclamation to the World," 23 September 1995, http://www.lds.org/family/proclamation, accessed 8 July 2014.

10. Seventh-day Adventist Church, "Statements, Guidelines, and Other Documents," http://www.adventist.org/fileadmin/adventist.org/files/articles/official-statements/Statements-2010-english.pdf, accessed 19 March 2014.

11. Ellen G. White, *An Appeal to Mothers: The Great Cause of the Physical, Mental, and Moral Ruin of Many of the Children of Our Time* (Battle Creek, MI: Steam Press, 1864).

12. It remains to be seen which direction each religion will take in regard to gender equity. The Family has institutionalized Karen Zerby's leadership, along with a trend toward greater democratization in the movement more generally. Since Karen Zerby and her current husband, Peter, institutionalized patterns for replacement of religious leadership, it seems likely that the movement will survive their deaths, though it will likely remain small. New recruits are limited, and birthrates have declined. Women will probably continue to prophesy in The Family, and the movement will probably continue to try to distance itself from its history of child sexual abuse. It would be difficult for Wicca to retreat from its feminism, for the reasons outlined above, though privatized religious experience always allows for variability between practitioners. Mormonism moderated its tone somewhat under the leadership of President Thomas S. Monson (b. 1927; he became president in 2008), but Elder Boyd K. Packer (b. 1924), his possible replacement, called feminists, with "homosexuals, and so-called intellectuals," the enemies of the church. Some Seventh-day Adventist conferences recently ordained women, but faced resistance from denominational leaders when they did. At least for the moment, Mormon and Adventist leaders continue to use gender to distinguish the movements from the larger social context.

13. The individual who resists or rejects religious ideas still forms her thinking and actions in a context informed by them—from birth and concomitant naming or other rites of passage through decisions about marriage and reproduction, work, and family life, to old age and death. Religion informs communities' norms, rules, policies, and laws. Even in modern secular pluralistic societies in which meaning is contested and fragmented, religions strive to inform and address questions of ultimate meaning. Gender, which permeates religious meaning systems, is critical to this process.

WORKS CITED

Adler, Margot. *Drawing Down the Moon*. Boston: Beacon, 1986.

Arrington, Leonard J. "Blessed Damozels: Women in Mormon History." *Dialogue: A Journal of Mormon Thought* 6, no. 2 (1971): 22–31. https://www.dialoguejournal. com/wp-content/uploads/sbi/articles/Dialogue_Vo6No2_24.pdf.

Arrington, Leonard J., and Davis Bitton. *The Mormon Experience: A History of the Latter-day Saints*. New York: Knopf, 1992.

Arthur, David T. "Joshua V. Himes and the Cause of Adventism." In *The Disappointed: Millerism and Millennialism in the Nineteenth Century*, edited by Jonathan M. Butler and Ronald L. Numbers, 2nd ed., 36–58. Knoxville: University of Tennessee Press, 1993.

Ashurst-McGee, Mark Roscoe. "Zion Rising: Joseph Smith's Early Social and Political Thought." Ph.D. diss., Arizona State University, 2008.

Baer, Hans. "The Limited Empowerment of Women in Black Spiritual Churches: An Alternative Vehicle to Religious Leadership." *Sociology of Religion* 54, no. 1 (1993): 65–82.

Bainbridge, William Sims. *The Endtime Family: Children of God*. Albany: State University of New York Press, 2002.

Bainbridge, William Sims, and Rodney Stark. "Sectarian Tension." *Review of Religious Research* 22, no. 2 (1980): 105–24.

Barrett, Ruth. *Women's Rites, Women's Mysteries: Intuitive Ritual Creation*. Woodbury, MN: Llewellyn, 2007.

Beauvoir, Simone de. *The Second Sex*. 1949. Reprint, New York: Vintage, 2011.

Beck, Julie B. "What Latter-day Saint Women Do Best: Stand Strong and Immovable." Church of Jesus Christ of Latter-day Saints General Relief Society session, 7 October 2007. https://www.lds.org/general-conference/2007/10/ what-latter-day-saint-women-do-best-stand-strong-and-immovable?lang=eng.

Beecher, Maureen Ursenbach, and Lavina Fielding Anderson, eds. *Sisters in Spirit: Mormon Women in Historical and Cultural Perspective*. Urbana: University of Illinois Press, 1992.

Beem, Beverly G. "Equality in Ministry: From 1881 to Now." N.d. http://aaw.cc/PDF_ files/AAW%20Equality%20in%20Ministry%20Beem%201.pdf.

Benson, Ezra Taft. "To the Mothers in Zion." Address delivered at the Fireside for Parents, 22 February 1987. http://fc.byu.edu/jpages/ee/w_etb87.htm.

Berger, Helen A. *A Community of Witches: Contemporary Neo-Paganism and Witchcraft in the United States*. Columbia: University of South Carolina Press, 1999.

———. Introduction to *Witchcraft and Magic: Contemporary North America*, edited by Helen A. Berger, 1–7. Philadelphia: University of Pennsylvania Press, 2005.

———. "Witchcraft and Neopaganism." In *Witchcraft and Magic: Contemporary North America*, edited by Helen A. Berger, 28–54. Philadelphia: University of Pennsylvania Press, 2005.

Berger, Helen A., and Douglas Ezzy. *Teenage Witches: Magical Youth and the Search for the Self*. New Brunswick, NJ: Rutgers University Press, 2007.

Berger, Helen A., Evan A. Leach, and Leigh S. Shaffer. *Voices from the Pagan Census: A National Survey of Witches and Neo-Pagans in the United States*. Columbia: University of South Carolina Press, 2003.

Berger, Peter L. *The Sacred Canopy: Elements of a Sociological Theory of Religion*. 1967. Reprint, New York: Anchor Books, Doubleday, 1990.

Bietz, A. L. "Why Homes Crumble." *Advent Review and Sabbath Herald* 132, no. 8 (1955): 12–13.

Bose, Christine E. "Dual Spheres." In *Analyzing Gender: A Handbook of Social Science Research*, edited by Beth B. Hess and Myra Marx Ferree, 267–85. Newbury Park: Sage, 1987.

Bradley, Martha Sonntag. *Pedestals and Podiums: Utah Women, Religious Authority and Equal Rights*. Salt Lake City: Signature, 2005.

Bradwell v. State, 83 U.S. 130 (16 Wall. 130, 21 L.Ed. 442). Available from Legal Information Institute, Cornell University School of Law. http://www.law.cornell.edu/supremecourt/text/83/130#writing-type-1-MILLER.

Braude, Ann. "Women's History *Is* American Religious History." In *Retelling U.S. Religious History*, edited by Thomas A. Tweed, 87–107. Berkeley: University of California Press, 1997.

Brekus, Catherine A. "Female Preaching in Early Nineteenth-Century America." Center for Christian Ethics at Baylor University, 2009. www.baylor.edu/content/services/document.php/98759.pdf.

Brigham Young University Book of Abraham Project. "Oliver Cowdery, 1806–1850." N.d. http://www.boap.org/LDS/Early-Saints/OCowd-AP.html.

Brodie, Fawn M. *No Man Knows My History: The Life of Joseph Smith, the Mormon Prophet*. 1945. Reprint, New York: Vintage, 1995.

Bromley, David G., and J. Gordon Melton. "Reconceptualizing Types of Religious Organization: Dominant, Sectarian, Alternative, and Emergent Tradition Groups." *Nova Religio* 15, no. 3 (2012): 4–28.

Budapest, Zsuzsanna Emese. *The Holy Book of Women's Mysteries*. 1980. Reprint, San Francisco: Red Wheel/Weiser, 2007.

Bushman, Claudia Lauper. "Introduction." *Dialogue: A Journal of Mormon Thought* 6, no. 2 (1971): 5–8. https://www.dialoguejournal.com/wp-content/uploads/sbi/articles/Dialogue_V06No2_7.pdf.

Bushman, Claudia L., and Richard L. Bushman. *Mormons in America*. New York: Oxford University Press, 1999.

Bushman, Richard L. *Joseph Smith: Rough Stone Rolling, A Cultural Biography of Mormonism's Founder.* New York: Vintage, 2005.

Butler, Judith. *Gender Trouble: Feminism and the Subversion of Identity.* 1990. Reprint, New York: Routledge, 1999.

Calvin, John. *The Institutes of the Chrstian Religion.* 1536. Reprint, Grand Rapids, MI: Christian Classics Ethereal Library, n.d. http://www.ccel.org/ccel/calvin/institutes. pdf.

Carroll, Jackson W., Barbara Hargrove, and Adair T. Lummis. *Women of the Cloth: A New Opportunity for the Churches.* San Francisco: Harper and Row, 1983.

Chancellor, James D. *Life in The Family: An Oral History of the Children of God.* Syracuse: Syracuse University Press, 2000.

Chaves, Mark. *Ordaining Women: Culture and Conflict in Religious Organizations.* Cambridge: Harvard University Press, 1997.

Christofferson, D. Todd. "The Moral Force of Women." Church of Jesus Christ of Latter-day Saints General Conference session, 5 October 2013. http://www.lds.org/ general-conference/2013/10/the-moral-force-of-women.

Church of Jesus Christ of Latter-day Saints. "Church Handbook of Instructions: Book 1, Stake Presidencies and Bishoprics." 1998. http://www.wikileaks.org/wiki/ Mormon_Church_Handbook_of_Instructions,_full,_2006.

———. "The Doctrine and Covenants." N.d. https://www.lds.org/scriptures/ dc-testament?lang=eng.

———. "Facts and Statistics: The Church of Jesus Christ of Latter-day Saints." N.d. http://www.mormonnewsroom.org/facts-and-stats.

———. "God Loveth His Children." 2007. http://www.lds.org/ldsorg/v/index.jsp?locale =0&sourceId=3e05c8322e1b3110VgnVCM100000176f620a____&vgnextoid=e1fa5f7 4db46c010VgnVCM1000004d82620aRCRD.

———. "Handbook 1: Stake Presidents and Bishops." 2010. http://ge.tt/5OcBdKQ/v/0.

———. "Handbook 2: Administering the Church." 2010. http://www.lds.org/manual/ handbook?lang=eng.

———. "LDS Church History: LDS History, 1818 Fall." N.d. http://lds-church-history. blogspot.com/2009/01/lds-history-1818-fall.html.

Clifton, Chas S. "Fort Hood's Wiccans and the Problem of Pacifism." Paper presented to the New Religious Movements Group at the annual meeting of the American Academy of Religion, Nashville, TN, 20 November 2000. http://www.chasclifton. com/papers/hood.html.

Coleman, Kristy S. *Re-Riting Woman: Dianic Wicca and the Feminine Divine.* New York: Altamira, 2009.

Compton, Todd. *In Sacred Loneliness: The Plural Wives of Joseph Smith.* Salt Lake City: Signature, 1997.

Cook, Mary N. "Seek Learning: You Have a Work to Do." Church of Jesus Christ of Latter-day Saints General Conference session, 24 March 2012. http://www.lds.org/ broadcasts/article/general-young-women-meeting/2012/03/seek-learning-you-

have-a-work-to-do?lang=eng&query=%E2%80%9Clearn+marketable+skill,%E2%8
0%9D.

Cornwall, Marie. "The Institutional Role of Mormon Women." In *Contemporary Mormonism*, edited by Marie Cornwall, Tim B. Heaton, and Lawrence Young, 239–64. Urbana: University of Illinois Press, 1994.

Cowan, Douglas E., and David G. Bromley. *Cults and New Religions: A Brief History.* Malden, MA: Blackwell, 2009.

Cunningham, Scott. *Wicca: A Guide for the Solitary Practitioner.* St. Paul, MN: Llewellyn, 2004.

Daily, Steven. "The Irony of Adventism: The Role of Ellen G. White and Other Adventist Women in Nineteenth Century America." Ph.D. diss., School of Theology at Claremont, 1985.

Daly, Mary. *Gyn/Ecology: The Metaphysics of Radical Feminism.* Boston: Beacon, 1978.

Dasher, Bertha. "Leadership Positions: A Declining Opportunity?" *Spectrum* 15, no. 4 (1984): 35–37.

David, Moses [David Brandt Berg]. "Ban the Bomb!" Mo Letter no. 1434 (March 1983). http://www.exfamily.org/pubs/ml/b5/ml1434.shtml.

———. "The Bloodless Coup" ("The New Revolution," pt. 4). Mo Letter no. 329A (18 February 1975). http://www.exfamily.org/pubs/ml/b4/ml0329A.shtml.

———. "Child Brides!" Mo Letter no. 902 (4 April 1977). http://www.exfamily.org/pubs/ml/b6/ml902.shtml.

———. "Come on Ma!—Burn Your Bra!" Mo Letter no. 286 (22 December 1973). http://www.exfamily.org/pubs/ml/b4/ml0286.shtml.

———. "FFing and Jealousy!" Mo Letter no. 603 (2 July 1977). In *The Mo Letters*, vol. 5, 4661–69. Geneva: Children of God, 1976. Graduate Theological Union Special Collections.

———. "Flirty Little Fishy!" Mo Letter no. 293 (3 January 1974). http://www.exfamily.org/pubs/ml/ml293.html.

———. "I Gotta Split." Pt. 1. Mo Letter no. 28 (22 December 1970). In *The Mo Letters*, vol. 1, 231–36. Geneva: Children of God, 1976. Graduate Theological Union Special Collections.

———. "The Law of Love!" Mo Letter no. 302c (21 March 1974). In *The Mo Letters*, vol. 3, 2413–15. Geneva: Children of God, 1976. Graduate Theological Union Special Collections.

———. "Love vs. Law!" Mo Letter no. 647 (23 July 1977). In *The Mo Letters*, vol. 5, 5006–13. Geneva: Children of God, 1976. Graduate Theological Union Special Collections.

———. "My Childhood Sex! Doin' What Comes Naturally." Mo Letter no. 779 (28 June 1977 and 11 August 1978). http://www.exfamily.org/pubs/ml/ml779.shtml.

———. "Nudes Can Be Beautiful!—Movement with Meaning!" Mo Letter no. 1006 (March 1981). http://www.exfamily.org/pubs/ml/b5/ml1006.shtml.

———. "The Old Church and the New Church." Mo Letter no. A (August 1969). http://www.exfamily.org/pubs/ml/mlA.html.

———. "One Wife." Mo Letter no. 249 (28 October 1972). In *The Mo Letters*, vol. 2, 1911–15. Geneva: Children of God, 1976. Graduate Theological Union Special Collections.

———. "The Re-Organization Nationalisation Revolution!" Mo Letter no. 650 (January 1978). In *The Mo Letters*, vol. 5, 5031–37. Geneva: Children of God, 1976. Graduate Theological Union Special Collections.

———. "Revolutionary Sex." Mo Letter no. 258 (27 March 1973). In *The Mo Letters*, vol. 2, 1988–2015. Geneva: Children of God, 1976. Graduate Theological Union Special Collections.

———. "Scriptural, Revolutionary Love-Making." Mo Letter no. N (August 1969). http://www.exfamily.org/pubs/ml/b4/mlo000N.shtml.

———. "Sex Jewels." Mo Letter no. 919 (May 1980). http://pubs.xfamily.org/text.php?t=919.

———. "Teens!—(The Future of Your Father!)—Jewels from Dad on Teens!" Mo Letter no. 2056 (September 1985). http://www.exfamily.org/pubs/ml/b5/ml2056.shtml.

———. "Trust the Lord!—On Husband/Wife Relationships." Mo Letter no. 2135 (29 November 1983). http://www.exfamily.org/pubs/ml/b5/ml2135.shtml.

———. "Women in Love." Mo Letter no. 292 (20 December 1973). http://www.exfamily.org/pubs/ml/b4/mlo292.shtml.

———. "You Are the Love of God!" Mo Letter no. 699 (5 June 1978). In *The Mo Letters*, vol. 5, 5409–13. Geneva: Children of God, 1976. Graduate Theological Union Special Collections.

Davies, Douglas J. *An Introduction to Mormonism*. Cambridge: Cambridge University Press, 2003.

Davis, Deborah, and Bill Davis. *The Children of God: The Inside Story*. Grand Rapids, MI: Zondervan, 1984.

Davis, Rex, and James T. Richardson. "The Organization and Functioning of the Children of God." *Sociological Analysis* 37, no. 4 (1976): 321–39.

Deutsch, Francine M. "Undoing Gender." *Gender and Society* 21, no. 1 (February 2007): 106–27.

Deweese, Charles W. *Women Deacons and Deaconesses: 400 Years of Baptist Service*. Macon, GA: Mercer University Press, 2005.

Drew, A. J. *A Wiccan Bible: Exploring the Mysteries of the Craft from Birth to Summerland*. Franklin Lakes, NJ: New Page Books, 2003.

Eller, Cynthia. *Living in the Lap of the Goddess: The Feminist Spirituality Movement in America*. New York: Crossroad, 1995.

Faludi, Susan. *Backlash: The Undeclared War against American Women*. New York: Crown, 1991.

Fielding, Lavina. "Problems, Solutions: Being a Latter-day Saint Woman Today." *Ensign*, March 1976. http://www.lds.org/ensign/1976/03/problems-solutions-being-a-latter-day-saint-woman-today?lang=eng.

Finnigan, Jessica, and Nancy Ross. "'I'm a Mormon Feminist': How Social Media Revitalized and Energized a Movement." *Interdisciplinary Journal of Research on Religion* 9, article 12 (2013). http://www.religjournal.com/articles/article_view.php?id=80.

First Presidency and Council of the Twelve Apostles of the Church of Jesus Christ of Latter-day Saints. "The Family: A Proclamation to the World." 23 September 1995. http://www.lds.org/family/proclamation.

Foltz, Tanice G. "The Commodification of Witchcraft." In *Witchcraft and Magic: Contemporary North America*, edited by Helen A. Berger, 137–68. Philadelphia: University of Pennsylvania Press, 2005.

Frost, Gavin, and Yvonne Frost. *The Good Witch's Bible*. 7th ed. New Bern, NC: Godolphin, 1999.

———. *The Witch's Bible*. Los Angeles: Nash, 1972.

Gates, Susa Young. "A Message from a Woman of the Latter-day Saints to the Women in All the World." *Improvement Era* 10, no. 6 (1907): 447–52.

Gimbutas, Marija. *The Language of the Goddess*. New York: Norton, 1989.

Gordon, Lynn D., ed. *Gender and Higher Education in the Progressive Era*. New Haven: Yale University Press, 1990.

Gottlieb, Robert, and Peter Wiley. *America's Saints: The Rise of Mormon Power*. New York: Harcourt Brace Jovanovich, 1986.

Griffin, Wendy. "Webs of Women: Feminist Spiritualties." In *Witchcraft and Magic: Contemporary North America*, edited by Helen A. Berger, 55–80. Philadelphia: University of Pennsylvania Press, 2005.

Habada, Patricia A., and Beverly J. Rumble. "Women in Seventh-day Adventist Educational Administration." In *A Woman's Place: Seventh-day Adventist Women in Church and Society*, edited by Rosa Taylor Banks, 100–112. Hagerstown, MD: Review and Herald Publishing Association, 1992.

Hales, Brian C. "Emma Smith, Eliza R. Snow, and the Reported Incident on the Stairs." *Mormon Historical Studies* 10, no. 2 (2009): 63–75. http://mormonhistoricsites.org/wp-content/uploads/2013/04/Emma-Smith-Eliza-R.-Snow-and-the-Reported-Incident-on-the-Stairs.pdf.

Haloviak, Bert. "Ellen White Endorsed Adventist Women Ministers." *Spectrum* 19, no. 5 (1989): 35–38.

———. "Longing for the Pastorate: Ministry in 19th Century Adventism." Unpublished paper, 1988. http://www.adventistarchives.org/docs/AST/Pastorate.pdf.

———. "Route to the Ordination of Women in the Seventh-day Adventist Church: Two Paths." March 1985. http://www.adventistarchives.org/docs/AST/Ast1985.pdf.

Hanks, Maxine, ed. *Women and Authority: Re-emerging Mormon Feminism*. Salt Lake City: Signature Books, 1992.

"Her Husband Also, He Praiseth Her." *Advent Review and Sabbath Herald* 82, no. 2 (1905): 13.

Hinckley, Gordon B. "Stand Strong against the Wiles of the World." Church of Jesus Christ of Latter-day Saints General Conference priesthood session, 7 October 1995. http://www.lds.org/general-conference/1995/10/stand-strong-against-the-wiles-of-the-world?lang=eng.

Hutton, Ronald. *The Triumph of the Moon: A History of Modern Pagan Witchcraft*. New York: Oxford University Press, 1999.

Institute for Religious Research. "Mormons in Transition: 1838 First Vision Account by Joseph Smith." N.d. https://irr.org/mit/first-vision/1838-account.html.

Jacobs, Janet Liebman. "Hidden Truths and Cultures of Secrecy: Reflections on Gender and Ethnicity in the Study of Religion." *Sociology of Religion* 61, no. 4 (2000): 434.

———. "Woman-Centered Healing Rites: A Study of Alienation and Reintegration." In *In Gods We Trust: New Patterns of Religious Pluralism in America*, edited by Thomas Robbins and Dick Anthony, 373–84. New Brunswick, NJ: Transaction, 2009.

Jensen, Sarah Elizabeth. "Women Proclaiming the Gospel on Missions: An Historical Overview." *Segullah* 2, no. 1 (2006). http://segullah.org/spring2006/sisterhistory.html.

Johnson, Benton. "Church and Sect Revisited." *Journal for the Scientific Study of Religion* 10, no. 2 (1971): 124–37.

Johnson, Ida M. "The Far-Reaching Influence of Christian Women." *Advent Review and Sabbath Herald* 132, no. 4 (1955): 12–13.

Judd, Wayne R. "William Miller: Disappointed Prophet." In *The Disappointed: Millerism and Millennialism in the Nineteenth Century*, edited by Jonathan M. Butler and Ronald L. Numbers, 2nd ed., 17–35. Knoxville: University of Tennessee Press, 1993.

Kimball, Spencer W. "President Kimball Speaks Out on Morality." Church of Jesus Christ of Latter-day Saints General Conference session, 5 October 1980. http://www.lds.org/general-conference/1980/10/president-kimball-speaks-out-on-morality?lang=eng&query=%22president+kimball+speaks+out+on+morality%22.

Koranteng-Pipim, Samuel. "Does the Bible Support Ordaining Women as Elders or Pastors?" Pt. 1. N.d. http://www.adventistsaffirm.org/article/157/women-s-ordination-faqs/2-does-the-bible-support-women-s-ordination.

Kramer, Bradley H. "Keeping the Sacred: Structured Silence in the Enactment of Priesthood Authority, Gendered Worship, and Sacramental Kinship in Mormonism." Ph.D. diss., University of Michigan, 2014.

Kress, D. H. "The Influence of a Godly Mother." *Advent Review and Sabbath Herald* 127, no. 19 (1950): 14–15.

Laake, Deborah. *Secret Ceremonies: A Mormon Woman's Intimate Diary of Marriage and Beyond*. New York: William Morrow, 1993.

Land, Gary. "Coping with Change, 1961–1980." In *Adventism in America: A History*, edited by Gary Land, 2nd ed., 208–30. 1986. Reprint, Grand Rapids, MI: Eerdmans, 1998.

Lattin, Don. *Jesus Freaks: A True Story of Murder and Madness on the Evangelical Edge*. New York: HarperOne, 2007.

Lawson, Ron. "Geopolitics within Seventh-day Adventism." *Christian Century* 107, no. 37 (1990): 1197–1203.

Lewis, James R., and J. Gordon Melton, eds. *Sex, Slander, and Salvation: Investigating The Family/Children of God*. Stanford, CA: Center for Academic Publication, 1994.

Lindén, Ingemar. *The Last Trump: An Historico-Genetical Study of Some Important Chapters in the Making and Development of the Seventh-day Adventist Church*. Frankfurt: Peter Lang, 1978.

Lloyd, Ernest. "I Want My Mother." *Advent Review and Sabbath Herald* 127, no. 12 (1950): 14.

Lorde, Audre. *Sister Outsider*. 1984. Reprint, Berkeley: Crossing, 2007.

Luckman, Thomas. *The Invisible Religion: The Problem of Religion in Modern Society*. New York: Macmillan, 1967.

Lunday, Berneice. "Please Stay Home with Me!" *Advent Review and Sabbath Herald* 137, no. 21 (1960): 12.

Luther, Martin. *First Principles of the Reformation, or The Ninety-Five Theses and Three Primary Works of Dr. Martin Luther*. Edited by Henry Wace and C. A. Buchheim. 1883. Reprint, Grand Rapids, MI: Christian Classics Ethereal Library, n.d. http://www.ccel.org/ccel/luther/first_prin.pdf.

Madsen, Carol Cornwall. "Mormon Women and the Temple: Toward a New Understanding." In *Sisters in Spirit: Mormon Women in Historical and Cultural Perspective*, edited by Maureen Ursenbach Beecher and Lavina Fielding Anderson, 80–110. Urbana: University of Illinois Press, 1992.

May, Frank O. "Correlation of the Church Administration." In *Encyclopedia of Mormonism*, 323–25. New York: Macmillan, 1992.

McGuire, Meredith B. *Religion: The Social Context*. 5th ed. Long Grove, IL: Waveland, 2002.

McKay, David O. "Safeguards against the Delinquency of Youth." *Conference Report*, October 1946, 111–17. http://scriptures.byu.edu/gettalk.php?ID=264&era=yes.

Monson, Thomas S. "The Women's Movement: Liberation or Deception?" *Ensign*, January 1971. http://www.lds.org/ensign/1971/01/the-womens-movement-liberation-or-deception?lang=eng.

Moore, Marvin. "Happy Homes Require Equal Effort." *Adventist Review* 167, no. 26 (1990): 18.

Morrill, Susanna. *White Roses on the Floor of Heaven: Mormon Women's Popular Theology, 1880–1920*. New York: Routledge, 2006.

Murray, Margaret. Introduction to *Witchcraft Today*, by Gerald B. Gardner, 15–16. New York: Citadel, 2006.

Newell, Linda King. "The Historical Relationship of Mormon Women and Priesthood." In *Women and Authority: Re-emerging Mormon Feminism*, edited by Maxine Hanks, 23–48. Salt Lake City: Signature Books, 1992.

Nietz, Mary Jo. "Queering the Dragonfest: Changing Sexualities in a Post-Patriarchal Religion." In *Feminist Narratives and the Sociology of Religion*, edited by Nancy Nason-Clark and Mary Jo Nietz, 29–52. Walnut Creek, CA: Altamira, 2001.

Nilsson, Sanja. "Rebooting The Family: Organizational Change within The Family International." *International Journal for the Study of New Religions* 2, no. 2 (2011): 157–78.

North American Division of the Seventh-day Adventist Church. "Theology of Ordination: Study Committee Report." November 2013. http://static.squarespace.com/static/50d0ebebe4b0ceb6af5fdd33/t/5277dee3e4b0878dc12abbad/1383587555021/nad-ordination-2013.pdf.

Northern Asia-Pacific Division of the General Conference of Seventh-day Adventists. "Biblical Research Committee Report and Recommendations: Theology of Ordination and the Ordination of Women to Gospel Ministry." 17 December 2013. https://mail.warren-wilson.edu/service/home/~/?id=171836&part=2&auth=co&view=html.

Numbers, Ronald L. *Prophetess of Health: A Study of Ellen G. White.* 3rd ed. Grand Rapids, MI: Eerdmans, 2008.

O'Dea, Thomas F., and J. Milton Yinger. "Five Dilemmas in the Institutionalization of Religion." *Journal for the Scientific Study of Religion* 1, no. 1 (1961): 30–39.

Olsen, Jeannine E. *One Ministry Many Roles: Deacons and Deaconesses through the Centuries.* St Louis: Concordia, 1992.

Oswald, Helen K. "Happier Homes in 1955." *Advent Review and Sabbath Herald* 132, no. 1 (1955): 12–13.

Otis, Rose. "Take Time to Be a Mother." *Review and Herald* 147, no. 8 (1970): 9.

Packer, Boyd K. "Talk to the All-Church Coordinating Council." 18 May 1993. http://www.zionsbest.com/face.html.

———. "To Young Men Only." Church of Jesus Christ of Latter-day Saints General Conference priesthood session, 2 October 1976. http://www.mormonstudies.net/html/packer/youngmen.html.

Pagels, Elaine. *The Gnostic Gospels.* New York: Vintage, 1989.

———. *On the Origin of Satan: How Christians Demonized Jews, Pagans, and Heretics.* New York: Random House, 1995.

Pearson, Michael. *Millennial Dreams and Moral Dilemmas: Seventh-day Adventists and Contemporary Ethics.* Cambridge: Cambridge University Press, 1990.

Petrey, Taylor G. "Toward a Post-Heterosexual Mormon Theology." *Dialogue: A Journal of Mormon Thought* 44, no. 4 (2011): 106–44.

Pike, Sarah M. *New Age and Neopagan Religions in America.* New York: Columbia University Press, 2004.

Poloma, Margaret M. *The Assemblies of God at the Crossroads: Charisma and Institutional Dilemmas.* Knoxville: University of Tennessee Press, 1989.

Priddy, Luella B. "Women and the Message." *Advent Review and Sabbath Herald* 87, no. 2 (1910): 11.

Puttick, Elizabeth. *Women in New Religions: In Search of Community, Sexuality, and Spiritual Power.* New York: St. Martin's, 1997.

Quinn, D. Michael. "LDS Church Authority and New Plural Marriages, 1890–1904." *Dialogue: A Journal of Mormon Thought* 18, no. 1 (1985): 9–105. https://www.dialoguejournal.com/wp-content/uploads/sbi/articles/Dialogue_V18N01_11.pdf.

———. "Mormon Women Have Had the Priesthood since 1843." In *Women and Authority: Re-emerging Mormon Femininsm,* edited by Maxine Hanks, 365–409. Salt Lake City: Signature Books, 1992.

Richardson, James T., Joel Best, and David G. Bromley, eds. *The Satanism Scare.* New York: Walter D. Gruyter, 1991.

Robbins, B. F. "To the Female Disciples in the Third Angel's Message." *Advent Review and Sabbath Herald* 15, no. 3 (8 December 1859): 21–22.

Robbins, Thomas, and David G. Bromley. "Social Experimentation and the Significance of American New Religions: A Focused Review Essay." In *Research in the
Social Scientific Study of New Religion*, edited by Monty Lynn and David Moberg,
1–28. Greenwich, CT: JAI, 1992.

Roberts, B. H. "The Church of Jesus Christ of Latter-day Saints at the Parliament of
Religions." *Improvement Era* 2, no. 12 (1899): 893–906.

Robinson, Ella M. "Little and Unimportant?" *Advent Review and Sabbath Herald* 137,
no. 6 (1960): 12–13.

Ruether, Rosemary Radford. *Goddesses and the Divine Feminine*. Berkeley: University
of California Press, 2006.

"The Sensible Girl." *Advent Review and Sabbath Herald* 66, no. 32 (1889): 501. http://
docs.adventistarchives.org/docs/RH/RH18890806-V66-32__B.pdf#view=fit.

Seventh-day Adventist Church. *Seventh-day Adventist Church Manual*. 17th ed. Hagerstown, MD: Review and Herald Publishing Association, 2005.

———. "Seventh-day Adventist World Church Statistics: Summary of Statistics 2012." N.d. http://www.adventist.org/information/statistics/article/go/0/
seventh-day-adventist-world-church-statistics-2012/.

———. "Statements, Guidelines, and Other Documents." June 2010. http://www.
adventist.org/fileadmin/adventist.org/files/articles/official-statements/Statements-
2010-english.pdf.

Seventh-day Adventist Church Office of Archives, Statistics, and Research. "1973 Role
of Women in the Church Committee: Mohaven Documents." N.d. http://www.
adventistarchives.org/1973-5-mohaven#.Un05440IZr6.

Shepherd, Gary, and Gordon Shepherd. "Accommodation and Reformation in The
Family/Children of God." *Nova Religio* 9, no. 1 (August 2005): 67–92.

———. "Reboot of The Family International." *Nova Religio* 17, no. 2 (November 2013):
74–98.

Shepherd, Gordon, and Gary Shepherd. *Talking with the Children of God: Prophecy and
Transformation in a Radical Religious Group*. Urbana: University of Illinois Press,
2010.

Sigerman, Harriet. "An Unfinished Battle, 1848–1865." In *No Small Courage: A History
of Women in the United States*, edited by Nancy Cott, 237–88. New York: Oxford
University Press, 2000.

Smith, Joseph. Papers. Church History Department, Church of Jesus Christ of Latter-
day Saints. http://josephsmithpapers.org.

Stanley, Caroline Abbott. "Homemaking: A Vocation." *Advent Review and Sabbath
Herald* 77, no. 25 (1900): 390.

Starhawk. *Dreaming the Dark: Magic, Sex, and Politics*. 1982. Reprint, Boston: Beacon,
1997.

———. *The Earth Path: Grounding Your Spirit in the Rhythms of Nature*. New York:
HarperCollins, 2004.

———. *The Empowerment Manual: A Guide for Collaborative Groups*. Gabriola Island,
British Columbia: New Society Publishers, 2011.

———. *The Pagan Book of Living and Dying: Practical Rituals, Prayers, Blessings, and Meditations on Crossing Over.* New York: HarperCollins, 1997.

———. *The Spiral Dance: A Rebirth of the Ancient Religion of the Great* Goddess. 1979. Reprint, New York: HarperCollins, 1999.

———. *Truth or Dare: Encounters with Power, Authority, and Mystery.* San Francisco: HarperSanFrancisco, 1987.

———. *Webs of Power: Notes from the Global Uprising.* Gabriola Island, British Columbia: New Society Publishers, 2002.

Stark, Rodney, and William Sims Bainbridge. *The Future of Religion: Secularization, Revival and Cult Formation.* Berkeley: University of California Press, 1985.

Stone, Jon R. "Nineteenth- and Twentieth-Century American Millennialisms." In *The Oxford Handbook of Millennialism,* edited by Catherine Wessinger, 492–514. New York: Oxford University Press, 2011.

The Story of Davidito. N.p.: The Family International, 1982. Excerpts available at http://www.xfamily.org/index.php/Story_of_Davidito#Advocating_sex_with_children.

Strong, June. "A New Kind of Women's Lib." *Advent Review and Sabbath Herald* 152, no. 15 (1975): 15–16.

Swatos, William H. "Church-Sect and Cult: Bringing Mysticism Back In." *Sociological Analysis* 42, no. 1 (1981): 17–26.

T. "The Man of the House." *Advent Review and Sabbath Herald* 72, no. 17 (1895): 261. http://docs.adventistarchives.org/docs/RH/RH18950423-V72-17__B.pdf#view=fit.

Tanner, N. Eldon. "No Greater Honor: The Woman's Role." Address delivered at the General Conference, 7 October 1973. http://www.lds.org/general-conference/print/1973/10/no-greater-honor-the-womans-role?lang=eng.

Taves, Ann. "Visions." In *Ellen Harmon White: American Prophet,* edited by Terrie Dopp Aamodt, Gary Land, and Ronald L. Numbers, 30–51. New York: Oxford University Press, 2014.

Todd, Jay M. "Improvement Era." In *Encyclopedia of Mormonism.* New York: Macmillan, 1992. http://eom.byu.edu/index.php/Improvement_Era.

Ulrich, Laurel Thatcher. "Mormon Women in the History of Second-Wave Feminism." *Dialogue: A Journal of Mormon Thought* 43, no. 2 (2010): 45–63. http://www.dialoguejournal.com/wp-content/uploads/sbi/articles/Dialogue_V43No2_53_2.pdf.

Vance, Laura. "Converging on the Heterosexual Dyad: Changing Mormon and Adventist Sexual Norms and Implications for Gay and Lesbian Adherents." *Nova Religio* 11, no. 4 (May 2008): 56–76.

———. "Evolution of Ideals for Women in Mormon Periodicals, 1897–1999." *Sociology of Religion* 63, no. 1 (2002): 91–112.

———. "Gender." In *Ellen Harmon White: American Prophet,* edited by Terrie Dopp Aamodt, Gary Land, and Ronald L. Numbers, 279–94. New York: Oxford University Press, 2014.

———. *Seventh-day Adventism in Crisis: Gender and Sectarian Change in an Emerging Religion.* Urbana: University of Illinois Press, 1999.

Van Zandt, David E. *Living in the Children of God*. Princeton: Princeton University Press, 1991.

Victor, Jeffrey S. *Satanic Panic: The Creation of a Contemporary Legend*. Peru, IL: Open Court, 1993.

Vogel, Dan, and Scott C. Dunn. "'The Tongue of Angels': Glossolalia among Mormonism's Founders." *Journal of Mormon History* 19, no. 2 (1993): 1–34. http://digitalcommons.usu.edu/cgi/viewcontent.cgi?article=1021&context=mormonhistory.

Vyhmeister, Nancy. "Deaconesses in the Church." Pt. 2. *Ministry: International Journal for Pastors*, September 2008. https://www.ministrymagazine.org/archive/2008/September/deaconesses-in-the-church.html.

Walker, Ronald W., David J. Whittaker, and James B. Allen. *Mormon History*. Urbana: University of Illinois Press, 2001.

Wallis, Roy. "Yesterday's Children: Cultural and Structural Change in a New Religious Movement." In *The Social Impact of New Religious Movements*, edited by Bryan Wilson, 97–133. New York: Rose of Sharon Press, 1981.

Watts, Kit. "An Outline of the History of Seventh-day Adventists and the Ordination of Women." SDAnet, April 1995. http://www.sdanet.org/atissue/wo/appendix5.htm#*.

Weber, Lynn. *Understanding Race, Class, Gender, and Sexuality: A Conceptual Framework*. 2nd ed. New York: Oxford University Press, 2009.

Weber, Max. *Economy and Society*. 1922. Reprint, Berkeley: University of California Press, 1978.

———. *On Charisma and Institution Building*. Chicago: University of Chicago Press, 1968.

———. *The Sociology of Religion*. 1920. Reprint, Boston: Beacon, 1991.

———. *The Theory of Social and Economic Organization*. Edited by Talcott Parsons. 1947. Reprint, New York: Free Press, 1964.

Welcome, S. C. "Shall the Women Keep Silence in the Churches?" *Advent Review and Sabbath Herald* 16, no. 14 (23 February 1860): 109–10.

Welter, Barbara. "The Cult of True Womanhood, 1820–1860." *American Quarterly* 18, no. 2 (1966): 151–74.

Wessinger, Catherine. "Charismatic Leaders in New Religions." In *The Cambridge Companion to New Religious Movements*, edited by Olav Hammer and Mikael Rothstein, 80–96. Cambridge: Cambridge University Press, 2012.

———. "Woman Guru, Woman Roshi: The Legitimation of Female Religious Leadership in Hindu and Buddhist Groups in America." In *Women's Leadership in Marginal Religions: Explorations outside the Mainstream*, edited by Catherine Wessinger, 125–46. Urbana: University of Illinois Press, 1993.

West, Candace, and Don H. Zimmerman. "Doing Gender." *Gender and Society* 1, no. 2 (1987): 125–51.

White, Ellen Gould Harmon. "Address and Appeal, Setting Forth the Importance of Missionary Work." *Advent Review and Sabbath Herald*, 19 December 1878. http://egwtext.whiteestate.org/publication.php?pubtype=Periodical&bookCode=RH&lang=en&collection=2&section=all&QUERY=%22Nothing+will+deter+this+class+fro

m+their+duty.+Nothing+will+discourage+them+in+the+work.+%22&resultId=3& isLastResult=1&year=1878&month=December&day=19.

———. *An Appeal to Mothers: The Great Cause of the Physical, Mental, and Moral Ruin of Many of the Children of Our Time*. Battle Creek, MI: Steam Press, 1864.

———. *Christian Education*. Battle Creek, MI: International Tract Society, 1894. https:// egwwritings.org/.

———. *Daughters of God*. Hagerstown, MD: Review and Herald Publishing Association, 1998. http://egwtext.whiteestate.org/publication.php?pubtype=Boo k&bookCode=DG&lang=en&collection=2&section=all&pagenumber=102& QUERY=%22be+set+apart+to+this+work+by+prayer+and+laying+on+of+ha nds%22&resultId=2.

———. "The Duty of the Minister and the People." *Advent Review and Sabbath Herald*, 9 July 1895. http://egwtext.whiteestate.org/publication.php?pubtype=Periodical&bo okCode=RH&lang=en&collection=2&section=all&QUERY=%22let+every+individ ual+labor%2C+privately+or+publicly%2C+to+help+forward+this+grand+work.+P lace+the+burdens+upon+men+and+women+of+the+church+%22&resultId=4&is LastResult=1&year=1895&month=July&day=9.

———. *Evangelism*. Washington, DC: Review and Herald Publishing Association, 1946. http://egwtext.whiteestate.org/publication.php?pubtype=Book&bookCode=Ev&lan g=en&collection=2&section=all&pagenumber=469&QUERY=%22women+to+do+ this+work%2C+and+it+will+feel+the+loss+if+the+talents+of+both+are+not+com bined%22&resultId=1.

———. "The Excellency of the Soul." *Advent Review and Sabbath Herald*, Art. B, para. 1 (9 May 1899). http://egwtext.whiteestate.org/publication.php?pubtype=Periodical& bookCode=RH&lang=en&collection=2&section=all&QUERY=%22man+and+ever y+woman+has+a+work+to+do+for+the+master%22&resultId=3&isLastResult=1& year=1899&month=May&day=9.

———. *The Great Controversy between Christ and Satan: The Conflict of the Ages in the Christian Dispensation*. 1888. Reprint, Washington, DC: Review and Herald Publishing Association, 1911. http://www.whiteestate.org/books/gc/gc.asp.

———. *Life Sketches of Ellen G. White*. Mountain View, CA: Pacific Press Publishing Association, 1915.

———. Manuscript Releases. Vol. 12. 1990. http://egwtext.whiteestate.org/publication-toc.php?bookCode=12MR&lang=en&collection=2&section=all.

———. Manuscript Releases. Vol. 13 (nos. 1000–1080). https://egwwritings.org/.

———. "The Need of Trained Workers." *Advent Review and Sabbath Herald* 70, no. 7 (14 February 1893): 97–98.

———. "Satan's Rebellion." *Signs of the Times*, 23 July 1902. http://text.egwwritings.org/ publication.php?pubtype=Periodical&bookCode=ST&lang=en&year=1902&mont h=July&day=23.

———. *A Sketch of the Christian Experience and Views of Ellen G. White*. Saratoga Springs, NY: James White, 1851. http://www.anym.org/SOP/en_ExV.pdf.

———. *Testimonies for the Church*. Vol. 4. 1881. https://egwwritings.org/.

————. *Welfare Ministry.* Washington, DC: Review and Herald Publishing Association, 1952. http://egwtext.whiteestate.org/publicationtoc.php?bookCode=WM&lang=en.

————. "Women as Christian Laborers." *Signs of the Times,* para. 8 (16 September 1886). http://egwtext.whiteestate.org/publication.php?pubtype=Periodical&bookCode=ST&lang=en&collection=2&section=all&QUERY=%22women+as+christian%22&resultId=3&isLastResult=1&year=1886&month=September&day=16.

————. "Women as Missionaries." *Advent Review and Sabbath Herald,* 10 December 1914. http://egwtext.whiteestate.org/publication.php?pubtype=Periodical&bookCode=RH&lang=en&year=1914&month=December&day=10.

————. "Words to Lay Members." *Advent Review and Sabbath Herald,* 26 August 1902. http://egwtext.whiteestate.org/publication.php?pubtype=Periodical&bookCode=RH&lang=en&year=1902&month=August&day=26.

White, Jean Bickmore. "Women's Suffrage in Utah." N.d. Utah.Gov Services: Utah History to Go. http://historytogo.utah.gov/utah_chapters/statehood_and_the_progressive_era/womenssuffrageinutah.html.

Whitman, Dale A. "Extermination Order." N.d. Brigham Young University Studies. http://web.archive.org/web/20061020144758/http://ldsfaq.byu.edu/emmain.asp?number=74.

Wilson, Bryan. "An Analysis of Sect Development." *American Sociological Review* 24, no. 1 (1959): 3–15.

————. *Magic and the Millennium.* New York: Harper, 1973.

————. *The Noble Savages: The Primitive Origins of Charisma and Its Contemporary Survival.* Berkeley: University of California Press, 1978.

Wilson, Ted N. C. "A Response to the Action of the Pacific Union Conference Constituency Meeting on Sunday, August 19, 2012." *Adventist Review,* 19 August 2012. http://www.adventistreview.org/article/5625/archives/issue-2012–1523/a-response-to-the-pacific-union-conference-constituency-vote.

————. "State of the Church." 14 November 2013. http://vimeo.com/79438041.

Wood, Kenneth H. "The Home Is in Big Trouble." *Adventist Review* 157, no. 2 (1980): 3, 16.

Wright, Jared. "Southeastern California Conference Executive Committee Votes to Ordain Women." *Spectrum,* 22 March 2012. http://spectrummagazine.org/blog/2012/03/22/southeastern-california-conference-executive-committee-votes-ordain-women.

Yinger, J. Milton. *Religion in the Struggle for Power.* 1946. Reprint, New York: Russell and Russell, 1961.

Zerby, Maria. "Flirty Little Teens, Beware!" Mo Letter no. 2590 (October 1989). http://www.exfamily.org/pubs/ml/b5/ml2590.shtml.

FOR FURTHER READING

Additional resources can be found on the companion website: http://nyupress.org/vance.

Banks, Rosa Taylor, ed. *A Woman's Place: Seventh-day Adventist Women in Church and Society*. Hagerstown, MD: Review and Herald Publishing Association, 1992.

Beecher, Maureen Ursenbach, and Lavina Fielding Anderson, eds. *Sisters in Spirit: Mormon Women in Historical and Cultural Perspective*. Urbana: University of Illinois Press, 1992.

Berger, Helen A., and Douglas Ezzy. *Teenage Witches: Magical Youth and the Search for the Self*. New Brunswick, NJ: Rutgers University Press, 2007.

Berger, Helen A., Evan A. Leach, and Leigh S. Shaffer. *Voices from the Pagan Census: A National Survey of Witches and Neo-Pagans in the United States*. Columbia: University of South Carolina Press, 2003.

Bradley, Martha Sonntag. *Pedestals and Podiums: Utah Women, Religious Authority and Equal Rights*. Salt Lake City: Signature, 2005.

Budapest, Zsuzsanna Emese. *The Holy Book of Women's Mysteries*. San Francisco: Red Wheel/Weiser, 2007.

Bushman, Claudia L., and Caroline Kline, eds. *Mormon Women Have Their Say: Essays from the Claremont Oral History Project*. Salt Lake City: Greg Kofford Books, 2013.

North American Division of the Seventh-day Adventist Church. "Theology of Ordination: Study Committee Report." November 2013. http://static.squarespace.com/static/50d0ebebe4b0ceb6af5fdd33/t/5277dee3e4b0878dc12abbad/1383587555021/nad-ordination-2013.pdf.

Puttick, Elizabeth. *Women in New Religions: In Search of Community, Sexuality, and Spiritual Power*. New York: St. Martin's, 1997.

Shepherd, Gordon, and Gary Shepherd. *Talking with the Children of God: Prophecy and Transformation in a Radical Religious Group*. Urbana: University of Illinois Press, 2010.

Wessinger, Catherine, ed. *Women's Leadership in Marginal Religions: Explorations outside the Mainstream*. Urbana: University of Illinois Press, 1993.

White, Ellen G. *Daughters of God: Messages Especially for Women*. Hagerstown, MD: Review and Herald Publishing Association, 1998.

INDEX

Mo. *See* Berg, David
Mokcsay, Zsuzsanna Emese, 104
Mo Letters: creation of, 80–81; Maria's
    voice in, 82
Monson, Thomas S., 33

Nauvoo Expositor, 29
Nauvoo, Illinois, 23, 24
Newell, Linda King, 27,
North American Division: decisions on
    gender equity, 68; and women's ordi-
    nation, 70, 74–75
Noyes, John Humphry, 2, 19
Numbers, Ronald L., 54

O'Dea, Thomas, 13
Ordain Women, 38, 39
Ordination: in Adventism, 59–60, 61,
    64–72, 74–75, 123, 125, 154n88, 155n95;
    debates regarding, 7. *See also* Kelly,
    Kate; Ordain Women
Organization of The Family: Chain of
    Cooperation, 82; The Family Inter-
    national, 91; Fellowship Revolution,
    157n19; loosening of membership
    rules (2004), 92–93; Reboot, 94–95,
    98–99; Reorganization National-
    ization Revolution (RNC), 82–83,
    158n37; "The Shake-up 2000," 92;
    and women in leadership, 96, 99–
    100

Patriarchy, 4, 5, 6, 15–16, 36
Peter Amsterdam. *See* Kelly, Steve
"Pink issue" of *Dialogue*, 35
Polarity: and gender binary, 107–108,
    110, 117–118; and God and Goddess,
    109–110
Polygamy: practice of, 24–26, 27, 28–29,
    140n21; repeal of, 30
Priesthood: in contemporary Mormon-
    ism, 39, 40–41, 44; in organization
    of Relief Society, 26; restoration of,
    22–23

Priesthood correlation, 35
Proclamation: criticisms of, 38; gender
    roles in, 37, 47; and same-sex marriage,
    144n76
Proposition 8, 37, 144n76
Provisioning, 81
Puttick, Elizabeth, 12, 138n33

Quinn, D. Michael, 28, 37
Quorum of Twelve Apostles, 29, 34, 40, 47

Reboot. *See* Organization of The Family
Relief Society: organization of, 26–27;
    and priesthood, 123, 142n55; and
    priesthood correlation, 35; and Utah
    suffrage, 30
Religious socialization, 4, 5, 6–7, 16, 41
Review (a.k.a. *Second Advent Review and
    Sabbath Herald*), 56–57, 61–64, 67–68
Rites of passage, 113–114, 167n13
Roberts, Sandra E., 70, 71
Rodriguez, Ricky: in The Family, 88,
    160n47; murder and suicide, 95,
    162n72. *See also* Sexual abuse

Sabbats: in Wicca, 109, 110, 112; sexuality
    in, 119
Same-sex attraction/same-gender attrac-
    tion. *See* LGBT
Same-sex marriage: Mormon response
    to, 37, 39; in Wicca, 165n48. *See also*
    Handfasting
Samhain, 110
Satanism, 105–106, 120
Second Great Awakening, 20, 27, 139n6
Second-wave feminism: and Adventism,
    73; defined, 141n46; and Mormonism,
    33; and The Family, 86–87; and Wicca,
    103–104, 115, 116–117, 120
Sexual abuse: in *Techi's Life Story*, 88; in
    Teen Training Camps, 93; in The Fam-
    ily, 88–91, 97, 159n44, 159n45, 160n49,
    160n52, 160n54, 160n55; in *The Story of
    Davidito*, 88, 90, 97, 98, 161n55, 160n48

ABOUT THE AUTHOR

Laura Vance is Professor of Sociology and directs Gender and Women's Studies at Warren Wilson College, where she specializes in the study of gender in new religious movements. Her publications include *Seventh-day Adventism in Crisis: Gender and Sectarian Change in an Emerging Religion.*